Events that Changed Great Britain from 1066 to 1714

Events that Changed Great Britain from 1066 to 1714

Edited by
Frank W. Thackeray
and
John E. Findling

GREENWOOD PRESS
Westport, Connecticut • London

Library of Congress Cataloging-in-Publication Data

Events that changed Great Britain from 1066 to 1714 / edited by Frank W.
   Thackeray and John E. Findling.
      p. cm.
   Includes bibliographical references and index.
   ISBN 0-313-31666-X (alk. paper)
   1. Great Britain—History—To 1485. 2. Great Britain—History—Tudors, 1485–
1603. 3. Great Britain—History—Stuarts, 1603–1714. I. Thackeray, Frank W.
II. Findling, John E.
DA32.E89 2004
941—dc21   2003045527

British Library Cataloguing in Publication Data is available.

Library of Congress Catalog Card Number: 2003045527
ISBN: 0–313–31666–X

First published in 2004

Greenwood Press, 88 Post Road West, Westport, CT 06881
An imprint of Greenwood Publishing Group, Inc.
www.greenwood.com

Printed in the United States of America

The paper used in this book complies with the
Permanent Paper Standard issued by the National
Information Standards Organization (Z39.48-1984).

10 9 8 7 6 5 4 3 2 1

Contents

Illustrations   **vii**

Timeline   **ix**

Preface   **xvii**

1.   The Norman Conquest, 1066   **1**

   Introduction   1
   Interpretive Essay by Frederick Suppe   6

2.   The Magna Carta, 1215   **19**

   Introduction   19
   Interpretive Essay by Linda E. Mitchell   24

3.   The Rise of Parliament, 1295–c. 1461   **39**

   Introduction   39
   Interpretive Essay by Mark K. Vaughn   44

4.   The Hundred Years' War, 1337–1453   **57**

   Introduction   57
   Interpretive Essay by Douglas Biggs   62

5.   The Wars of the Roses, 1455–1485   **75**

   Introduction   75
   Interpretive Essay by Kristen Post Walton   81

6. **The English Reformation, 1529–1536**   **95**

    Introduction   95
    Interpretive Essay by Kenneth L. Campbell   99

7. **Elizabethan England, 1558–1603**   **115**

    Introduction   115
    Interpretive Essay by Connie Evans   119

8. **Civil War and Restoration, 1642–1660**   **131**

    Introduction   131
    Interpretive Essay by William T. Walker   136

9. **The Plague and the Fire, 1665–1666**   **147**

    Introduction   147
    Interpretive Essay by Robert Landrum   151

10. **The Glorious Revolution, 1688–1689**   **165**

    Introduction   165
    Interpretive Essay by Steven E. Siry   171

Appendix A: Glossary   **185**

Appendix B: Ruling Houses and Dynasties   **191**

Index   **193**

About the Editors and Contributors   **199**

Illustrations

William (the Conqueror) of Normandy routed King Harold's army
at the Battle of Hastings in 1066   2

King John signed the Magna Carta on June 15, 1215   20

A contemporary view of the Houses of Parliament from the Thames
River   40

Mounted knights in armor attacked lightly armed infantry   58

Richard III was killed at the Battle of Bosworth Field in 1485   76

King Henry VIII is shown here wooing his lover, Anne Boleyn,
at the residence of his adviser, Cardinal Wolsey   96

In 1587 Queen Elizabeth I signed the death warrant for her cousin,
Mary, Queen of Scots   116

King Charles I received the last rites before his execution in
January 1649   132

In 1666 the Great Fire swept London, destroying much of the
city's center including 13,000 houses   148

William III became king of England in 1689 after driving his
father-in-law, James II, from the throne   166

Timeline

c. 2500 B.C.E.	First migrants from continental Europe arrive in England
55 B.C.E.	Julius Caesar first appears in England
43 C.E.	Rome conquers England
122–128	Hadrian's Wall constructed
407	Rome abandons England
c. 600	Christianity comes to England
664	Synod of Whitby
787	Danes invade England
871–899	Alfred the Great rules
1042–1066	Edward the Confessor rules
1066	Norman Conquest of England; William I (the Conqueror) king of England
1070	Lanfranc appointed Archbishop of Canterbury
c. 1080	Bayeux tapestry made
1086	Domesday Book
1087	William I dies; William II (Rufus) ascends throne
1093	Anselm appointed Archbishop of Canterbury

1100	William II dies; Henry I ascends throne
1135	Henry I dies; Stephen ascends throne
1154	Stephen dies; Henry II ascends throne
1162	Thomas Becket named Archbishop of Canterbury
1164	Constitutions of Clarendon
1166	Assize of Clarendon
1170	Thomas Becket murdered in Canterbury Cathedral
1171	Henry II conquers much of Ireland
1188	Saladin Tithe
1189	Henry II dies; Richard I (the Lion-Hearted) ascends throne
1190–1193	Richard I on the Third Crusade
1199	Richard I dies; John ascends throne
1202–1204	John defeated by Philip II of France
1214	Battle of Bouvines
1215	Magna Carta
1216	John dies; Henry III ascends throne
1249	University College at Oxford founded
1258	Provisions of Oxford
1263	Battle of Lewes
1264	Battle of Evesham
1272	Henry III dies; Edward I ascends throne
1275–1290	The Statutes of Edward I
1282–1284	Edward I subjugates Wales
1284	Peterhouse College at Cambridge founded
1290	Jews expelled from England
1295	Model Parliament
1297	Confirmation of the Charters
1298	Battle of Falkirk
1307	Edward I dies; Edward II ascends throne

1314	Battle of Bannockburn
1327	Isabella and Mortimer overthrow Edward II; Edward III ascends throne
1337–1453	Hundred Years' War
1340	Battle of Sluys
1346	Battle of Crécy
1348–1349	Black Death (bubonic plague) ravishes England
1351	Statute of Laborers
	Act of Provisors
1353	Act of Praemunire
1356	Battle of Poitiers
1360	Treaty of Bretigny
1376	Black Prince dies
	"Good" Parliament
1377	Edward III dies; Richard II ascends throne
1381	Wat Tyler's rebellion
1382	John Wycliffe translates Bible into English
1399	Richard II deposed; Henry IV ascends throne
1400	Geoffrey Chaucer dies
1413	Henry IV dies; Henry V ascends throne
1415	Battle of Agincourt
1420	Treaty of Troyes
1422	Henry V dies; Henry VI ascends throne
1431	Joan of Arc burned at the stake
1450	Jack Cade's rebellion
1455	Battle of St. Albans
1461	Battle of Towton Moor
	Henry VI deposed; Edward IV ascends throne
1470	Thomas Mallory writes *Morte d'Arthur*
1471	Battle of Tewkesbury

1476	First printing press in England
1483	Edward IV dies; Edward V ascends throne
	Edward V deposed; Richard III ascends throne
1485	Richard III killed at battle of Bosworth Field; Henry VII ascends throne
1494	Poynings Law
1499	Erasmus in England
1509	Henry VII dies; Henry VIII ascends throne
1513	Battle of Flodden
1516	Thomas More writes *Utopia*
1521	Pope Leo X names Henry VIII "Defender of the Faith"
1527–1534	Reformation in England
1534	Act of Supremacy
1535	Thomas More executed
1536	Anne Boleyn executed
1539	The monasteries dissolved
1540	Thomas Cromwell executed
1547	Henry VIII dies; Edward VI ascends throne
1549	Book of Common Prayer published
1553	Edward VI dies; Mary I (Bloody Mary) ascends throne
1556	Archbishop Thomas Cranmer executed
1558	Mary I dies; Elizabeth I ascends throne
	Calais lost to France
1563	Statute of Apprentices
	Book of Martyrs published
1576–1587	The voyages of Martin Frobisher
1578–1580	Francis Drake circumnavigates the globe
1587	Mary Stuart (Mary, Queen of Scots) executed
1588	England defeats the Spanish Armada
1600	East India Company chartered

1603	Elizabeth dies; James I (James VI of Scotland) ascends throne
1605	Gunpowder Plot
1607	Jamestown colony founded in Virginia
1608	Ulster Plantation begun
1611	King James version of the Bible
1616	William Shakespeare dies
1620	Pilgrims found Plymouth colony
1625	James I dies; Charles I ascends throne
1626	Francis Bacon dies
1628	Massachusetts Bay Company established
	William Harvey publishes *On the Motion of the Heart and Blood in Animals*
1633	William Laud named Archbishop of Canterbury
1638	Scotland rebels
1640–1660	The Long Parliament
1642–1646	First Civil War
1644	Battle of Marston Moor
1645	Battle of Naseby
1647	Second Civil War
1648	Pride's Purge
1649–1651	Third Civil War
1649	Charles I executed
	England declared a Commonwealth under the leadership of Oliver Cromwell
	Cromwell invades Ireland
1650	Thomas Hobbes publishes *Leviathan*
	First Navigation Act
1652	First Dutch War
1653	Cromwell named Lord Protector
1658	Cromwell dies

1660	Restoration of the monarchy; Charles II ascends throne
1661–1679	Cavalier Parliament
1661–1665	Parliament enacts the Clarendon Code
1662	The Royal Society chartered
1663	John Milton publishes *Paradise Lost*
1665–1667	Second Dutch War
1666	The Great Fire devastates London
1670	Treaty of Dover
1672–1674	Third Dutch War
1673	Test Act
1679	Habeas Corpus Act passed
1685	Charles I dies; James II ascends throne
1687	Isaac Newton publishes *Principia*
1688–1689	Glorious Revolution; James II deposed
1689–1697	War of the League of Augsburg
1689	William and Mary begin joint rule
	Bill of Rights enacted
	John Locke publishes *Treatises on Government*
1690	Battle of the Boyne
1694	Mary II dies
	Bank of England founded
	Triennial Act
1696	Treasons Act
1697	Peace of Ryswick
1699	Trading post at Canton established
1701–1713	War of Spanish Succession (Queen Anne's War)
1701	William III dies; Anne ascends throne
	Act of Settlement
1704	Battle of Blenheim
	England seizes Gibraltar

1706   Battle of Ramillies

1707   Act of Union unites England and Scotland

1711   South Sea Company established

1712   Treaty of Utrecht

1714   Anne dies; George I ascends throne

Preface

This volume, which describes and evaluates ten of the most important events in Great Britain before 1714, is the second in a two-volume series on events that changed Great Britain. The first volume treated events that occurred between 1714 and the present. This volume is a kind of historical cousin to our two other series of books, Events That Changed the World, which consisted of five volumes published between 1995 and 2001, and Events That Changed America, which consisted of four volumes published between 1996 and 2000.

In a sense, those series and the positive response to them provided the inspiration for this series. Great Britain has loomed large in the history of the world since at least the sixteenth century, and it has, of course, also played a pivotal role in the early development of the United States. As a consequence, volumes in our two other series make frequent references to British history, and when Barbara Rader, our former editor at Greenwood Press, suggested that we do a two-volume series on events that changed Great Britain, it seemed an excellent idea. We hope that this book and its companion on the later events that shaped British history will enable students and lay readers to place Great Britain in its proper world historical context and also to appreciate the fascinating history of Britain itself.

The current volume is designed to serve two purposes. First, the editors have provided an introduction that presents factual material about each event in a clear, concise, chronological order. Second, each introduction is followed by a longer interpretive essay by a specialist exploring the ramifications of the event under consideration. Each essay concludes with a selected bibliography of the most important works about the event. The ten chapters are followed by two appendices that provide additional information useful to the reader. Appendix A is a glossary of names, events, organizations, and terms mentioned but not fully explained in the introductions and essays. Appendix B charts the ruling houses and monarchs of Great Britain. A timeline of important events in British history before 1714 appears on page ix.

The events covered in this volume were selected based on our combined teaching and research. Of course, another pair of editors might have arrived at a list somewhat different from ours, but we believe that we have assembled a group of events that truly changed Great Britain over the first several centuries of its recorded history.

As with all published works, numerous people behind the scenes deserve much of the credit for the final product. Barbara Rader encouraged us to begin the project, and Kevin Ohe has been an exemplary editor through the process of turning our manuscript into a book. The staff of the Photographic Division of the Library of Congress provided genial assistance to us as we selected the photographs that appear in the book. Our student research assistant, Megan Renwick, helped us out in numerous ways, and we are grateful to Indiana University Southeast (IUS) for providing funds to hire her and to pay other project-related costs. We are especially grateful to Brigette Colligan, who was always there to type or retype material. Various staff members at the IUS computer center cheerfully unscrambled disks and turned mysterious word-processing programs into something we could work with. Special thanks to Roger and Amy Baylor and Kate Lewison for making their establishment available to us, enabling us to confer with colleagues and former students in a congenial atmosphere. Among those who helped us make this a better book are John Newman, Sam Sloss, Sheila Anderson, Kim Pelle, Yu Shen, and Glenn Crothers. And, most important, we thank our authors, whose essays were well conceived and thoughtful, and whose attention to both detail and scholarship was much appreciated.

Finally, we wish to express our appreciation to our spouses, Carol Findling and Kathy Thackeray, and to our children, Jamey Findling and Alex and Max Thackeray, whose patience with us and interest in our work made it all worthwhile.

Frank W. Thackeray
John E. Findling

1

The Norman Conquest, 1066

INTRODUCTION

Sometime around 2500 B.C.E., the first migrants from continental Europe arrived in Britain. By 1500 to 1000 B.C.E., groups of people had come together and created a fairly unified society of farmers and traders that historians have termed Celtic, best known to contemporary society for their excellent work in bronze tools and decorative items. Some five hundred years later, a new wave of immigrants came to Britain and introduced the Iron Age. Many of them had ties with France (then known as Gaul), and when Julius Caesar's Roman armies conquered Gaul in 56 B.C.E., it was only natural that the Romans would proceed on to Britain.

The Roman invasion and conquest of Britain came in the year 43 C.E. and inaugurated four hundred years of Roman presence there. The Romans saw Britain as their outermost line of defense, but the island also presented economic benefits. British farmers grew significant amounts of grain for export to other parts of the empire, and miners extracted tin and iron ore from deposits in the southwest. Rome's interest in Britain as a defensive outpost led to the construction of Hadrian's Wall between 122 and 133. The wall, made from stone and rubble, stretched seventy miles across England between present-day Newcastle and Carlisle and was named for the emperor at the time, Hadrian, a skilled military engineer.

Under Hadrian and his successors, the Romans developed a system of local government organized around towns, the villas of the rich, and the small villages of the poor. The economy remained based on agriculture and mining and was relatively prosperous.

William of Normandy's claim to the English throne was tenuous at best. However, this strong, resolute, warrior prince routed King Harold's exhausted army at the Battle of Hastings in 1066 and took the English crown for himself. (Reproduced from the Collections of the Library of Congress.)

By the third century, pirates began to threaten towns along the coasts, and in the fourth century, barbarian invasions began. In these waning days of the Roman Empire, defending everything proved impossible, and between 383 and 407, many soldiers were taken out of Britain and sent to crisis points in other parts of Europe, the Middle East, or North Africa. They never returned. By the year 500, most of the Roman social and economic organization had disappeared, although two significant legacies remained: a road system that converged on London, confirming its role as the most important town in Britain, and the presence of Christianity, which took root in the fourth century.

The period from the end of the fourth century to the Norman Conquest in 1066 is known as the era of Anglo-Saxon England. Saxon soldiers first came to Britain from what is now Germany as mercenaries fighting Britain's enemies, but as more of them arrived, the Saxons became the enemy. Despite courageous British resistance, they had conquered most of the island by about the year 600. The Saxons (or, more correctly, Anglo-Saxons) developed a militaristic society based on the *comitatus*, a bond between a regional warlord and his followers. Although armies were small by modern-day standards, these armies fought frequently and fiercely, especially in the early part of the era.

Beginning in the seventh century, various warlords achieved a semblance of authority over the others and were called *bretwealdas,* a corruption of the Latin *Rex Britannica,* or king of Britain. The earliest bretwealdas were from Northumbria, the northernmost kingdom. Their culturally diverse society (because of the wide variety of immigrants) held sway for about a century, during which time Theodore, archbishop of Canterbury in the 670s, united and strengthened the Catholic Church in Britain.

By the middle of the eighth century, the kingdom of Mercia in west central Britain was predominant. Mercian kings, especially Offa (758–796), produced impressive defensive works and implemented a more sophisticated administrative system. A succession of weaker kings in the ninth century, however, allowed the southwestern Kingdom of Wessex, the third of the great kingdoms, to gain control. A Saxon-dominated region, Wessex had to deal with serious invasions from Scandinavia, especially Denmark. These were particularly troublesome during the reign of Alfred (871–899). Despite the frequent wars, Alfred managed to improve the military, encourage education, and revamp the legal system to strengthen the social order.

Dutch invasions continued in the tenth and early eleventh centuries, and in 1013, Danish king Swein drove British king Aethelraed from power (and from the country) and launched thirty years of Danish rule. Swein soon died and was replaced by his son Cnut (sometimes spelled Canute), who reigned from 1016 until 1035. Under Cnut's rule, English affairs became more ordered and the throne more secure. But Cnut was a Dane and continued his involvement in Danish politics, a fact not to the liking of English landholders. At this time, England was split into four earldoms, three of which had been kingdoms in the Middle Ages: Northumbria, East Anglia, Mercia, and Wessex. Northumbria and East Anglia were firmly under Danish control, whereas Mercia and Wessex were more independent. Each of the four earls was a powerful political figure, so it is no surprise that when Cnut died in 1035 without a clear successor, a power struggle ensued between Cnut's two sons, each by a different wife. Both of these sons were dead by 1042, however, and out of the confusion, a son of Aethelraed, Edward (known as Edward the Confessor) emerged as king in 1042. With his accession to the throne, Danish influence in Britain ended.

Edward the Confessor ruled for twenty-four years and, although not considered a great king, he did manage a well-organized government (for the day) with strong local institutions in the sheriff and the shire court and an effective tax system. In addition, a military system based on the *fyrd*, or local militia, was in place. Edward, a strongly religious individual, also began the rebuilding (and enlarging) of Westminster Abbey as the monarchial church.

After about 1050, it was clear that Edward would have no children, and the question of succession arose once again. Among numerous possible claimants to the English throne, the most likely heir was in the lineage of the duchy of Normandy, across the English Channel in northern France. Edward had lived in exile in Normandy for many years before becoming king, and he at one time promised the throne to young William, son of Duke Robert of Normandy.

In England in the 1050s, Edward's greatest rival was Godwin, earl of Wessex, who had been responsible for the death of Edward's brother Alfred in 1036. Conflict that stopped short of war resulted in Godwin's exile in 1051, and his death in 1053 elevated his son Harold to the earldom of Wessex. After successfully rebuffing a Welsh revolt in the early 1060s, Harold was arguably the most powerful figure in England.

In Edward's last years, internal conflict, especially between Harold and his brother Tostig, earl of Northumbria, weakened the English crown. Edward died in January 1066, and Harold became king, only to face a summer invasion from Norway. This invasion, led by Harald Hardrada and abetted by Tostig, climaxed in Yorkshire at the battle of Stamford Bridge on September 24–25. Harold won a clear victory, and, with the deaths of Tostig and Hardrada, reached the height of his power and popularity in England.

Unfortunately, Harold's time in the sun was brief. William of Normandy, now the duke following the death of his father and perhaps looking to enforce the alleged promise Edward had made years earlier, had moved his own troops across the English Channel, landing at Pevensey on September 28. Only then did William learn of Harold's preoccupation with the Norwegian invasion and the fighting that had recently concluded in Yorkshire. William established his forces in defensive positions on the peninsula near Hastings and near his fleet, should a hasty withdrawal become necessary. Here news of Harold's decisive victory at Stamford Bridge reached William, and although some military historians have questioned the strategy of locating his forces where supplies were limited, it may be that William lacked the confidence to confront Harold farther inland and risk having his escape route cut off.

Harold likely learned of William's landing a few days after the battle of Stamford Bridge, while his army was resting from that engagement. But he was a determined leader. He rallied his army, found reinforcements, and set off toward the south. By October 8 or 9, Harold's army passed through London, and three days later camped in Sussex near Hastings. Harold, knowing that the Normans were a highly mobile army, quickly moved nearer to Hastings in order to block William from spreading his forces throughout more of southern England.

As October 14 dawned, Harold probably intended to keep the Normans at bay until his forces could destroy William's fleet and attack with a clearly stronger force. William, on the other hand, needed to force the issue immediately, lest his troops be starved into submission on the narrow peninsula. Food would soon be a problem for the Normans, and the likelihood of bad weather increased daily. Thus William attacked the English forces at dawn on October 14, and although Harold's forces were tired from their rapid march to Hastings, they gathered themselves into a strong defensive position on a ridge, forming what was known as a shield wall. Each army had about 7,000 men, and by all accounts they were evenly matched. The English army staved off the first major attack, forcing the Normans back, but then, English troops began to break ranks—whether by orders or not is unclear—and pursued the Normans. William managed to halt his army's retreat and bring his troops around to a point where they could counterattack on the left flank of the English army.

This was the turning point of the battle, which continued into late afternoon. The Normans fought intensely during the afternoon, perhaps aware that if the battle were prolonged for even a day or two, reinforcements would reach Harold. Moreover, ships loyal to Harold were said to be on their way to destroy the Norman fleet. During the long battle, Harold was killed, apparently from an arrow in the eye. This was a devastating blow to the English; upon hearing the news, their discipline weakened and many soldiers fled. By nightfall, the Normans had secured victory. William continued his conquest, capturing Winchester, Canterbury, and London, and confirming his triumph on Christmas Day with his consecration as king of England.

More than five years passed before William's tenure as king of England was secure. An invasion from Norway, abetted by forces from the north of England, challenged William in 1069, and revolt erupted in Scotland in 1072, but neither succeeded in dislodging the Norman king. William ruled until 1087 when he died from an injury suffered while horseback riding during a punitive expedition to France.

Out of William's accession and reign came two remarkable cultural treasures: the Bayeux Tapestry and Domesday Book. The Bayeux Tapestry, more than 200 feet long, tells in word and picture the story of the Battle of Hastings. It was probably made in the 1080s for William's half-brother Do, bishop of Rochester but originally from Bayeux, in Normandy.

Domesday Book relates back to the system of taxation in place during Edward's reign. In 1086, William convened a conference of the provincial leaders of England to discuss the economic strength of the kingdom. The result was an extensive survey, almost like a census, of the shires of England, with an enumeration of people, farm animals, and other economic assets. This was all recorded in what became known as Domesday Book, so-called because it suggested what God might have at his disposal on Judgment Day, or Domesday. At any rate, it has provided scholars ever since with a magnificently detailed picture of English life in the late eleventh century.

INTERPRETIVE ESSAY
Frederick Suppe

Most books that cover all of English history use the year 1066 to begin a new chapter, because the Battle of Hastings, which occurred in that year, drastically changed the course of English politics, government, and society. However, the events of that year are more complex than this, for there were two major battles in England during that year. What happened at each, and what did not happen, were decisive in shaping England and its inhabitants for the next several hundred years.

Some background information will help to understand why these two battles occurred, whose armies were involved in them, and what the issues were. From 1042 until his death on January 6, 1066, King Edward the Confessor ruled England. However, the king had no children, so for much of his reign the question of who would succeed him as king was a major political issue. The most powerful nobles of Anglo-Saxon England were the earls, and in 1066 the most powerful of the English earls was Harold Godwinson, the earl of Wessex. Harold was extremely ambitious and hoped to succeed Edward as king, but there was also another powerful figure with claims on the throne of England.

Across the English Channel from the southern coast of England was the French province of Normandy. Its name derives from the Viking "Northmen" who had settled it in 911. By 1066 the descendants of these Viking settlers had become French-speaking nobles, but they were among the toughest soldiers in western Europe. The ruler of Normandy in 1066 was Duke William, who had become duke in 1035 when only seven years old and who had survived several rebellions to become an experienced ruler and military commander. Before Edward the Confessor became king of England, he had been an exile in Normandy, and he retained strong connections with that French duchy. In 1051 Edward had designated Duke William his successor as king of England, and in 1064 he sent Harold, the earl of Wessex, over to Normandy to confirm this. Harold's ship was blown off course, and he was captured by a subordinate of Duke William's, who delivered him to the duke. Despite his own political ambitions, Harold was forced to take an oath acknowledging Duke William's claim to the English kingship and pledging to help William gain that claim. Harold later claimed that an oath extorted under duress was not a valid one.

King Edward the Confessor died on January 6, 1066. Shortly before his death, the old king was persuaded to designate Harold as his successor, and Harold had himself crowned king within days of Edward's death. Duke William immediately began making preparations to invade England to enforce his own claim to the throne of England. However, Harold also had to deal with his younger brother, Tostig, who had been earl of Northumbria, the northernmost earldom in England. Tostig had been forced into exile by a rebellion in 1065. Looking for allies to help him regain his position, Tostig enlisted the help of the king of Norway, Harald

Hardrada. Since Viking raiders had attacked England repeatedly during the late tenth century and Cnut, king of Denmark, had also been king of England from 1016 until 1035, Harald Hardrada believed that he also had a reasonable claim to the English kingship.

Considering Duke William's pending invasion from Normandy to be his most pressing problem, King Harold assembled an army on the southern English coast to defend against it. However, this force exhausted its provisions by September 8 and Harold was forced to disband it. Soon thereafter, however, he received the news that King Harald Hardrada and Tostig had landed an army in Yorkshire and had defeated local forces there. Harold reassembled his army, raced north, and defeated the Norse king at the Battle of Stamford Bridge on September 25. If the English army had lost this battle, then it is possible that England would have been ruled by a Scandinavian king and that the country would have become culturally and linguistically part of the Scandinavian world.

While Harold was in northern England defending the kingdom against the Norse invasion, William landed his forces on the south coast of England. Harold hastened back to London within a week and mustered what forces he could assemble to oppose William's army. The decisive battle between these two rivals for control over England occurred on October 14, 1066, about nine miles north of the port city of Hastings. Harold deployed his force of foot soldiers atop a commanding ridge. The core of his force consisted of housecarls, heavily armored infantrymen with tall shields, battle-axes, and swords. These were supplemented by as many less well-equipped footmen as Harold had been able to assemble from southern England during the short time available to him. Harold's basic tactic was the shield wall, a line of footmen protected by the barrier of their interlocking body-length shields, against which his opponents would have to charge. William had a large number of armored knights mounted on horseback and a significant number of archers, as well as many footmen. William's initial uphill attacks did not succeed, but then the course of the battle changed. Thinking that a wave of the Norman knights was retreating in confusion, some of Harold's men charged down the hill after them, thus breaking the shield wall. At this point in the battle, a high-arching arrow struck Harold in the eye, killing him. The knights in William's army now took the offensive against the leaderless English forces. By the end of the battle many of the English nobles who had supported Harold were killed or had fled.

Although William did not actually conquer all of England on that day, the outcome was inevitable. Harold and his brothers had been killed and most of his supporters were gone. William worked his way through southern England and was crowned king in London on Christmas day of 1066. There was some scattered resistance to his rule, but he ruthlessly suppressed all opposition, and by 1072 all of England was firmly under his control.

The Battle of Hastings and William's subsequent conquest of all of England brought immediate changes to the country. England now had a new ruler—a French-speaking noble. His conquering army had consisted of French speakers from Normandy, the neighboring province of Brittany, and other regions of northern France. To reward them for their military service to him and to establish the basis for maintaining in England an army loyal to him, William confiscated lands that had belonged to English nobles and distributed these to his followers. By doing this he introduced the feudal system to England.

Feudalism was a system by which a nobleman who possessed a large amount of land would grant a piece of it called a fief to a knight. In this relationship the fief-granting noble was called a lord and the recipient knight was called a vassal. The fief was large enough to support the knight and his family so that he could be a full-time warrior. In return for his fief the knight was expected to provide forty days of military service each year to his noble lord whenever summoned. By granting enough fiefs to individual knights, a lord would have the potential to muster a small but potent military force when needed. During the twenty-one years that he ruled England, William the Conqueror distributed large amounts of territory to his principal followers. These men in turn granted some of these lands as fiefs to their own knights. Within a generation the ownership of most lands in England had changed hands. Toward the end of his reign William wanted to know who actually possessed every single bit of property in England and what it was worth. The result of his wish is called "Domesday Book."

In 1086 the king sent officials to every shire (county) of his kingdom with a list of questions for every manor in England. These included who had owned that property in 1066 before the Conquest, who now owned it, what it had been worth and what it was now worth, and how many people lived on the property and how many animals and other resources they possessed. The officials summoned knowledgeable local men in each shire to respond to these questions. Within a year, the responses were compiled into the enormously informative Domesday Book; the explanation for the name given on p. 6 conforms to that in the OED.

The Anglo-Saxon Chronicle, an English-language annual account of events kept for many years before 1066 and continued for a generation afterwards, complained vehemently about how intrusive and detailed the Domesday Book inquiries were. The Chronicle complained that the king's officials asked about every single pig! While modern readers may sympathize with the chronicler's complaints, they do show how effectively and efficiently King William and his French-speaking successors ruled over England. Domesday Book also reveals that William kept about one-fifth of all the lands in England as his own personal property, making him not only the richest man in that country, but also one of the most powerful rulers in all of Europe.

Domesday Book is a great source of information about what England was like during the late eleventh century and how much changed as a result of the Battle of Hastings and the Norman Conquest. For example, it shows that in manor after manor the owner in 1066, a man with an English name like Ethelwulf, had been replaced by 1086 by someone who had a Norman French name like Robert or William or Richard.

Another striking piece of evidence about the Battle of Hastings itself and the events that led up to it is the Bayeux Tapestry. This woven tapestry, about twenty-three feet in length, uses cartoon-like characters and captions in Latin to depict the story of King Edward the Confessor, Harold, Duke William, and scenes from the battle. Although it is sympathetic to the victorious Norman side of the conflict, the tapestry does provide some visual details about armaments and clothing.

Although William had effectively destroyed most potential military opposition to him at Hastings, he and his army were essentially a few thousand French speakers trying to control an English-speaking country with some 1.5 million inhabitants. To solidify his military control, William and his followers built castles all over the country. The most famous of these was the Tower of London, a large rectangular stone tower that William erected at the east end of London as a base from which to control that city. Later kings of medieval England added more elaborate fortifications to the Tower of London, but present-day visitors can still see the original stone tower at the heart of this complex. However, most of the early castles built during William's reign were earthen and timber fortifications called "motte and bailey" castles that could be erected more quickly than stone ones. A motte and bailey castle consisted of an earthen mound topped by a timbered watchtower and surrounded by a wall of upright logs anchored in the ground. Within a century many of these motte and bailey castles were replaced by more durable and more expensive ones constructed of stone. That visitors to Britain today can still see many of these castles suggests just how firm and determined the new French-speaking noble class was to establish their control over England.

After he conquered England, William was not only king of that country, but also continued to be the Duke of Normandy. Because Normandy was a province of France, William was theoretically a subordinate to the king of France. The next several centuries of English kings continued this politically anomalous pattern. As nobles with lands in France they should have obeyed the French kings, but as kings of England they were independent rulers and were powerful enough to contend against the French kings. This pattern continued from William the Conqueror's reign until the end of the "Hundred Years' War" in 1453, and it meant that most English kings during this long period became entangled in wars in France.

Although France is larger geographically than England and had a larger population, the kings of England were able to hold their own in these struggles because England was probably the most efficiently governed country in medieval western Europe, and its rulers could therefore marshal their resources effectively. Before 1066 England had been divided into separate districts called shires, which were local units of government. Each shire had a local official called a sheriff (shire-reeve) who would receive written orders from the king and would carry these out. William the Conqueror inherited this system and used it in compiling Domesday Book. William's successors continued to develop the English administrative system. William's youngest son, who became King Henry I (1100–1135), established an effective financial auditing system called the Exchequer. The Exchequer was named for a cloth with a checked or grid pattern of stripes draped over a counting table. The vertical columns on the table provided places to account for pounds, shillings, and pennies—the units of medieval English currency—while the two horizontal rows kept track of money collected and money spent. Each year the sheriff of each shire was summoned to London and directed to bring with him copies of all written orders to collect money or to spend it, along with all the money he had left at the end of the year. Markers were placed on the Exchequer table to show first how much money the sheriff should have collected in response to each of the orders he had received, and then how much of that money he had been ordered to spend. When the process was completed, everyone around the table could easily see how much money the sheriff should have remaining to hand over to the royal government. Because of this sophisticated system, it was difficult for an English sheriff to cheat the king's government. Today the chief financial official in the United Kingdom is still called the Chancellor of the Exchequer.

Because King William had clearly conquered all of England and had granted parts of it to his followers, he and later English kings could exert the legal aspects of rulership over the whole country. King Henry II (1154–1189) spent almost as much time in France as he did in England but wanted a legal system that would function even when he was out of the country. He and his judges of the royal court began to evolve a system of "common law"—so called because it was common to the whole country. Under this system, groups of royal judges would travel from one shire to the next in a regular circuit or pattern. When they arrived in a shire, the local sheriff would convene everyone in that shire who had legal business to bring before the royal judges. To reach decisions in trials the judges would assemble groups of respected local men who were called juries because they swore an oath in court that, after hearing all the evidence, they would determine the truth. ("Jury" comes from the French word for swearing an oath—*jurer*—and the word "verdict" comes from the Latin words for telling the truth.) Englishmen who were victims of crime or who were accused of a crime were willing to pay small fees to Henry II's royal government to have their cases heard by a jury because this method seemed so much fairer and more reasonable than the variety of previously existing methods. Common law continued to develop in England and eventually became the basis for the American legal system.

Although the feudal system was an effective way for William and his successors to reward his followers, to support an army, and to therefore control the country, it also could limit a king from exercising total unlimited power. A feudal relationship between a lord and a vassal included responsibilities and obligations for both parties, even if the lord was king of England. King John (1199–1216) discovered this in 1215 at the meadow of Runnymede just west of London. Constantly in need of money, he exploited his barons (his major vassals) in ways they regarded as unfair. One of their principal complaints was that John kept increasing the fees a young baron had to pay to the king to inherit the family lands after his father died. Incensed by this and by many other grievances, the barons collected their armies and confronted the king. Essentially, they threatened to wage war against their own king unless he agreed to sign a formal document agreeing to end a long list of abuses and to treat them and all other English people fairly. This document is called Magna Carta (the "Great Charter") and showed that everyone in the kingdom, even the king himself, was subject to the law. One of its most important provisions was the guarantee that every free Englishman could have the right to a trial by jury—and thus could not be arbitrarily punished by the king.

Although many Americans may occasionally sympathize with the desire to rebel against the government, this is hardly the most efficient way for differences of opinion about political matters to be resolved. King John's military confrontation with his barons in 1215 is part of the context for understanding how much more effectively an English king later that century handled this same problem. King Edward I (1272–1306) fought wars against the Welsh, the Scots, and the king of France—expensive undertakings that required revenues far beyond the customary amounts the nobles and other inhabitants of England were used to providing to their kings. Over the course of his reign Edward developed a custom of assembling his major nobles and representatives from each shire and each major town for discussion sessions to consider his requests for new taxes. These discussions were called "parliaments" from the French word *parler*—to talk. During them the king would describe the problems he faced and the need for more funds, the assembled nobles and representatives would bring up problems and grievances, and eventually the parliament would compromise about new taxes. These discussion sessions gradually evolved into the fundamental British governmental institution called Parliament. The American system of government, in which the elected representative Congress must cooperate with the chief executive in determining taxes and passing laws, is based on this pattern developed in medieval England.

William the Conqueror and his Norman followers had taken an entire country by military force. During the generations after 1066 the French-speaking nobles he had settled all over England (and who are therefore usually termed "Anglo-Norman" because of their English residence) continued their aggressive and ambitious ways by conquering neighboring parts of the British Isles. These Anglo-Norman nobles began carving out territories along the southern and northern coasts of Wales in the late eleventh century, and subsequent English kings waged many military campaigns against the Welsh. Finally, in the late thirteenth century, King Edward I completely conquered that region in three great wars and erected in northern Wales some of the most impressive castles in all of Britain to solidify his control. Wales was not officially incorporated into the English kingdom until the reign of King Henry VIII in 1536, but by then it had been under effective English control for two centuries.

In the mid-twelfth century ambitious English nobles were invited to Ireland by an exiled Irish king. Fearing that these nobles might carve out independent territories there, King Henry II brought a large army to Ireland to establish his authority over that island. The relationship between

England and Ireland has been a changing and often difficult one ever since. Henry VIII proclaimed himself King of Ireland in 1541, and that country officially became part of the United Kingdom in 1801. In 1922, Ireland was divided into two parts: an independent country now called the Republic of Ireland, and six counties of Northern Ireland that are still part of the United Kingdom.

English domination of Scotland was more complicated. During the twelfth century the younger sons of many ambitious Anglo-Norman noble families were invited to settle in Scotland and were given land. They built castles and brought with them many other aspects of the culture that they had developed in England. (The Stuart family, who later became the royal family of Scotland, is an example of this pattern.) King Edward I tried to conquer Scotland during the late thirteenth century and failed, but cultural and political links between the two countries persisted. In one of history's ironies, after the death of the English Queen Elizabeth in 1603, her closest relative was her cousin, James VI, king of Scotland, who immediately traveled to England to rule over both countries simultaneously. This led to the combination of the two countries into the United Kingdom in 1707. Although it took centuries for all four of these regions to combine, one can argue that the Norman Conquest created the conditions that led to their combination.

However, not all of the long-term effects of the Norman Conquest involve politics and law. One of the most striking changes happened to the English language. Prior to 1066 the language of England was Old English—a language very similar to modern German in its grammar, although many of its basic words (like "fire" and "house") are still part of the modern English language. At that time Old English was the official language of government and was spoken by English people in ordinary conversation. William the Conqueror, his followers, and their families who settled in England were all French speakers. Although the majority of the population continued to speak English, French was now the language of the new ruling class and therefore the language of government. This change in status for the English language allowed its grammar to change drastically. Since English no longer appeared in government documents, its grammar and vocabulary were freer to change to reflect the way English speakers were using their language. Intermarriage and other sorts of social relationships between native speakers of the two languages promoted the easy absorption of French vocabulary into the English language. The results can be seen in Geoffrey Chaucer's *Canterbury Tales*, a work written in the late fourteenth century in what scholars call Middle

English. Although this stage of English is clearly different from contemporary English, a reader of modern English can understand most of what Chaucer wrote.

Because French was the official language in England for several centuries after the Norman Conquest, English adopted many words from French during this period. Surveying some of the new words English gained at this time gives an idea of the areas of life in which the French-speaking nobles dominated English society and customs. New words in the arenas of politics and government include: "government" itself, "prison," "castle," "country," "court," "crime," "royal," "army," "lieutenant," "sergeant," and "soldier." Other words of French origin show that its influence extended to many other areas of life. These include: "beef," "pork," "veal," "boil," "fry," "question," "second," and "language." It is instructive to compare the first three words in this list with "cow," "pig," and "calf," which are all words in Modern English based on the Old English words. That native English words continued to be used for the animals reveals that most of the people in post-Conquest England who worked with these animals on farms were English speakers. However, once the animals had been butchered and converted to meat to be used in cooking for the households of the new nobles, French words were used. Because the French-speaking nobles could more easily afford to eat expensive meats more often than could poorer English speakers, French words came to predominate in this area.

Fashions in personal names also changed after the Conquest. It was quite natural for the Norman conquerors of England to continue to give French names to their offspring who were born in England. When the French-speaking nobles married Anglophone English natives, the higher prestige of French caused such couples to bestow French names on their children. And within a century not only English noble families but also quite ordinary people were giving their sons French names such as Robert, Richard, and William—an indication that the two linguistically distinctive cultures were beginning to meld. Interestingly, it took a few more generations before French names came to be fashionable for daughters in England.

It is therefore reasonable to view 1066 as a decisive year in English history. It can also be fascinating to speculate about what might have happened if the results of the two battles had been different. If the Norwegian Harald Hardrada had defeated King Harold at the Battle of Stamford Bridge, then England would have been ruled by Scandinavian kings. If Harold had won both Stamford Bridge and Hastings, then the country would probably have continued as it had been—fairly well governed but without the need for castles. It seems likely that in this case England would probably not have become so entangled with the wars and political affairs of France and other continental European countries.

However, Duke William of Normandy did prevail at Hastings. This victory and his subsequent conquest of the whole English kingdom did bring immediate changes, including replacement of the old ruling class by a new one, construction of hundreds of castles, and English kings who were frequently out of the country because of their involvement in French affairs. However, the long-term changes initiated by the Norman Conquest make the year 1066 significant. The new kings developed a system of government that gave them very effective control over the resources of their country, including the ability to tax those resources. While striving to extend legal aspects of royal control throughout all of England, King Henry II and his royal judges developed the beginnings of common law. Inherent within that legal system was the concept that everyone, including the king, should abide by laws and be subject to them. King John was forced to acknowledge this in 1215 by signing the Magna Carta. Edward I was guided by this principle to develop Parliament, which today is still an essential component in the government of the United Kingdom and was the inspiration for the U.S. Congress. The influx of French speakers enriched English vocabulary, with a new layer of French words supplementing the fundamental Germanic Old English ones. The result for modern English is a wealth of synonyms that delights poets and allows anyone writing in the language to easily express subtle differences in meaning and connotation.

SELECTED BIBLIOGRAPHY

Barlow, Frank. *Edward the Confessor.* Berkeley: University of California Press, 1984. A well-written biography of the next to last Anglo-Saxon king and a description of his times.

Chibnall, Marjorie. *Anglo-Norman England, 1066–1166.* New York: Basil Blackwell, 1986. Surveys the political, social, and economic changes in England during the century after the 1066 Conquest.

_____. *The Debate on the Norman Conquest.* Manchester, UK: Manchester University Press, 1999. The author lucidly explains the scholarly debates about the significance of 1066 and the kinds of changes it brought to England.

Darby, H.C. *Domesday England.* Cambridge, UK: Cambridge University Press, 1977. A systematic discussion and analysis of the wealth of information about the people and resources of England contained in Domesday Book.

Davies, Norman. *The Isles, A History.* New York: Oxford University Press, 1999. An integrated treatment of the history of all the British Isles; chapter 5 provides a thought-provoking geographic context for 1066.

DeVries, Kelly. *The Norwegian Invasion of England in 1066.* Rochester, NY: Boydell Press, 1999. Describes the invasion of northern England by Harald Hardrada in 1066 and its context.

Douglas, David C. *William the Conqueror.* Berkeley: University of California Press, 1967. A political biography of William that includes his rise as Duke of Normandy and his conquest of and rule over England.

Douglas, David C. and George Greenaway, eds. *English Historical Documents.* Vol. 2 (1942–1189). New York: Oxford University Press, 1953–1955. An edited collection of a huge variety of primary sources that describe England during this period, including excerpts from the Anglo-Saxon Chronicle, other chronicles, and illustrations of the entire Bayeux Tapestry.

Green, Judith. *The Aristocracy of Norman England.* Cambridge, UK: Cambridge University Press, 1997. Examines the new dominant social class in post-Conquest England.

Hollister, C. Warren. *The Military Organization of Norman England.* New York: Oxford University Press, 1965. Describes how William the Conqueror and his successors and nobles organized the military resources of post-1066 England.

Holt, J.C. "Feudal Society and the Family in Medieval England," *Transactions of the Royal Historical Society,* 5th series, vol. 32 (1982), 193–212; vol. 33 (1983), 193–220; vol. 4 (1984), 1–26; and vol. 35 (1985), 1–28. A four-part article examining various aspects of the new feudal landed ruling class in post-1066 England.

Jackson, Peter, ed. *Words, Names, and History. Selected Writings of Cecily Clark.* Rochester, NY: D.S. Brewer, 1995. A series of studies about patterns and changes in personal names and place-names in England after the Norman Conquest.

Morillo, Stephen, ed. *The Battle of Hastings: Sources and Interpretations.* Rochester, NY: Boydell Press, 1996. Combines selections from primary sources from the period that describe this battle with twelve articles on various aspects by experts and an introduction by the author.

Pounds, J.J. G. *The Medieval Castle in England and Wales. A Social and Political History.* Cambridge, UK: Cambridge University Press, 1990. Part 1 examines the social and political effects of castles on England during the century after 1066.

Stenton, Frank. *Anglo-Saxon England.* 3rd ed. Oxford: Clarendon Press, 1971. A thorough treatment of the period of English history before the Norman Conquest.

Swanton, Michael, ed. and trans. *The Anglo-Saxon Chronicle.* New York: Routledge, 1998. An excellent translation into modern English of the whole text of this important primary source, which supplies an English perspective on the events of 1066 and Domesday Book.

Walker, David. *The Normans in Britain.* Oxford, UK: Blackwell, 1995. Considers the impact of the events of 1066 on Ireland, Scotland, and Wales, as well as on England.

Walker, Ian W. *Harold, the Last Anglo-Saxon King.* Stroud, Gloucestershire, UK: Sutton, 1997. An account of the life and brief reign of William the Conqueror's opponent at Hastings.

Whitelock, Dorothy, David C. Douglas, Charles H. Lemmon, and Frank Barlow, *The Norman Conquest, Its Setting and Impact*. New York: Charles Scribner's Sons, 1966. Four separate articles on the Anglo-Saxon achievement, William the Conqueror, the campaign of 1066, and the effects of the Norman Conquest.

Wilson, David. *The Bayeux Tapestry*. London: Thames & Hudson, 1985. An excellent study of this remarkable artifact from the eleventh century, with colored illustrations of the entire tapestry.

2

The Magna Carta, 1215

INTRODUCTION

Feudalism, the political system of the Middle Ages, featured a ceaseless contest for domination among that epoch's three major competitors—the Church, the monarchy, and the nobility or aristocracy. At the outset of the modern era—roughly A.D. 1500—the monarchy (at least in western Europe) had begun to emerge triumphant. However, the ultimate success of western Europe's monarchies had not been preordained; in fact, at various times during the Middle Ages the monarchy had been the clear loser. This certainly was the fate of England's King John I, who ruled from 1199 to 1216. King John not only lost his battles with the Church, in 1215 his nobility forced him to sign the famous Magna Carta. In the English-speaking world, the Magna Carta has become synonymous with the rights and liberties of the individual vis-a-vis the state.

In England, the nobles and their putative leader, the king, had struggled against each other almost nonstop since the Norman Conquest of 1066. As early as 1075, William the Conqueror had crushed a rebellion among his own nobility who objected to the restraints that the king had imposed upon them. However, William was a strong ruler; he not only centralized royal authority in England but also subordinated the unruly nobility to the monarchy.

William's two immediate successors were also strong rulers; nevertheless, both William II and Henry I experienced periodic difficulties with their barons who chafed under royal control. When Henry I died in 1135, a power struggle for the throne ensued between Matilda, Henry I's

Almost universally regarded as England's worst king, John signed Magna Carta on June 15, 1215. John's unhappy barons—with the support of Church officials—forced this famous document on the reluctant monarch. (Reproduced from the Collections of the Library of Congress.)

daughter, and Stephen, son of William I's daughter Adela. Although Stephen triumphed, his weak personality and contested claim to the throne inspired increased baronial unrest. The nobility successfully challenged the monarch on several fronts, and England descended into near anarchy.

With Stephen's death in 1154, the English monarchy's fortunes improved significantly. The new king, Henry II, proved as capable and determined as his earlier ancestors. In particular, he developed a uniform and effective system of justice that laid the foundations of England's present legal system. Henry blended and modified traditional courts with courts and offices controlled by the king such as the forerunners of the King's Bench and court of Common Pleas, and royal itinerant justices who made annual circuits throughout the kingdom.

Henry also brought England's sheriffs, the king's most important local agents, under much closer royal control, and in 1166 he issued the Assize of Clarendon that established the rough equivalent of today's grand jury, also under royal supervision. Simultaneously, Henry expanded the king's power to adjudicate land disputes, a lucrative and important area of the law given the economic and social importance attached to landownership at the time. Moreover, the confused nature of land tenure and transfer under the often incoherent feudal system ensured thousands of cases always pending.

Not coincidentally, by extending royal jurisdiction to every nook and cranny of his kingdom Henry immeasurably strengthened the monarch's hand at the expense of his medieval rivals—the nobility and the Church. However, it was said of Henry that he could rule every house except his own, and it was under Henry's sons that the nobility and Church would stage a dramatic comeback.

Henry and his wife, Eleanor of Aquitaine, who came to oppose her husband at every step because of his infidelities and abuse, had four grown sons—Henry, Geoffrey, Richard, and John. Toward the end of Henry's life, these sons actively conspired against their father and made common cause with his rival Philip Augustus, king of France. Although Henry and Geoffrey preceded their father in death, Richard inherited the crown upon Henry's passing in 1189.

Richard I, better known as Richard the Lion-Hearted, has enjoyed a good press thanks in no small measure to his attractive personality (Richard was the archetype of the valiant, chivalrous "knight in shining armor") and the outpouring of stories and films that the Robin Hood legend has spawned. In truth, Richard proved a practically worthless king of England. As was the case with many medieval knights, he was obsessed with fighting. The Crusades provided an early outlet for his fixation, and during the latter half of his reign he engaged in almost constant warfare defending his French holdings against the ambitious Philip Augustus. In fact, during his ten-year reign Richard spent only a few months' total time in England. Nevertheless, this did not deter him from impoverishing England in order to pay his ransom when the Holy Roman Emperor captured him on his return from the Third Crusade and to raise and maintain his armies in France. That Richard achieved this was more a tribute to the efficient governmental system his father had bequeathed him and to loyal and competent administrators in England than to anything he himself did. While on campaign in France in April 1199, Richard was killed and the crown passed to John, his younger brother.

John is widely regarded as England's worst king; however, this is not to say that he lacked certain positive attributes. By almost universal agreement John was highly intelligent and much evidence shows that he was a superb administrator who took a keen interest in his kingdom's affairs. Nevertheless, even if one allows for the deluge of negative propaganda that his enemies (and they were legion) disseminated, the picture of John that emerges is singularly negative. Cruel, brutal, arbitrary, capricious, treacherous, untrustworthy, inconstant, tyrannical, grasping—all these pejorative adjectives have been applied to John with real justification. For example, it appears that he murdered his nephew Arthur in a drunken rage, frequently killed his hostages instead of turning them over for ransom, starved to death his enemies' captured relatives, regarded every woman in the kingdom as his personal possession, exacted ever increasing sums from his nobility, and broke his word almost as soon as he gave it. Individually, these disreputable acts would not necessarily have enraged a monarch's aristocracy; after all, this rough and tumble age featured a good deal of what today is characterized as antisocial behavior. However, taken cumulatively, John's actions crossed the proverbial line; he appeared to threaten the very code—distorted though it might have been—that governed medieval society. His behavior was so outrageous and his personality so repellant that by the time of Magna Carta, John had managed to alienate almost all of England.

Not only did John's nobility detest him for his personality and behavior, they disrespected him for his military shortcomings. In this era much was excused or overlooked if the man who held the throne proved to be a successful warrior. While John occasionally exhibited personal bravery, his military adventures were almost always crowned with failure. Failure breeds contempt, and it was no accident that John's barons began to refer to him as "Softsword."

At the start of his reign, John found himself matched against Philip Augustus of France. Although he won some initial victories and defeated his nephew, Arthur, whom Philip backed, John's indolence, abusive treatment of his vassals, numerous breaches of the feudal "code," and apparent lack of concern for his inheritance spelled disaster. When John directly confronted Philip, a growing number of his French knights abandoned him. By 1204 John's holdings in France had been reduced to a portion of Aquitaine. Among other territories, John surrendered Normandy, Anjou, and Maine to Philip.

Several years later, John roused himself to again challenge Philip. In preparation for renewed hostilities, John extracted huge sums from his English barons, much to their displeasure. For example, within a decade John arbitrarily tripled the scutage—a fee that the king's vassals could pay in lieu of performing their military service obligations—and imposed that levy on his nobles seemingly at will. Furious, many noblemen refused to pay the sums that John demanded. Moreover, many simply did not respond to his calls to join his military entourage.

Much of John's war chest went to create an anti-French alliance. This required significant bribes and subsidies. Nevertheless, the prospect of defeating Philip and regaining at least some of his lost French lands greatly appealed to John. Disaster rather than success ensued. In July 1214, at the Battle of Bouvines in Flanders, Philip handily defeated John's ally, Otto, who had laid claim to the Holy Roman Empire. John, who had committed himself to aid Otto, instead floundered in France as his contemptuous barons turned their collective backs on him. This humiliating defeat cost John what little remaining prestige and respect he enjoyed.

Not nearly as damaging as Bouvines but still harmful to John was his extended battle with the Church. Just as he found an exceptional opponent in Philip Augustus, John had the misfortune to cross swords with Innocent III, perhaps the strongest of the medieval popes. With the death in 1205 of Hubert Walter, the secularized archbishop of Canterbury who also served as an effective royal administrator for John, a struggle ensued to name his successor. In short order, John found himself locked in battle with Innocent. The dispute reached such proportions that England was placed under an interdict and John was excommunicated. Ultimately, the papacy triumphed with the appointment of Stephen Langton as archbishop of Canterbury and head of the Church in England.

As it turned out, Langton was instrumental in rallying the English barons and forcing Magna Carta upon the reluctant but friendless king. Universally hated and reeling from the defeat at Bouvines, John now faced increasing discontent at home. As early as 1213, the English nobility had gathered at St. Paul's in London to voice their unhappiness with John. There Langton read to them Henry I's coronation charter that contained the king's promise to refrain from abusing the nobility as his ancestors had.

The situation grew even more serious in the following year, and early in 1215 the rebellious barons, especially those from the northern part of the country, gathered at Stamford. From there they marched to London, which opened its gates to receive them. Cornered, John opted for compromise over conflict. In June 1215, he met his angry nobility at Runnymede meadow alongside the Thames River outside of London. There, on June 15, John signed Magna Carta, or the Great Charter.

Magna Carta contained sixty-three clauses arranged in no particular order. It dealt with specifics rather than generalities, and its focus ranged from the profound (the administration of justice, royal abuses, feudal dues and payments) to the mundane (bridge building, weights and measures, riverine fishing concerns). Whatever its importance at the time, over the centuries Magna Carta evolved to have a monumental impact on the world's English-speaking nations.

INTERPRETIVE ESSAY
Linda E. Mitchell

According to historian Doris Mary Stenton, "The common law received in Magna Carta its first generally recognized statute, written law, authoritative at the date of its publication." Possibly the most famous document of the medieval world, the original version of the Great Charter, dated 1215 and signed by King John, was not actually a legal document: the king's seal had been coerced by barons whose rebellion had negated their feudal oaths of loyalty. The "legal" version of Magna Carta is actually the revised version of 1225, published by King Edward I in 1297 as a "Statute of the Realm." The 1215 Charter was not even called "Great": the designation *magna* appears in 1217 to differentiate it from a shorter royal charter, the Charter of the Forest, also issued in 1217.

Historians focus on a number of questions that address the importance of Magna Carta from the thirteenth century to the present day. Why did the kings of medieval Britain consider it important to reissue and confirm a charter that gave away so many of the rights and privileges they enjoyed? Why were reissues and confirmations of the charter also so important to the medieval baronage? Why did confirmation of Magna Carta become a royal requirement according to the emerging class of "parliamentary knights" who formed the fourteenth and fifteenth-century House of Commons? Finally, in the seventeenth century, why did the anti-Stuart party before and after the English Civil War consider Magna Carta the foundation for a "constitution," unwritten but pervasive, that guaranteed the kinds of civil liberties the framers of the United States Constitution took for granted in 1789?

The importance of Magna Carta for all of Britain's political community is incalculable. From the very beginning the charter had a unique resonance not only for the nobles but for free commoners as well. Nevertheless, it is difficult to assess its actual impact on the legal and political experiences of medieval English people. Despite regular confirmations by kings after 1215, mention of the Charter occurs infrequently in venues such as the law courts, where legal precedent determined the shape of judicial decisions throughout the thirteenth and fourteenth centuries. Although some petitioners to Parliament referred to Magna Carta in their complaints, these references tended to use the Charter as an icon of good governance, rather than as having a specific legal impact.

Magna Carta must thus be discussed in multiple contexts, among them its mythic significance. By the late fourteenth century, although largely superceded by royal statutes, the Charter maintained its mythic power to inspire efforts to regulate the Crown. Even though it suffered a decline in significance in the years of Lancastrian and Tudor dominance, it was revived by the ideologues of "civil" government who needed a standard to combat the enormous success of absolutist systems in the seventeenth century. By this time, however, Magna Carta had taken on a biblical aura; it had become a universal manifesto of liberal egalitarianism and collective governance, able to be interpreted infinitely. All of these issues must be addressed individually, but it is important to emphasize the historical significance of the Charter on the medieval political and legal community of the thirteenth and fourteenth centuries—the era in which both common law and Parliament developed.

The original Charter of 1215 contains sixty-three clauses. By 1225, these clauses had been reduced to roughly half that number through a process of emendation and reduction. The Charter of Liberties of 1215 was itself an emendation of a draft charter now known as "The Articles of the Barons." Although clerical editors attempted to group the sixty-three clauses into general categories, they are not consistently organized. Clauses relating to the Church, for example, include the famous first clause guaranteeing that the "liberties" of the Church will be preserved, a reiteration of this promise in Clause 63, and a reference to the guardianship of abbeys being maintained in the hands of the founding families—not specifically a Church-related clause but, rather, one that upheld a customary privilege of the baronage. In the 1225 version of the Charter, a clause was added. Clause 36 states that any lands given by a layperson to the Church must owe its traditional military and customary services, as if it were still held by a layperson. Thus, even though these clauses relate either directly or tangentially to the relationship between the Church in England and the Crown, they are not grouped together in a separate section.

A significant number of clauses in the 1215 Charter relate specifically to problems between King John and the baronage. John's treatment of hostages and prisoners was notoriously savage; for example, he starved the wife and eldest son of Baron William de Braose to death when they were hostages in his custody. As a result, Clauses 49 and 56 to 59 all deal with the safe return of hostages held by the king—English, Welsh, and Scots alike. Similarly, John's reliance on followers from the southern French region of Poitou, his use of mercenaries to prosecute the war against his barons, and the need to adjudicate the disseisins, or the appropriation of someone's land without legal cause or right, which John had engaged in at the expense of his barons, had to be addressed in the charter: Clauses 50 to 52 and 55 deal with these issues. Finally, in Clause 53, those men who pledged to accompany John on Crusade to the Holy Land were granted respites, or protection from prosecution in the royal courts until the recipient returned homes. All of these clauses ceased being relevant as soon as John died; therefore, they were deleted from later versions of the Charter.

Other clauses in the 1215 Charter were combined and re-edited in order to delete redundancies. Clauses 7 and 8 were reduced to one clause, numbered 7 in the 1225 Charter, which secured the privileges of widows in receiving their marriage portions, dower, and inheritances promptly upon the death of their husbands and without having to pay cash for the privilege. Similarly, the extensive protections of 1215 against royal forces appropriating horses, carts, goods, wood, and provisions without paying for them were compressed into fewer clauses in the 1225 version.

The 1225 Charter also attempted to address some issues that had been neglected in 1215, such as clarifying the frequency of county assizes and the personnel required to participate. One thing the 1225 version did not do, however, was retain the Baronial Council of Twenty-five. This was, in fact, deleted as early as the 1216 version of the charter introduced by William Marshal, earl of Pembroke, as regent for the young king, Henry III. As a result, there were no clauses in the "official" version of the Great Charter that mandated a method of enforcement, something many historians see as a real detriment to the constitutional nature of the document.

The main difference between the 1215 original and the 1225 version that became the foundation of the "English constitution" was thus the difference between a document created by and for a powerful faction of rebellious subjects and a document created by and for a royal administration intent on reducing motivations for further rebellion while at the same time preserving the autonomy of the Crown. The version of the Charter that became law, therefore, was the one that represented the interests of the Crown while still preserving the intentions of the baronial original.

One of the most interesting uses of Magna Carta is as a model for developing royal statute. Between 1216 and 1225, the editing of the Charter created the precedent not only that such refinements could be made—thereby preserving it as a "living" document—but also demonstrated the mechanism by which further statutory innovations could be accomplished.

Magna Carta achieved a status different from earlier legal texts; it was not merely "confirmed," it was assumed as part of each successive king's body of law. This process divorced the document from its historical origins and placed it in a context that was perpetually present, much like the United States Constitution. As such, later statutes and provisions both of the Crown and of rebellious barons, from the Statute of Merton in 1236 and the Provisions of Oxford in 1258 to the Ordinances of 1311, could be seen as emendations of the Great Charter in spirit, if not always in substance.

The era between 1216 and 1388 is significant in that a number of baronial rebellions occurred, accompanied by charters of "liberties" that sought to limit the power of the Crown by mandating the sharing of such power with a council of barons. In addition, the kings of this era—Henry III, Edward I, Edward II, Edward III, and the regency council of Richard II—all promulgated royal statutes that clarified points of law and created precedents based upon judicial action. Both phenomena owe a significant debt to the existence and rhetorical use of Magna Carta.

The most significant baronial documents of the era are the Provisions of Oxford of 1258 and the Ordinances of 1311. In both cases, prominent barons were rebelling against the king (Henry III and Edward II, respectively) because of perceived abuses against baronial power and the perception of the dependence of both kings on "aliens" and "foreigners." These are precisely the charges against King John in 1214 that led to the 1215 Charter. Moreover, like the original version of Magna Carta, the Provisions of Oxford and the Ordinances of 1311 were both nullified when the Crown regained control following the failure of the rebellion. It should be obvious that Magna Carta was not only the model for these two later documents, but that the sentiments expressed in both—shared authority between the king and a representative council; the expulsion of foreign-born courtiers who had the ear of the king; protection for populations at risk of being abused by the Crown, such as widows and royal wards; demands for judicial restraint and reasonable monetary fines and dues— were largely the same as those found in 1215. While the Provisions of Oxford do not specifically mention Magna Carta, many of the clauses refer to issues that parallel those in the Charter, such as the need for competent ministers appointed to the judiciary. Perhaps more importantly, the statute that ended the Barons' Wars, the "Dictum of Kenilworth" (1266), specifically mentions that the king will uphold the requirements of the Great Charter. In 1311, the ordinances against Edward II explicitly mention Magna Carta in the sixth clause, which states that "the Great Charter shall be observed in all its particulars...."

This need to reiterate the privileges and constraints contained in Magna Carta suggests that the relationship between the Crown and the baronage had not really improved between 1215 and 1311. In fact, it had not improved; rather, it had developed along the very lines that the original charter had tried to prevent. Such developments, however, were influenced by the people engaged in governance—and Henry III and Edward II were notoriously problematic rulers. Other kings, such as Edward I and Edward III, were able to balance the growth of royal power and the necessary relationship with the baronage more effectively.

It is easy to see how rebellious barons would turn to the Great Charter as their model for further charters of liberties. It is not as simple to discuss the ways in which Magna Carta influenced the development of royal statute. Perhaps the most straightforward influence occurred in kings' willingness to reissue and confirm the Charter. As a result, the important legislation of the era can be seen as continuations of the reissued Great Charter, from Henry III's Statute of Merton to Edward III's establishment of justices of the peace.

Perhaps the most useful example of this process is the confirmation of Magna Carta and the Charter of the Forest that King Edward I made in 1297. Firstly, it was this confirmation that was included in the *Statutes of the Realm.* Secondly, the 1297 confirmation included a promise to confer with the baronage and representatives of the realm—the invention of a formal parliamentary system—whenever fiscal circumstances required the king to request a special "aid" (a medieval form of taxation). Thirdly, the confirmation required that the Great Charter be read aloud by every sheriff in every county—in Latin *and* English—so that all the people could be made aware of the privileges and mandates contained therein.

The kings most actively engaged in legislation of this kind—Edward I and Edward III—were fully aware of the need to act in concert with the baronage. They consistently called for the election of "parliaments" whenever they mandated a change in legal statute such as when they refined the relationship between common law and local custom, or clarified provisions for the transfer of property to future generations, or limited the amount of land that could be transferred into Church hands, and so on. Although judicial reforms of earlier kings also served as models for the development of these statutes, the way they were written, as well as the kinds of concessions made within them, suggest that they were written with the Great Charter in mind.

Thus, the existence of the Charter as a living document enabled the royal and baronial creators of English common law to use it as a foundation for everything from the topics of legislation to the actual language used in the statutes.

In the area of "private" law, Magna Carta sought protection for those who were most easily dispossessed through "bad lordship": widows, free minors in wardship, baronial heirs, and subfeoffees and tenants. The result was a comprehensive standardization of the relationship between such figures and the Crown. In 1215, the baronage had experienced more than a decade of King John's abuse of the disenfranchised in order to gain revenue, and they were thoroughly tired of it. Consequently, relief was standardized; minor heirs under wardship were exempted from paying relief upon achieving their majority; and widows were guaranteed that they would receive their dower, inheritance, and *maritagium* upon the death of their husbands without extraordinary delay and without having to pay a relief. Moreover, widows were guaranteed that they would not have to pay an extortionate amount to gain control of their remarriage. There was nothing revolutionary about these particular clauses in the Charter; nevertheless, they had the most long-lasting practical effects.

By standardizing relief to £100 for a barony and £5 (100 shillings) for a knight's fee, the creators of the Great Charter attempted to prevent the king from abusing heirs in order to fill royal coffers. What is amazing about this particular clause was not that it was retained in future versions of the Charter, but that it *worked*. Moreover, the standard of £100 and £5 was lowered—possibly because of a clerical error—in the 1297 confirmation of the Charter to 100 marks and 5 marks, respectively (a mark was two-thirds of a pound). This change made it even more difficult for the Crown to use feudal inheritance to generate income. As a result, kings were forced to negotiate fiscal agreements through the development of a parliamentary system.

By standardizing the payment for the transfer of feudal property from one generation to another, Magna Carta also thereby made such transfers *automatic*. This principle runs counter to the ideology behind feudal lands—that they belong to the liege lord and cannot be transferred except by formal oaths of homage and fealty, which are regulated by the lord not by the vassal. With a standard payment, the control over such transfers of property came to be regulated by the central court system; it was no longer possible for the lord to prevent an heir from entering his or her inheritance for nonpayment of the relief. This combination of precedents effectively converted property held in formal life tenure to virtual private property. The only way the lord could recover such land was either by the biological failure of the family to which it had been conveyed or by forfeiture of the property and the dissolving of the feudal ties of homage.

Another innovation—this time concerning widows' dower—resulted from another possible clerical slip of the pen. In the early thirteenth century, most baronial marriages mandated a "nominated" (named) dower for the bride; that is, specific properties were designated for the wife, should she survive her husband. Another form of dower, "reasonable" dower, used the standard formula that a widow was entitled to life use of one-third of her late husband's estate at the time of his death. This form of dower is emphasized in the Great Charter, although the nominated form is also mentioned. In 1225, however, the reissued Magna Carta defines "reasonable" dower as one-third of the husband's estate held by him *at any time during the marriage*. Although this alteration might indeed have been a clerical error, its effects were tremendous. Within a decade, widows were suing heirs and tenants for reasonable dower using the revised formula.

This new definition of "reasonable" dower potentially placed a significantly larger share of the heirs' estate in the hands of the widow. Any property alienated by her husband during their marriage could be claimed as owing dower, and the heir had to compensate the widow out of his or her share. Not only did this prove to be lucrative for widows—

especially noble widows—it also proved lucrative for the royal courts. There was a tremendous increase in the number of dower cases heard after 1225, many of which involved widows suing tenants for dower in alienated land. In fact, by the end of the thirteenth century kings sought actively to limit widows' access to inherited property, with limited success until the statutory "strict settlement at marriage" of the sixteenth century reinstated a nominated form of dower that constituted substantially less than the "reasonable" one-third enjoyed by medieval widows.

Thus, Magna Carta provided a framework whereby feudal property would not be seized by rapacious lords, families would not be beggared by outrageous levels of royal or baronial extortion, and both widows and minor heirs would be protected and financially stable. The Charter not only made royal abuse more difficult, its status as a living document also provided the means for further limitations on royal power.

Some of the most famous clauses of the Great Charter involved social-political issues: the marriage of minors in wardship "without disparage-ment;" judgment by one's peers; the appointment of royal administrators based upon competence and local knowledge rather than favoritism; guarantees that royal courts would not abrogate the powers of local courts; guarantees of speedy and economical justice; the requirement of gaining baronial consent should the king wish to exact an "extraordinary aid" or levy scutage; and so on. Interestingly, those clauses found most compelling by later political theorists were virtually unenforceable in the thirteenth and fourteenth centuries.

Scholars have debated the term "disparagement" when referring to royal control of marriage, but no one has been able to define it to anyone's satisfaction. If disparagement meant that the guardian could not marry his or her ward to someone of lower social status, this would have nulli-fied virtually all the marriages of the highest levels of the baronage for the next three hundred years. If disparagement referred to the marriage of wealthy minors to royal foreign favorites, then some of the most signifi-cant marriages of the thirteenth century would never have occurred. Although these marriages did excite baronial criticism, they could not be prevented from occurring; Magna Carta was powerless in the face of royal prerogative.

Judgment by one's peers in the Middle Ages did not mean a jury made of fellow citizens. It meant that, for example, a dispute between a Welsh-man and an Englishman would be investigated by a "jury" made up of equal numbers of Welshmen and Englishmen. Due process in the modern sense of the term—even the concept of a speedy trial—was completely unknown in the unwieldy legal system of medieval England. Civil litigation could drag on for years, even decades, because of official malfeasance, questionable delaying tactics, and the enthusiasm medieval people felt for "self-help"—the often violent feuding among neighbors that royal legislation attempted to limit. In addition, justices after Magna Carta were as prone to corruption as before, despite its assurances that fair and equitable justice would prevail. For example, Edward I, under pressure to ameliorate the high level of corruption among the justices of the bench, was able to achieve little to improve the level of the royal court's integrity.

Clauses such as these carried no real political power because they were never defined in terms that could be interpreted as statute. Instead, they acted as brakes on royal ambition and provided a context for baronial opposition. Historically, the most significant effect of these particular kinds of clauses in Magna Carta was the abandonment of regular courts "in eyre" during the reign of Edward I. However, a modified version of such circuit courts can be seen in the establishment of "Peace" justices by Edward III in the mid-fourteenth century. "Peace" justices were a hybrid of royal and local administration; they were enrolled by the Crown but were supposed to derive from local authorities.

It is also significant that the development of a "parliamentary" structure, attributed substantially to the reign of Edward I (1272–1307), seems to have had little to do with Magna Carta. Nevertheless, it played a significant *ideological* role in the development of the parliamentary system. Edward I was the first king to summon a broadly representative body to Westminster, but it was nothing like the council of twenty-five barons described in the 1215 Charter. It was also nothing like the baronial council mandated in the 1258 Provisions of Oxford. Instead, Edward summoned not only the baronage to meet in "parlement" (literally, a talk-fest), he also instituted a summons for two "knights of the shire" to be elected to represent each county and representatives from the major cities and towns that had royal charters of incorporation. Thus, although the original Charter might have influenced Edward to enact such a parliamentary system, it cannot be considered the impetus for the structure he devised.

The development of a coherent structure for legislation; the clarification of the relationship between the Crown and the baronage; the ideological foundations of what constituted "good governance": all these were affected by the Great Charter. Magna Carta did not, however, alter the basic social relationships between lords and vassals, lords and tenants, free people and villeins, or the rural aristocracy and the urban elites. Disenfranchised groups, such as women, wards, and the unfree, experienced neither a change in status nor any significant empowerment. Nevertheless, both some of the specific clauses and the ideology behind the charter did provide mechanisms by which the political and judicial systems could be manipulated. Women, for example, could pursue larger dower settlements on the basis of the 1225 redefinition of "reasonable" dower. Welshmen could complain that they were being judged by Englishmen during the Edwardian conquest of Wales in the late thirteenth century. Peasants in the fourteenth century could claim the right to judgment by their peers on the basis of such a mandate in the Great Charter. All free people could petition "Parliament" in the late thirteenth and fourteenth centuries on the basis that the Great Charter was not being respected by people in authority.

Kings and ruling elites in the two centuries following John's reign were also aware of—and concerned about—less advantaged groups gaining opportunities by exploiting the Great Charter. Some of the statutes enacted by rulers such as Edward I, Edward III, and Richard II were designed to limit the impact of Magna Carta's innovations once they had become apparent. The challenge to reasonable dower begun in the fourteenth century had its origins in Edward I's De Donis statute of 1290. The fourteenth-century Statute of Laborers was a response to the inflation of wages following the Black Death, but it also denied to the peasantry the opportunity to use Magna Carta to achieve free status. As "backlashes," such enactments do not implicate the Great Charter as the sole culprit, but they do point to the rhetorical use of Magna Carta as it will come to be conceived by early modern political theorists critiquing the growing absolutist power of the seventeenth-century Stuart kings.

In 1628, Sir Edward Coke, former Chief Justice of both the Common Pleas and the King's Bench, wrote that Magna Carta was "the fountain of all the fundamental Laws of the Realm and therefore it may truly be said of it that it is 'great matter in small content.'" The great nineteenth-century constitutional historian, William Stubbs, claimed, "The Great Charter is the first great public act of the nation, after it has realised its own identity . . . the whole of the constitutional history of England is little more than a commentary on Magna Carta." The opinion of Coke and Stubbs has been shared by virtually every historian and analyst of the British liberal tradition since the 1600s. What makes this one document, which by the seventeenth century was thoroughly anachronistic, so vitally important? Simply put, by the end of the Tudor era Magna Carta achieved the status of myth—the myth of a document that prevents tyranny.

The political climate of seventeenth-century England was extremely volatile. Elizabeth I, the last Tudor monarch, had stabilized her kingdom through a combination of clever manipulation and dedication to the notion of ideological pluralism. Not only were English people permitted to interpret the doctrines of the Church of England broadly (ranging from radical "Puritans" to conservative Anglo-Catholics), they were also able to interpret the relationship between king and government—by this time a bicameral parliamentary system with houses of Commons and Lords—as a fluid and integrated system. When she died, however, her heir was James VI, king of Scotland, whose idea of appropriate royal power clearly reflected the influence of French absolutism rather than English parliamentary monarchy. James I (his title in England) mounted the throne determined to impose his royal will on his new kingdom. He succeeded in doing so, but only by refusing to call a parliamentary election in order to gain tax revenue, and instead filling the royal treasury through short-term solutions such as inventing and selling noble titles.

James' absolutist tendencies in the political arena also appeared with respect to the Church of England. Parliamentary leaders of the House of Commons, locked out of political decision making, were also religious reformers; they desired to "purify" the Church of England of its Catholic ritual and traditions. Although this community was unable to gain advantage during the reign of James I, it came to power during the reign of his son, Charles I, whose royal treasury was full of debts rather than cash.

The clash between Charles I and the House of Commons resulted in a civil war during which a parliamentary army led by the radical Puritan Oliver Cromwell ousted the monarchy and established two decades of military dictatorship. However, Cromwell's death ended the interregnum period; Charles II returned from exile in France and the monarchy was reestablished. Conflict between the "Restoration" monarchy and Parliament did not end, however, and it was exacerbated by the unpopularity of Charles' brother, James II, who succeeded him. Ultimately, a virtually bloodless coup forced James to abdicate in favor of his eldest daughter, Mary, and her husband, William Prince of Orange, who were both thoroughly Protestant and willing to rule in conjunction with a representative Parliament. This was the so-called "Glorious Revolution" of 1688–1689.

It is possible to see many parallels between the chaotic relationship of the King and the baronage in the thirteenth and fourteenth centuries and similarly chaotic relationships between the Stuart kings and Parliament in the seventeenth century. Unlike the earlier era, however, the later period experienced a lively vocal and literary debate as to the relevance of monarchy, the nature of legitimate government, and the role of representative systems in the governance of the realm. Central to this debate was the notion of a "Social Contract" between government and "The People." Both absolutists—conservative and radical alike—and liberals, or "Whigs," posited this idea of a contract, although each had different views of what it constituted.[1] The Whig position was the victor. It justified the overthrow of one monarch—James II—on the basis of his failure to adhere to the demands of the social contract and replaced him with rulers who would reestablish the contract between themselves and the people.

The Whig position could not, however, claim this process as innovation. In the early modern world, innovation was not valued in and of itself; instead, the "liberal" ideologues of the revolution of 1688–89 had to establish their position as one bounded by tradition and precedent. They chose Magna Carta as the perfect instrument to demonstrate the legitimacy of their claims. Their use of the Great Charter, rather than focusing on the specific provisions of the document or its historical context, established it as a kind of icon illustrating a system in which power was vested in the "community of the realm" through "consent of the governed." Thus, the Whigs originated their "constitutional" position with the 1215 document.

Constitutional doctrine in the seventeenth century focuses on specific ideological positions. First, that a reciprocal social contract exists between the ruler and the people: the ruler protects the inalienable rights of life, liberty, and property for the good of the people, and the people agree to relinquish their autonomy and absolute liberty for the sake of such protection. Second, that if a ruler fails to abide by the contract, the people have an obligation to remove him and replace him with someone who will reestablish the appropriate parameters of the contract. Third, that if an individual breaks laws that protect the people from depredations against their lives, liberty, or property, that individual can be removed from the population protected by the social contract and can be punished. Fourth, that the relationship between the ruler and the people is overseen by the principles of due process and consent of the governed through parliamentary representation.

Whig philosophers such as John Locke and Whig historians such as Edward Coke, William Blackstone, and William Stubbs "found" all of these principles extant in Magna Carta. To them, it formed a primitive verification of the existence of a social contract even in the era they termed the "Dark Ages." Looking with hindsight, they traced their own political agenda back to the bad old days of King John and the barons, ignoring the anachronisms inherent in such a view and thereby calcifying Magna Carta into an icon of early modern political liberalism. And there it has remained to this day.

NOTE

1. The terms *conservative* and *liberal* are used in their classical sense. Conservatives favored a traditional approach to monarchy and traditional fiscal institutions, such as state-owned monopolies and mercantilism. Liberals favored a greater share of power between the Crown and Parliament as well as a fiscal policy based on competition in the marketplace and minimal government intervention. Neither group questioned the social and political hierarchies that existed in the early modern world.

SELECTED BIBLIOGRAPHY

Adams, George Burton. "The Origin of the English Constitution, II." *American Historical Review* 13 (1908): 713–730. A classic in the study of the Great Charter, Adams is useful in identifying the relationship between the Charter and the Provisions of Oxford during the reign of Henry III.

Carpenter, D. A. *The Minority of Henry III.* Berkeley and Los Angeles: University of California Press, 1990. There are several useful discussions in this larger work of the role of the regency council headed by Stephen Langton and William Marshal on the reissuing and emendation of the 1215 Charter in 1216, 1217, and 1225.

Holt, James C. *Magna Carta.* 2nd ed. Cambridge: Cambridge University Press, 1992. Holt is the acknowledged expert on Magna Carta and its history, and this is the gold standard of books on the subject.

———, ed. *Magna Carta and the Idea of Liberty.* New York: John Wiley & Sons, 1972. A collection of readings that also includes a good translation of the 1215 Charter, this provides excerpts from the most important analyses of Magna Carta's impact on British history and political theory.

Howard, A. E. Dick. *Magna Carta, Text & Commentary.* rev. ed. Charlottesville: University Press of Virginia, 1998. This is a good analysis with an excellent translation of the 1215 Charter, written specifically for students.

Maddicott, J. R. "Magna Carta and the Local Community 1215–1259." *Past & Present* 102 (1984): 25–65. Places the Great Charter in the context of the conflicts occurring during the reign of Henry III; sees the document as a rallying point for the airing of local grievances and the development of the "gentry's" local political authority.

Painter, Sidney. "Magna Carta." *American Historical Review* 53 (1947): 42–49. A published version of an address made to members of the Medieval Academy of America and the American Historical Association. In this article Painter assesses the impact that King John; William Marshal, Earl of Pembroke; and Stephen Langton, archbishop of Canterbury had on the creation of the 1215 Charter.

Reynolds, Susan. "Magna Carta 1297 and the Legal Use of Literacy." *Historical Research* 62 (1989): 233–244. An important article about the change in the amount of relief from £100 to 100 marks that makes a cogent argument in favor of the change being the result of a clerical error.

Smith, J. Beverley. "Magna Carta and the Charters of the Welsh Princes." *English Historical Review* 99 (1984): 344–362. This article focuses specifically on the clauses in the 1215 Charter that refer to the Welsh nobility.

Stenton, Doris Mary. *After Runnymede: Magna Carta in the Middle Ages.* Charlottesville: University Press of Virginia, 1965. Based on a series of lectures by a noted constitutional historian, this is one of the most accessible analyses of Magna Carta's impact in the hundred years following 1215.

Thompson, Faith. *Magna Carta, Its Role in the Making of the English Constitution 1300–1629.* Minneapolis: University of Minnesota Press, 1948. Thompson's work deals with the impact of Magna Carta in the later Middle Ages and the ways in which the Charter was interpreted as to contain elements of constitutional law such as the concept of *habeus corpus* and the ideas of the Whig party in the seventeenth century.

_____. "Parliamentary Confirmation of the Great Charter." *American Historical Review* 38 (1933): 659–672. Thompson, one of the most important early twentieth-century American historians to study Magna Carta, examines the ways in which Magna Carta was used in petitions to Parliament in the fourteenth century and the confirmations of the Charter made by Parliaments in the later Middle Ages.

Warren, W. L. *King John.* Berkeley and Los Angeles: University of California Press, 1961. A classic study of the last Angevin king, Warren includes a cogent discussion of the events leading to the Charter, the Charter itself, and the resulting disputes between the king, the baronage, and the Church.

3

The Rise of Parliament, 1295–c.1461

INTRODUCTION

Webster's dictionary defines the word *parliament* as "an official or formal conference or council, usually concerned with government or public affairs." The word is derived from the French verb *parler,* meaning to talk or discuss. The Westminster (British) Parliament is sometimes called the "mother of parliaments" because it is the oldest continually functioning deliberative body in the world. As important as Parliament has become, its rise to prominence in the English-speaking world was not rapid; rather, it was a gradual process covering several centuries.

The origins of Parliament are shrouded in the mists of early medieval English history. Most observers trace the modern Parliament to the Anglo-Saxon witenagemot, an advisory body to the kings of that era. At irregular intervals, the monarch called the witenagemot into session. It consisted of the monarch, his closest advisers, and the realm's most important nobles and prelates as selected by the king. Among its limited and ill-defined duties, the witenagemot advised the king and served much like the highest court of the land. It also collaborated with the king in issuing statements that had the force of law. The witenagemot acted as regent when necessary and validated the crowning of the monarch.

With the Norman Conquest of 1066, the Anglo-Saxon witenagemot morphed into the Norman Great Council. As before, the Great Council met irregularly, and both its composition and its responsibilities remained largely unchanged. However, during the thirteenth century the Great Council began its transformation into today's Parliament. By the middle

Arising from obscure origins, the English—later British—Parliament eventually evolved into the oldest and most respected deliberative body in the world. The current House of Parliament was constructed toward the middle of the nineteenth century in a neo-Gothic style designed to evoke memories of Parliament's earliest years. (Reproduced from the Collections of the Library of Congress.)

of that century, the term *parliament* was being used to describe meetings of the Great Council. Moreover, the composition of the Great Council had begun to change. As early as 1254, King Henry III began to summon knights of the shire to attend the Great Council. Although Henry's father, King John, had first summoned the knights in 1213, their attendance at the Great Council became more frequent after 1254. While the knights of the shire belonged to the nobility, they were far removed in wealth and power from the barons, or magnates, who automatically received invitations to the Great Council. Usually of comparatively modest means, the knights of the shire represented the interests of the lower ranks of the nobility and the shires where they resided.

Controversy between Henry III and his barons resulted in another important addition to the Great Council's composition. When Henry and his magnates clashed over the question of money (Henry, having overspent his revenues, demanded that his barons assent to a special tax), the resulting dispute degenerated into civil war. For a time, Simon de Montfort, the king's brother-in-law, eclipsed Henry as the power in England.

During this short period, Simon called a parliament in 1265 to bolster his position. In addition to the usual array of magnates and prelates, Simon also issued invitations to knights of the shire and to burghers, or wealthy and prominent but non-noble residents of England's towns.

At this time, parliament was still an occasion rather than an institution; however, this would soon change. The reign of Edward I (1277–1307) ushered in significant parliamentary modifications. Edward, a competent ruler, loved the intricacies of politics and administration. Consequently, he continually tinkered with Parliament in order to govern England more effectively. Although Edward was by no stretch of the imagination a democrat, he did see advantages in gaining the consent of the governed (or, at least, the upper crust of the governed) in his quest for more revenues and greater support of his policies.

The date commonly given as the beginning of Parliament is 1295. In that year Edward summoned an assembly that became known as the Model Parliament, although it actually served no prototypical function. It included magnates, prelates, and members of the lower clergy; however, the clerics gradually withdrew from attending Parliament in favor of dealing with the monarch through ecclesiastical convocations comprised solely of clergy. The Model Parliament also included two knights from each of England's 40 shires, or counties, and two burgesses, or burghers, from 114 chartered towns or boroughs. London also sent representatives.

With the Model Parliament, the future composition of Parliament became a bit clearer. Two years later, in 1297, the domain of parliamentary competency became a bit clearer as well. Dating back to at least the Norman Great Council, that body had confirmed the monarch's levying of taxes and had given its approval to any extraordinary taxes the monarch wished to impose. Although the king almost always got his way, this parliamentary responsibility had both deepened and broadened during the thirteenth century as the monarchs and the Great Council/Parliament skirmished frequently over money issues. At the 1297 meeting of Parliament, Edward I issued the Confirmation of the Charters. In desperate need of monies for his military campaigns in Scotland and France, Edward reaffirmed the Magna Carta, including its directive that "scutage and aid shall be levied in our kingdom only by the common council of our kingdom," and promised not to levy extraordinary taxes or duties "without the common consent of the realm." Gradually, Parliament was acquiring for itself the power of the purse.

At this time and into the first few decades of the fourteenth century, another important development was under way. Gradually, the knights of the shire came to realize that their interests could best be advanced in alliance with the burghers rather than with the barons. Consequently, the knights and the burghers drew close, hastened in part by the frequent intermarriage that took place between these two different social groups. By about 1340, both the amalgamation of these two groups and their separation from the prelates and magnates were almost complete. The phrase "men of Commons" began to appear. Thus Parliament divided into what would become the House of Commons and the House of Lords.

Parliament's importance increased dramatically during the fourteenth century thanks to the skyrocketing cost of war. During that century and beyond, the English kings found themselves engaged in almost constant warfare. This is particularly true after 1340, when the Hundred Years' War inspired a series of English monarchs to mount military campaigns in France. While England won most of the battles, France won the war. All of this proved costly, and generating money to prosecute the war required the English kings to rely increasingly on Parliament, but especially on Commons.

By virtue of both tradition and documents such as Magna Carta and the Confirmation of the Charters, Parliament exercised some control over the realm's finances. Now, with the huge expenditures associated with fielding an army, the monarchy repeatedly had to request additional or extraordinary taxes from Parliament. Parliament soon came to realize the powerful position it occupied and began to refuse these requests for money unless or until the king met other demands that Parliament put forward. In other words, grants of money to the king not only had to be approved by Parliament, they were also contingent upon the king doing Parliament's will. By the end of the century, Parliament was also taking an active role in auditing the king's funds and designating precisely the purposes for each grant. Meanwhile, the House of Commons gradually overshadowed the House of Lords in matters concerning money. By 1395 parliamentary grants of money were being made to the king "...by the Commons with the advice and assent of the Lords." Commons' ascendancy over money matters was now almost complete.

During the fourteenth century, Parliament also greatly expanded its heretofore almost nonexistent legislative function. For many years Parliament and its predecessors had passed on to the king private petitions from individuals or groups seeking redress of grievances. Beginning in 1327, however, Parliament began to draw up its own petitions regarding matters of general interest to the realm. Passing them on to the king, Parliament expected him to consider these petitions seriously. From this beginning, it was only a short step for the House of Commons to begin to link these petitions to its grants of money. In short order, a quid pro quo developed whereby the granting of the king's request for money required the king to accept Parliament's petitions, which usually dealt with matters other than money.

However, all too frequently the monarch ignored or in some way subverted Parliament's petitions. This spurred Parliament to substitute statutes, or bills, for petitions. Traditionally, England's kings had been able to issue royal ordinances on their own. However, from at least the time of Edward I, royal statutes, dealing with matters of fundamental importance, replaced royal ordinances in importance. Although Edward and those who followed him might draft the statutes, they were usually careful to make certain that Parliament gave its assent. For years, Parliament routinely rubber-stamped these royal statutes. However, during the fourteenth century—in response to the king's mishandling of parliamentary petitions—Parliament began to initiate the process of statute making. By the end of the century, Parliament (specifically the House of Commons) began the legislative process. As the procedure evolved, bills or statutes would originate in the House of Commons and, if successful there, move to the House of Lords for approval and then on to the king for his signature.

During the fourteenth century, Parliament also first assumed something of a policy-making function for the kingdom. Of course, controlling the purse had a significant effect on royal policy, but beginning with the so-called "Good Parliament" of 1376, Parliament took more proactive steps. Specifically, it invoked a heretofore unknown "right" of impeachment. Under impeachment, Commons could indict the king's ministers for a variety of actions including "high crimes and misdemeanors" and pass the accused along to the House of Lords for trial where conviction might result in the death penalty. Such parliamentary power had a chilling effect on royal behavior, including the making and execution of policy.

Many regard the year 1399 as marking the height of Parliament's power. In that year it ratified the deposition of Richard II and his replacement by Henry IV, a usurper from the House of Lancaster. Certainly Parliament continued to flex its muscles through the first six decades of the fifteenth century when Lancastrian kings sat on England's throne. During those decades, Parliament secured for its members freedom of speech during parliamentary debate and freedom from arrest on civil charges during that body's sessions and while traveling to or from Parliament. Parliament also began to set standards for the selection of members to the Commons.

In 1430 it ruled that any freeholder possessing land generating an annual income of forty shillings had the right to elect the knights of the shire. Each town that had representation in Parliament was given the right to set its own electoral regulations.

The era of Parliament's ascendancy came to an end with the arrival of the Yorkist kings and their successors from the House of Tudor. Under these monarchs, Parliament found itself eclipsed until the seventeenth century when it repeatedly and successfully challenged the absolutist claims of the Stuart kings. Nevertheless, by the middle of the fifteenth century the foundations of the Parliament that exists today were firmly established.

INTERPRETIVE ESSAY
Mark K. Vaughn

The image of Parliament conjures up visions of an august body of common folk in conflict with the king or at the very least trying to restrain the king, but the rise of Parliament was actually very different. Parliament was an extension of royal authority, a tool of the king designed to assist in routine governmental business that threatened to overwhelm an increasingly centralized monarchy. Parliament also served as a means to pry money out the newest class of moneyed people in England. Parliament did not arise out of some baronial need to control the king, but rather as an attempt by the barony to retain their feudal prerogative to counsel the king and as a royal means to more efficiently run the kingdom.

The rise of Parliament was not a single, datable event. Rather it was a series of events that, taken together, form an evolution not a revolution. The slow, vacillating development of Parliament does not detract from its importance, as it is one of the most significant events in the history of Britain and the world. Its impact can be seen more so in the centuries since the Middle Ages as the English Parliament has been used time and again as the prototype for parliamentary forms of governments throughout the world. In short, the rise of Parliament is as noteworthy for the social changes it signifies as for the changes that it initiates.

The rise of Parliament heralded significant economic, social, and political changes in Britain that had taken place over the previous two centuries. The economic changes of the twelfth century brought about dramatic changes in feudal society. Accompanying these changes in society were changes in warfare that necessitated larger and larger expenditures that strained the traditional sources of royal revenue. The king took advantage of these economic and social changes to find new sources of money. In turn, the changes in feudal society necessitated changes in the political structure of England; in return for money a say in political affairs was demanded. These essential developments all came together to effect change in the thirteenth century. The evolution of Parliament began as a result of the rise of towns and a dramatic increase in the medieval English economy, which led to the restructuring of feudal society and a change in the relationship between the crown and community of the realm.

It was the economic recovery—ongoing since the twelfth century—that prompted many of the changes in feudal society and the accompanying political transformations. The new importance of towns best reflected the new economic trends. Towns such as Bristol and Chepstow were established originally as market towns; others, such as Kingston-upon-Hull and Montgomery, were established for their strategic location. Some thirteenth-century towns were built for military reasons. Royal towns such as Deganwy, Flint, Aberystwyth, Rhuddlan, Caernarfon, and Conway were built in Wales to secure English rule there, while Berwick and Carlisle were built to supply English armies on campaign in Scotland. Other towns were relocations of existing towns. Winchelsea, one of the Cinque Ports threatened by the encroaching sea, was moved; Portchester relocated to Portsmouth to take advantage of a deeper, more accessible harbor. Not all of the towns were new, as some of them had existed since Roman times. Towns and cities such as London, York, Lincoln, and Chester underwent a renaissance with the upswing in trade.

What these towns all had in common was that they provided a focal point for the new economy. They were centrally located places where merchants could sell goods collected in the surrounding countryside or brought in from afar to be traded, bought, or sold. Another common trait was that these towns were usually granted charters that guaranteed the towns' liberties and trading privileges and encouraged merchants to settle.

The merchants were the architects of and power behind the economic revival. Their efforts to increase their personal wealth through the acquisition and sale of goods began a new commercial revolution. In the early eleventh century, merchants had operated individually, collecting and selling their goods; by the twelfth century, these merchants now worked within guilds, operating vast mercantile enterprises importing and exporting goods from all over Europe. For England the wool trade represented the foundation of the economy. Sheep, raised throughout the north of England and Wales, produced between fifteen and twenty million pounds of wool per year for the cloth manufacturers of Flanders. This represented an enormous source of wealth for England and her merchants. But for all their money and power, they were still considered members of the third estate and unceremoniously lumped with the peasants. A new "middle class" was forming, but it did not yet have a place in feudal society.

Joining the merchants in the middle class was another new group composed of educated, nonreligious professionals—lay clerks and lawyers. These royal officials were educated as their clerical predecessors had been, but they were not members of the first estate—the clergy. Beginning in the twelfth century, the government bureaucracy was becoming increasingly professional and centralized. New clerks and lawyers were a welcome addition to the royal court as the routine business of government began to overwhelm the existing structure. In the courts, the king assumed control over the entire judicial system under a common law and sought to extend his income through fines. As with the merchants, a middle class found no place in the tripartite feudal societal scheme, but that feudal framework was rapidly declining.

The rise of the merchant and professional urban bureaucrat class (burgesses) was not without difficulty. The class system, or more appropriately the "status system" in England, was based on three orders or estates. The first estate was composed of those who pray—the clergy, ranging from the wealthiest archbishops and abbots down to the poorest monks and parish priests. The second estate was composed of those who fight—the landed aristocracy who also provided the military might of the realm and ranged from the wealthiest earls down to poorer, landless knights. Finally, the third order was composed of everybody else—mainly the peasants and of course the new merchants and professionals. Mobility between the classes was almost nonexistent. As the twelfth and thirteenth centuries progressed, the burgesses, with their new money and prestige, did not fit into the traditional class system. Additionally, lay clerics sought the same recognition and recompense that their religious "brethren" enjoyed. Both groups felt themselves far above the peasants and on a par with the lesser clergy or nobles. The feudal society, based on these three orders, was obsolete and could not easily accommodate the merchant and professional class. In order to fit in a middle class there would have to be some societal adaptations. As social mobility was not a realistic option, the new middle class sought a voice for the power they associated with their money. While it was true that the merchants had considerable amounts of money, in thirteenth-century England that did not necessarily translate into social mobility or political power; or at least that was the case until the king developed an insatiable need for money.

In addition to the changes in the third estate, the second estate was also going through a major transformation. Minor rural landowners, the gentry, were achieving a sense of financial independence and a voice of their own. The gentry represented a new, educated, and politically active social stratification within their order. Additionally, major landowners, the barons, were also in the midst of great social change. The barons, with the fracturing of their order and the rise of merchants, were quickly losing their voice at the king's court.

The feudal offices, originally held by the major landowners, were gradually being filled by professional, nonlandholding ministers friendly to the crown. The offices of the Exchequer, Chancery, Wardrobe, and the Justiciary were no longer occupied by men who had held them by hereditary title. The nature of the offices, in fact the entire king's court, was changing. England was becoming a centralized, bureaucratic monarchy. The holders of these major offices began to replace the barons in the king's council and left them without a say in either the routine or major foreign or domestic decisions of the realm. These trends in aristocratic leadership were clearly evident during the reigns of John and Henry III as the contempt the kings felt for the magnates led to a breakdown in relations between the king and his new ministers on one side and the barons on the other. The break was most clearly evident in the series of civil wars, known as the "Barons' Wars" that plagued both of their reigns.

John and Henry III had attempted many schemes to maintain the lands they ruled and to extend the prestige of their kingship. Many, if not most, of these schemes did not meet with much success. John lost Normandy (1204), Anjou (1205), and Brittany (1206) and witnessed the defeat of his allies at Bouvines (1214). Henry III's reign saw the loss of Poitou (1224), the abortive and costly attempt to secure the throne of Sicily for his second son, Edmund (1254–1257), and repeated defeats in Wales. Increasingly distressed by the monarchy's defeats, the barons attributed much of the problem to the king's failure to consult with them. In response to these debacles, the barons of the realm refused to participate in these royal adventures or to contribute any further money unless the king agreed to accept their counsel. In fact, Magna Carta (1215) and the Provisions of Oxford (1258) both contained clauses designed to secure the barons' prerogative to counsel and advise the king in matters pertaining to the administration of the realm.

Thus, during the reigns of John and Henry III the significance of Parliament's rise was linked to the struggle of the hereditary holders of the great offices to retain their positions. Meanwhile, the king moved to replace barons with professional ministers or, in some instances, royal favorites who served at his pleasure. The king's actions removed the great office holders from the royal council but not from the newly developing Parliament. The main results of this move were the establishment of a centralized government headed by appointed, professional ministers who also served on the royal council and a Parliament where the major barons met to advise and counsel the king. The barons were unhappy with the new arrangements and their discontent helped to establish a tradition of opposition to the king in the newly evolving Parliament.

The tradition of opposition to the king remained fairly muted, only gaining importance during the rule of weak monarchs such as John or Henry III. For example, it is clearly evident in the baronial factions of the Barons' War and the period of Simon de Montfort's rule between the Battle of Lewes (1264) and the Battle of Evesham (1265). However, this does not mean that Parliament developed a true sense of an opposition role. In fact, throughout the remainder of Henry III's reign after 1265, Parliament became an extension of royal power and a tool of the crown to garner support for royal projects. It should be noted that during this period, Edward, the future king, carried out many edicts in his father's name. Parliament in the hands of a strong ruler was a tool for the monarchy, but in the hands of a weak ruler it served to provide a necessary restraint.

Following the Battle of Lewes, where Simon de Montfort captured Henry III, the reform movement collapsed as the individual barons pursued their self-interests. As de Montfort began to lose both the support and the money of his baronial allies, he sought to bolster his position through the summoning of a Parliament as had been proposed in the Provisions of Oxford. To this Parliament de Montfort invited many of the third estate's wealthier members. In short, de Montfort sought support—financial and political—from the merchants, especially those of London. In return he would grant them a say in the affairs of the realm—political power. It was a desperate ploy, but one that would be tried again in a more deliberate manner by Edward I. With de Montfort's defeat at the Battle of Evesham and the restoration of Henry III, the initiative failed; but Edward, soon to be king, learned that the support of *all* the estates was critical to success in domestic policy, diplomacy, and war. During Edward I's reign, the concept of Parliament as a tool of the crown became more firmly established as Edward sought to use Parliament to generate support and money from the new merchant class.

Throughout the thirteenth century, the costs for almost every venture the king embarked upon rose dramatically. The new economy made the cost of administering the kingdom that much more expensive. In addition to the government, the military was also becoming more professional. Wars had always been one of the most expensive ventures a king might undertake, but in the thirteenth century the expense of waging war and the frequency in which it was waged became the crucible for social and political change.

As noted, the relative lack of success that both John and Henry III experienced in diplomacy and on the battlefield did not inspire the nobility's confidence. As a result, the barons were less likely to continue to contribute cash to causes doomed to fail. The accession of Edward I in 1272 changed this. Edward, in the years since 1265, had matured and earned a reputation as a decisive and efficient military leader. After his coronation, he immediately began to correct the ills of the previous two administrations. He maintained the professional, centralized administration of the major offices, but he frequently summoned the major landholders to discuss affairs of the realm. In military matters Edward was completely successful, managing to conquer Wales in two campaigns (1276–1277 and 1282–1283). The wars of conquest that Edward waged were remarkably more expensive then any in the past. Edward's success could be attributed to the overwhelming force that he brought to bear on an enemy. Moreover, this large army was always well supplied. Following the campaigns, Edward undertook an extensive castle-building program throughout Wales to secure his conquests. Both the huge, well-supplied armies and the castle-building program were expensive, and Edward quickly exhausted all his revenues.

Thirteenth-century royal finances rested upon many different sources of income, including long-established feudal ones such as knighting of the eldest son, marriage of the eldest daughter, judicial fines, escheats and wardships, and scutage (payment in lieu of military service). These ancient feudal rights only provided a small part of the income the king required. The meager royal income could be augmented by imposing a tallage (tax) on the royal lands and towns, or by the occasional request of grants of an aid from the nobility (based on moveable property) or the clergy (based on rental income from real estate). Prior to the reign of Edward I, these last forms of taxation were used infrequently and only when the realm faced a dire threat as Parliament had to consent to each grant. With the triple threat from the French, the Welsh and the Scots in 1294, Edward had to go beyond even these emergency measures.

In 1294, having already exhausted both the normal revenues and baronial and clerical grants, Edward desperately needed to raise new funds. As Edward's predecessors had already discovered, it was rather difficult to squeeze the barons and clergy continually for more money; consequently, a new source of funds had to be found. At this point Edward began to look at the merchants again. He decided to impose a new sales tax, a new import and export tax, and a new customs tax on wool. Edward approached the barons with these new revenue-generating ideas and they approved, as they would not be impacted directly. The merchants, however, were alarmed at the extent of the new taxes and protested. As he still needed to fight a war, Edward wanted to gain the merchants' cooperation rather than alienate them since they were to play a significant role in helping to transport and supply his troops. Edward reduced the amount of the wool tax and decided to summon Parliament the following year. He was intent on making the successful prosecution of the war a matter that concerned the entire realm.

The Parliament of 1295, known as the "Model Parliament," set the standard by which future Parliaments were summoned. Following the procedure first implemented by Simon de Montfort in 1265, Edward summoned the burgesses and gentry (knights of the shire) in addition to the usual clerical and lay representatives to Parliament. The estates met together and eventually consented to grants of approximately ten percent from the clergy, the barons, and the towns. By summoning people other than barons and clergy, Edward created a major precedent and helped to establish an atmosphere of cooperation among the three estates under the king.

War in Gascony, and the Welsh and Scottish campaigns that it triggered, placed unprecedented demands on the king to raise sufficient funds from the realm. Edward requested and was granted several taxes between 1294 and 1297. With the threatened loss of Gascony and Edward's record of military success, the barons felt compelled to contribute. They were worried, however, that the regularity of the demands for contributions would create a precedent for an annual tax. Edward had to be able to outspend the French if he were to compete successfully with King Philip of France. Phillip had a richer kingdom at his disposal, but he did not have the developed tax system that the English had. Although the barons were unhappy contributing as much money as Edward demanded, they could hardly refuse the king; it was difficult to argue with Edward's success and, besides, he was looking out for the interest of the realm. In order to get the consent required, Edward summoned Parliament nine times between 1294 and 1297. One of the most interesting aspects of the rise of Parliament is that the implementation of new taxes did not become a precedent; rather, the summoning of Parliament—one consisting of members from all three estates—to consent to the new taxes became the precedent.

Throughout Europe in the thirteenth century, Roman law was rediscovered and reintroduced into the Church and courts of the various realms. This was the result of the reappearance of Aristotle's works, namely *Politics*, and the consequent summary and evaluation of his writings by Christian philosophers such as Thomas Aquinas. Aquinas' *Government of Princes* (1270) was one of the most influential. It discussed the two important Roman maxims; "that which touches all should be agreed upon by all" (*Quod omnes tangit ab omnibus approbetur*) and "that which pleases the prince has the force of law" (*Quod principi placuit, legis vigorem habuit*). These two maxims seem to contradict each other, but in the mindset of the thirteenth century they actually complemented each other. A king, although he was responsible to no one but God, was expected to rule justly and not seek personal profit. Kings should rule according to law and with the counsel of the realm's wise men. In England the evolution of Parliament, with its history of limited opposition to the king, followed this maxim closely. There was never any question of approving a request based on a threat to the realm, but there was, however, a great difference of opinion over what actually constituted a threat and what was personal enrichment for the king. The rise of Parliament then, symbolizes the change in the doctrine of authority that was taking place all over Europe.

England was not the only European state to develop a parliament. The reintroduction of Roman law was also accompanied by an evolution of royal courts into various kinds of class-based representative assemblies throughout Europe. Feudal society was changing as monarchies centralized power and sought new financing from the merchants and gentry. The aristocracy did not give up power willingly and the kings frequently empowered the national assemblies to help them consolidate royal authority. These assemblies, in addition to the granting of taxes, also dealt with similar items of business such as judicial and legislative matters, domestic and foreign policy issues and the resolution of royal succession matters. With so many similarities between the various national assemblies, it is hard to see how the English Parliament becomes the "mother of all parliaments."

There were two main differences between the English Parliament and the other national assemblies. One was the separation of Parliament into two separate houses. In the mid-fourteenth century, after the lower clergy had already begun to hold their own assemblies (convocations), the gentry found that they had more in common with the burgesses than with the larger landowners. As a result, the burgesses and gentry began to meet separately from the barons. This led to the development of a bicameral (that is, two-house) parliamentary system.

The other difference was the tradition of opposition that had evolved in the English parliamentary system. Limited opposition to the king and taxation, evident since the reigns of John and Henry III, had solidified during the crisis of 1297. Parliament, fearing the precedent of a yearly tax, refused Edward's request for another round of taxation. Eventually, Edward was able to convince Parliament to consent to a tax on the condition that he confirm the charters (the Charter of the Forests and the Magna Carta with its reissues) and guarantee that the tax would not become an annual occurrence. This opposition to regular taxation continued on through the reigns of Edward II and Edward III. The practice of opposition, especially to taxation, was somewhat contradictory as the Parliament was a royal expedient and it would be expected that if the king called Parliament to consent to his taxes, then the assembly had to cooperate.

With Parliament, England now had a mechanism to tax the burgesses and gentry of the realm legitimately, and the burgesses now had a say in royal foreign and domestic decision making. Furthermore, it was in both Parliament and the king's interest to keep the economy moving forward as a stronger economy meant more income for both. This mechanism gave the English the advantage when, in 1337 (during Edward III's reign), the Hundred Years' War began. England could mobilize the financial and physical resources of the realm more efficiently than France could. Additionally, it was through Parliament that the war became a common endeavor for the entire realm.

Frequently, when Parliament did grant a tax it placed requirements on the king in return. As a result, the consent to taxation became equated with the presentation of petitions and eventually the passage of legislation. These additional obligations that Parliament imposed on the king led to a reduction in the number of Parliaments summoned. As a result, the fifteenth- and sixteenth-century Yorkist, Lancastrian, and Tudor kings summoned fewer and fewer Parliaments.

Following the fourteenth century, the problems that the king faced with Parliament caused him to summon that body only at times of extreme emergency. In fact, through the end of the fifteenth century the idea of the king "living of his own," that is financing his household and personal expenditure through his own income and not that derived from national taxation, became the objective for both the king and Parliament. Even though the statutory regulations stipulated that there be three Parliaments a year, kings frequently summoned Parliament only when absolutely necessary to avoid interference with domestic and foreign policy. This trend peaked during the reigns of Henry VII (1485–1509), who only called seven

Parliaments in his twenty-four year reign, and Henry VIII (1509–1547), who only summoned twenty-eight Parliaments in his thirty-eight year reign. Parliament was not distinct from the king; it was a tool he employed at his pleasure. Later, when in dire need of money the seventeenth-century Stuart kings had to summon Parliament, it came with a greater political cost.

The medieval Parliament was not the same as its fifteenth- and sixteenth-century successors. The medieval doctrine of consent was replaced with the early modern concept of absolutism. The maxim of "that which pleases the prince has the force of law" supplanted the maxim of consent. Additionally, the medieval Parliament was not self-perpetuating; it could not control its future as it was summoned and dismissed at the pleasure of the king. Following the successful reigns of the Tudors, in the seventeenth century the Stuarts ascended the English throne with a decidedly Scottish view of kingship. These monarchs believed that they embodied the state's sovereignty, ruled by divine right, and summoned Parliament only when it was absolutely necessary.

The definitive break between the proto-Parliament of the Middle Ages and the sovereign Parliament of the Early Modern period occurred in 1688 when Parliament offered the throne of England to Mary Stuart, the Protestant daughter of the current king, James II, and her husband, William of Orange. In accepting the offer, William and Mary also accepted the supremacy of Parliament over the crown. Britain had instituted a constitutional monarchy, one where the king ruled by the consent of the governed and shared power with Parliament as determined by rule of law. The doctrine of consent of the governed replaced absolute rule. Parliament passed the Bill of Rights guaranteeing freedom of speech, the right to hold elections, and respect for the rule of law. Even though the institution of monarchy had been preserved with the help of the aristocracy, the middle class had also managed to establish a permanent voice in the domestic and foreign policies of Great Britain.

The rise of Parliament was one of the most significant events in the history of Britain. Parliament was a contrivance of government, designed to get the consent required for taxation, however, it had the additional benefit of giving voice to a new group of people, the burgesses and gentry, that would eventually form the middle class. Once the middle class gained a voice, it was not long before it leveraged a stronger say in political matters. These early Parliaments were responsible for promoting legislation, assisting in legal rulings, advising the king on important matters of the realm, and, more importantly, consenting to taxation. This close cooperation, although it would go through some serious trials, would result in a government favorable to economic stability and growth.

In some ways, allowing the new middle class to have a voice in the decision-making process permitted the earlier resolution of social issues and interclass conflict. However, it did not end the threat of an absolute monarchy. Nevertheless, instead of civil insurrection and social revolution in the manner of the French Revolution, the rise of Parliament resulted in the English Civil War and the Glorious Revolution. While traumatic events, the civil war and the Glorious Revolution were not nearly as bloody, disruptive, and bitter as the French Revolution, nor did they plunge all of Europe into war.

One lesson to be learned from the rise of Parliament is that power is both desired and elusive. In the case of England, kings such as Edward I were willing to share a bit of power with a representative institution (Parliament) in order to achieve something resembling a national consensus and, more importantly at that time, to gain access through taxation to new sources of wealth. In turn, the new members of Parliament were willing to part with considerable amounts of cash to achieve a voice in political affairs. Later, as Parliament grew in stature and became a fixture in the British political system, the king drew it into close cooperation to help him centralize the government and establish a form of government that could mobilize the people and their money to support domestic and foreign policies favorable to economic development.

The stability and promotion of the new middle class was key to the success of the British parliamentary system. The system, which by its very nature favored the middle class and a strong economy, resulted in the creation of an extensive empire. The empire's colonies, after they achieved their independence through peaceful means or revolt, sought to replicate the parliamentary system. Even the United States has a political system that features a bicameral legislative national assembly. In 1999 at the close of the twentieth century and just over seven hundred years after the Model Parliament met, Britain established a Welsh National Assembly and a Scottish Parliament. These devolved "parliaments" (technically the Welsh body is not quite a parliament) may be joined by a representative assembly for Northern Ireland (implemented but suspended in 2002) and even an English Parliament all under the auspices of the British Parliament. In larger terms, as the British Empire spread across the globe, the parliamentary system spread with it. The ultimate legacy, then, was the proliferation of Britain's parliamentary system throughout the world. The sun may have set on the British Empire, but it has not yet set on the legacy of its parliamentary system.

SELECTED BIBLIOGRAPHY

Brown, A. L. *The Government of Late Medieval England, 1272–1461.* London: Edward Arnold, 1989. Discusses the development of government in England between the reign of Edward I and the end of Henry VI's first reign.

Carpenter, D. A. "King, Magnates, and Society: The Personal Rule of King Henry III, 1234–1258." *Speculum,* 60 (1985): 39–70. Details the relationships between Henry III and the community of the realm.

_____. *The Reign of Henry III.* London: Hambledon Press, 1996. This important work provides a detailed analysis of Henry's government and the Barons' War.

Clarke, M. V. *Medieval Representation and Consent.* New York: Russell and Russell, 1964. A detailed analysis of the doctrine of consent and its role in the development of Parliament.

Davies, R. G., and Jeffrey H. Denton, eds. *The English Parliament in the Middle Ages.* Manchester: Manchester University Press, 1981. An excellent collection of essays from the leading scholars of the history of Parliament, this book focuses on the twelfth through early sixteenth centuries.

Frame, Robin. *The Political Development of the British Isles, 1100–1400.* Oxford: Oxford University Press, 1990. This book compares and contrasts political developments in England, Scotland, Wales, and Ireland.

Fryde, N. M., and Edward Miller. *Historical Studies of the English Parliament.* Vol. 1, *Origins to 1399.* Cambridge: Cambridge University Press, 1970. Covering the period from the origins of Parliament through the accession of Henry IV, this volume contains a series of essays from the leading scholars of the history of Parliament.

Harriss, G. L. *King, Parliament, and Public Finance in Medieval England to 1369.* Oxford: Clarendon Press, 1975. This work traces the centralization of the English government, the development of taxation, and the evolution of Parliament as a result of military requirements.

Jenks, Edward. *Edward Plantagenet: The English Justinian or the Making of the Common Law.* London: G. P. Putnam, 1902. This work details the role of Edward I in the centralization of the English legal system under the crown and the consolidation and standardization of English common law.

Jolliffe, J. E. A. *The Constitutional History of Medieval England: From the English Settlement to 1485.* 4th ed. New York: W. W. Norton, 1961. This classic volume covers the constitutional history of England from the Saxons through the deposition of Richard III. One of its most important aspects is its treatment of feudalism and the changing nature of the king's relationship to the community of the realm.

Keir, David L. *The Constitutional History of Modern Britain Since 1485.* 4th ed. New York: W. W. Norton, 1960. This venerable volume covers the constitutional history of England from the deposition of Richard III through the early twentieth century.

Maddicott, John R. "The English Peasantry and the Demands of the Crown, 1294–1341." In *Landlords, Peasants, and Politics in Medieval England,* 285–359. Edited by T. H. Aston. Cambridge: Cambridge University Press, 1987. This essay details the crown's relationship to the peasantry, stressing the impact on the peasants of royal exactions for war and daily requirements.

Miller, Edward. "Government Economic Policies and Public Finance: 1000–1500." In *The Fontana Economic History of Europe: The Middle Ages,* 339–373. Edited by Carlo M. Cipolla. London: Collins/Fontana Books, 1972. This important work details the relationship between taxation and its impact on the English economy and the royal administration.

————. "War, Taxation and the English Economy in the Late Thirteenth and Early Fourteenth Centuries." In *War and Economic Development,* 11–31. Edited by J.M. Winter. Cambridge: Cambridge University Press, 1975. Focusing on the critical period from Edward I's reign to the opening phase of the Hundred Years' War, this essay discusses the impact of taxation for war on the English economy.

Pollard, A.F. *The Evolution of Parliament.* 2nd ed. New York: Russell and Russell, 1920. This classic text covers the various aspects of the medieval English Parliament. In some of the more controversial essays it argues against the concept of the three estates and peerage as well as Edward I's Model Parliaments.

Powicke, Frederick Maurice. *King Henry III and the Lord Edward: The Community of the Realm in the Thirteenth Century,* 2 vols. Oxford: Clarendon Press, 1947. This classic work details the relationship that Henry III and Edward I had with the barons, and describes the descent of England into the Barons' Wars.

Prestwich, Michael. *Edward I.* New Haven: Yale University Press, 1988. This seminal work dissects the reign of Edward I. It is also contains a noteworthy chapter on the Council and Parliament.

————. *War, Politics, and Finance, under Edward I.* London: Faber and Faber, 1972. This important volume examines the impact of war on political developments that occurred during the reign of Edward I. It details the methods that Edward I employed to mobilize his resources and finances for war.

Sayles, George O. *The King's Parliament of England.* New York: W.W. Norton, 1974. Part of Norton's Historical Controversies Series, this book details the evolution of Parliament, focusing on the judicial aspects of its role in government.

Spuford, Peter. *Origins of the English Parliament.* New York: Barnes and Noble, 1967. Part of the Problems and Perspectives Series, this is one of the most important collections of essays detailing the origins and development of Parliament. The essays, written by the field's leading scholars, are accompanied by primary sources.

Tout, T.F. *Chapters in the Administrative History of Mediaeval England: The Wardrobe, the Chamber and the Small Seals,* 4 vols. Manchester: Manchester University Press, 1937. This classic work details the evolution of the English government. It is comprehensive and manages to explain all of the various offices in great detail.

4

The Hundred Years' War, 1337–1453

INTRODUCTION

The Hundred Years' War pitted England's kings against their French counterparts in an intermittent struggle that extended through the better part of two centuries. It affords an excellent example of a country winning the important battles yet, nevertheless, losing the war. Most of the major battles—Crécy (1346), Poitiers (1356), and Agincourt (1415)—resulted in spectacular victories for the English forces, but when the Hundred Years' War petered out in the middle of the fifteenth century, France emerged triumphant.

Although 1337 is the traditional starting date for the conflict, its origins extend back at least several decades earlier. Toward the end of the thirteenth century, problems that had long plagued Anglo-French relations grew more serious. At that time, the French king, Philip the Fair, entered into an alliance with Scotland directed against England. This inaugurated a Franco-Scottish relationship that was to last for almost three centuries. Acting through its Scottish ally, France could not only outflank England but also stir up trouble and even menace England's vulnerable northern regions.

France also posed an increased threat to England's economic stability. Much of England's prosperity depended upon its ability to export raw wool to Flanders to be woven into cloth and reexported back to England. While the merchants and artisans of Flanders enjoyed warm relations with their English producers and shippers, the ruling counts of Flanders were vassals of the French crown. This proved worrisome to the English, especially in light of royal France's policy of expanding and centralizing

Throughout the Middle Ages, mounted knights in armor usually enjoyed great success when attacking lightly armed infantry. During the Hundred Years' War, however, the English used the longbow and skilled pikemen to inflict crushing defeats
on mounted French noblemen at the Battles of Crécy (1346), Poitiers (1356), and
Agincourt (1415). (Reproduced from the Collections of the Library of Congress.)

the state. The potential absorption of Flanders into France frightened the
English.

However, the most important irritant in Anglo-French relations was the
question of English holdings in France proper. Dating back to the Norman
Conquest of England in 1066, those who wore the English crown also
ruled territories in France as vassals of the French king. Specifically, at the
start of the fourteenth century the English king, Edward I, held Gascony,
Anjou, Guyenne, and other French lands as fiefs from the French king. Put
simply, the French monarchy wanted to absorb these lands into an
expanding French state while the English crown was determined to hang
onto its valuable French territories at all costs.

During the first few decades of the fourteenth century, a dynastic mud-
dle brought these smoldering issues to a head and provided an excuse for
a war that the monarchs and much of the nobility of both England and
France had rather eagerly anticipated. At that time, feudalism was still the
dominant political system and, accordingly, birthright meant everything.
In 1314 Philip the Fair died. The French crown then passed in succession
to his three sons, each of whom died without male heirs. By 1328 the
French ruling house of Capet was extinct. Under primogeniture, the
crown should have gone to Philip's grandson by his daughter Isabella; but
this grandson was King Edward III of England, and the French nobility
would have none of that. Instead, they supported the claim of Philip's

nephew from the House of Valois. This nephew claimed the French throne in 1328 as Philip VI. A reluctant Edward of England accepted this outcome, but in 1337, when Philip VI attempted to confiscate Edward's French holdings, the English king resisted and war, which probably would have come about anyway, broke out. Three years later, citing his relationship to Philip the Fair, Edward made formal claim to the French throne. For the next 400 years, subsequent English monarchs would make this claim repeatedly if only ceremonially.

The first battle of any consequence during this initial phase of what would become the Hundred Years' War occurred at sea. In 1340, at the Battle of Sluys, what passed at that time for the English fleet defeated its French opponent, thereby giving England control over the English Channel and an opportunity for repeated invasions of France.

Six years later, in 1346, England achieved one of its most electrifying military triumphs. Edward, leading a marauding band of English raiders numbering perhaps 10,000, the vast majority of whom were yeoman archers, met a French force of three to four times this size at the Battle of Crécy in northern France. Taking a defensive position, the English annihilated the attacking French knights. The English relied on the longbow, a five-foot bow made of yew wood capable of shooting a three-foot arrow that could pierce a knight's armor at 200 yards. Using the longbow to disorganize and unhorse the French knights, the English foot soldiers destroyed their aristocratic adversaries. The contemporary French chronicler Jean Froissart noted that the English fired their bows with such force and frequency that their arrows fell like snow upon the hapless French.

Having learned nothing from this defeat, the French suffered its repeat ten years later at the Battle of Poitiers. This time Edward's eldest son, the famous "Black Prince," led the English. Although the French outnumbered the English by perhaps ten to one, the results were the same. The English were so successful at Poitiers that they even captured the French king, John II, and many of his retainers and held them for ransom.

For France, the situation was now bleak: their king was captive; English raiders devastated the French countryside; peasants rose in revolt; noblemen challenged royal authority, and Paris asserted its independence. A shaken France sued for peace in 1360. The Treaty of Bretigny marked a signal triumph for England. By its terms, Edward was recognized as absolute master of Gascony, Poitou, Limousin, Calais, Guyenne, and Ponthieu; no longer would he have to pay homage to the French king for these lands. Furthermore, France paid a kingly ransom of three million gold crowns for John II. In return for these concessions, Edward relinquished his claim to the French throne.

Although the English king now found himself in nominal possession of about one-third of France, his position was quite precarious. England was grossly overextended, and although most French disliked their monarchy they hated the English even more. Under John's successor, the able Charles V, France employed a primitive form of guerrilla warfare to eat away slowly but methodically at England's gains. At the time of Edward's death in 1377, English holdings in France had shrunk to the ports of Calais, Bordeaux, Cherbourg, and Bayonne. Exhausted and bankrupt, the English and French kings now placed their feud on the back burner in order to confront more pressing domestic matters.

Beginning in 1347, the Black Plague swept through Europe like the very wrath of God. Neither England nor France was spared; it is estimated that fully one and a half million of England's total population of four million died between 1348 and 1350. The plague brought about significant social and economic disruption: labor became scarce, and the decimated nobility scrambled to maintain its traditional hold over a now more assertive peasantry.

Financing the war presented another problem. Waging war is an expensive proposition under the best of circumstances, and the Hundred Years' War proved no exception. During the course of the conflict, the English kings yielded to Parliament greater control over the kingdom's purse strings in return for funds to conduct their operations in France. Consequently, Parliament—a sort of national assembly that represented the interests of the merchants and petty nobles as well as the great magnates—found itself with enhanced authority, while the monarchy's power declined.

In order to defray the costs of the seemingly never-ending French adventure, in 1380 Parliament introduced a poll (head) tax on all Englishmen. Designed to shift the burden of paying for the war from the propertied classes to the common man, the poll tax provoked a revolt among the already discontent peasantry. This peasant revolt, sometimes called Wat Tyler's Rebellion after one of its leaders, was quickly suppressed, but it clearly reflected the turbulent state England found itself in toward the end of the fourteenth century.

Even more dramatic evidence of England's dysfunction came with the reign of Richard II. In 1377 Richard, the ten-year-old eldest son of the Black Prince, inherited the throne. His twenty-two-year reign featured a significant intensification of the chaotic, centuries-long conflicts between the monarchy and the nobility and amongst the nobles themselves. These struggles threatened the entire kingdom with anarchy and rendered it virtually ungovernable. The destructive internecine warfare among England's most wealthy and important families barely subsided when Richard was deposed and murdered in 1399.

Richard II's successor, the usurper Henry IV, wrestled unsuccessfully with the fractious nobility as his dubious claim to the throne proved a major handicap. Upon Henry's death in 1413, his son and successor, Henry V, determined to renew the French conflict at least in part to give his unruly barons something to do with their time other than to challenge the king. However, Henry V, the rambunctious Prince Hal of Shakespeare fame, was also the epitome of the feudal warrior-king. He loved the military life, and growing factional chaos within France gave him the opportunity not only to indulge his warlike instincts but also to regain England's lost French lands.

In 1415 Henry renewed the conflict against France, and within a few months he inflicted a crushing defeat upon the French at the Battle of Agincourt. At Agincourt, Henry's wet, hungry, and tired army of about 8,000, three-fourths of whom were archers, met a French force at least five times its size. It was Crécy and Poitiers all over again. Helped by French tactical errors, the English bowmen and pikemen slaughtered the French knights, including many taken prisoner. English losses totaled fewer than 300 men.

In the flush of victory, Henry pressed forward over the next few years to capture Caen, Falaise, Cherbourg, and Rouen. A disaffected segment of the French nobility greatly aided his progress. Dynastic quarrels within France had divided that country into two warring factions: the Armagnacs, or Orleanists, who were tied to old and incompetent King Charles VI, prone to periods of insanity, and the Burgundians headed by the Duke of Burgundy, member of a lesser branch of the royal family who harbored ambitions for the throne. The Burgundians aligned themselves with the English and in 1418 seized Paris. Two years later, in 1420, Henry and his French allies forced the humiliating Treaty of Troyes on the defeated and insane Charles VI.

By the terms of the treaty, Henry was named regent of France for Charles and recognized as heir to the French throne. He also married Charles' daughter, Catherine, with the understanding that any male children from this marriage would succeed to both the English and French thrones. Charles' son, the dauphin of France, was declared illegitimate. However, not surprisingly, chaos ensued when in 1422 thirty-five-year-old Henry unexpectedly followed his father-in-law to the grave. The crown of both countries now passed to Henry and Catherine's infant son who was to rule England as Henry VI.

Lack of a strong hand at the helm virtually invited a renewal of hostilities and, indeed, supporters of the disinherited dauphin rallied to his cause. Foremost among these was the famous peasant girl of Domremy, Joan of Arc. Inspired by "voices from God," in 1429 Joan led a French army that lifted the English siege of Orléans. Later that year the dauphin was crowned king of France at Reims as Charles VII.

Although the Burgundians captured Joan in 1430 and sold her to the English, who burned her at the stake in the following year, England's fortunes were in terminal decline. Hated by the French, abandoned by its Burgundian ally, exasperated by the skyrocketing costs of its French adventure, and sucked into the vortex of destructive domestic political rivalries, England could not maintain its French position. Slowly but surely, a revitalized French crown drove the English from its territory. By 1453 all that remained of England's presence in France was the port of Calais. The Hundred Years' War was over.

INTERPRETIVE ESSAY
Douglas Biggs

In approaching a conflict as great and diverse as that which arose between France and England in the fourteenth and fifteenth centuries, some general considerations need to be made at the outset. First, contemporaries were not conscious of their participation in a "hundred years' war." This may seem to be stating the obvious, but it is a point worth making. Nearly constant warfare was not unusual to the minds of contemporaries in the fourteenth and fifteenth centuries. The English and French had been fighting since the time of the Norman Conquest in the eleventh century and they continued to do so for decades and centuries after 1453. For example, the first Yorkist king, Edward IV (1461–1483), invaded France in the late fifteenth century and so did his Tudor successors, Henry VII (1485–1509) and Henry VIII (1509–1547), in the sixteenth century. Second, even the dates of the "hundred years' war" are open to debate and discussion. Traditionally, the dates for the wars run from 1337 (when Edward III first invaded France) to 1453 (the fall of Bordeaux—the last English stronghold in Gascony). Yet, some modern historians have begun to push the dates of the wars to as early as 1300, claiming that the wars with France were nothing more than part of a Plantagenet policy of expansion begun by Edward I. Other historians claim that the wars ended not in 1453, but rather in 1455, when the first battles of the fifteenth-century English civil war known as the Wars of the Roses occurred. Third, the nature of the conflict itself continues to be debated. Some historians interpret the wars as nothing more than a continuation of the feudal conflict between lord (the French king) and vassal (the English king) over the latter's possession of the province of Gascony in southwestern France. Others perceive the conflict as being a dynastic struggle over the French throne, and still others see the "hundred years' war" not as a single conflict, but as a series of related struggles in which the antagonists possessed shifting goals and objectives depending on the decade under study. Whether one perceives the conflict between England and France in the period from 1337 to 1453 as a feudal conflict, a dynastic conflict, or merely as a series of glorious, if ultimately futile, wars interrupted by occasional outbreaks of peace, no one can debate that this one-hundred-year period of intermittent warfare of widely fluctuating fortune wrought great change in the social, cultural, and political fabric of England.

These changes may be grouped into two main categories with several points under each. The first category consists of those changes on which the wars had either no impact, such as the Black Death, or those already existing trends in government and society that the wars enhanced or accelerated, such as the "militarization" of the gentry, a growing sense of English and French "nationalism," and the negligible effect of the wars on the majority of the English population. The second main category consists of those changes in government and society that were more overt, and were more consciously instituted by contemporaries, such as the growth of centralization in government, the evolution of Parliament, and the growing independence of the English church from the papal curia.

Although the century of warfare had a profound impact on English society and politics, it should not be taken as the measure by which all things in the period are defined. In many areas of English life and culture the wars had little impact. The Great Plague, or Black Death, for example, would have ravaged Europe in the middle of the fourteenth century whether or not the English and French waged war. Percentages of those killed by the plague differ, but at least one-third and possibly as much as one-half of the populace of Europe was killed by the bubonic plague, which first struck in Italy in 1346 and ravaged across the continent of Europe in the following decade. Even though the first wave of the great plagues had died out by the middle of the 1350s, sporadic outbreaks continued until the end of the century and beyond.

The loss of so much population in so short a period of time accelerated a growing change in English society as a whole. To claim, as the nineteenth-century historian James E. Thorold Rogers did, that the plague introduced a "complete revolution in the occupation of the land," is an oversimplification of the Black Death's effect on English society, but it is nonetheless a good point from which to begin. The decline of serfdom that had begun in the thirteenth century continued and increased in pace throughout the fourteenth and fifteenth centuries. Part of this was the result of overpopulation before the Black Death, and part was the result of depopulation after the plague. Although the plague most affected the lower orders of society, no one was immune to its effects and, when one combines the plague along with death in war and from natural causes, room for social advancement was greatly enhanced. At the top of the social scale there was a large turnover in the great families of England. Of the twenty-one families who started the period as members of the titled nobility, only three were still members of that elite group by the time the wars ended. Thus, for Englishmen of lesser means social mobility and advancement were readily possible. In a relatively small number of cases, young men of little means went off to war and through good fortune came home with great wealth and rose into the ranks of the gentry, baronage and even into the titled nobility. For more Englishmen, the road to social advancement lay in making sound purchases of land at the right time, and in taking advantage of royal service. To fund the wars, the English government found it necessary to centralize its bureaucracy and administration in order to realize as much income from the populace as possible. This centralization led to an increase in the number and type of local government offices, and many richer peasants and gentry rose to social and political prominence in their counties through service to the Crown.

In other areas of English life, the war accentuated or accelerated already evolving dynamics. The wars completed a "militarization" of the gentry that began during the wars of Edward I (1272–1307). Throughout the Welsh and Scottish wars of the late thirteenth and early fourteenth centuries, Edward I and Edward II (1307–1327) had worked to encourage men of knightly rank to partake in their campaigns with limited success. One of Edward III's (1327–1377) great achievements was his ability to build on the military establishment created by his grandfather and to use his personality to "sell" his continental wars to large numbers of the titled nobility and gentry who had not found participation in earlier conflicts to be desirable. Whether through the promise of profit, loyalty to the king, or pursuit of personal glory, more and more gentry men (men of esquirely rank, especially) adopted coats of arms and were proud to pass to their sons not only a tradition of armigerous pursuits but often the very material of war itself: swords, armor, and lances.

The promise of wealth and power attracted many lesser gentry and even members of the peasantry to the dangers of war. For some Englishmen, their military careers were spectacularly profitable, if not always honorable or commensurate with the ideas of chivalry. For example, Sir Robert Knolles began his career as a valet and rose to the rank of knight through profit from wars when serving his king and also through service as a mercenary in Spain and France. Another such success story was that of Sir John Hawkwood, an Englishman of insignificant birth who used the wars to become the leader of the White Company, one of the fourteenth century's most infamous mercenary bands. In the last decades of the fourteenth century, Hawkwood and his band roamed across France and Italy, holding prominent local civilians for ransom and forcing towns to pay protection money before moving on to greener pastures.

Yet, for most Englishmen military service in France featured long hours of boredom. Opportunities for great wealth were few and far between. Battles were not entered into lightly, and the majority of a medieval soldier's time was taken up in the most mundane of duties such as garrisoning castles, and towns, or waiting under arms for an expedition to begin. Although soldiers were supposed to be paid in a timely fashion, this was not always the case, and troops could become intractable and surly and take out their frustrations on whomever was close at hand. Often these were local people who found themselves held for ransom, or found their towns and villages ransacked. One of the most scandalous examples of this occurred during the ill-starred Portuguese campaign of 1381–1382 led by Edmund, Earl of Cambridge. Without pay from home, the English troops turned to extorting money and goods from the local Portuguese peasants and gentry, the subjects of their ally, the king of Portugal; and Earl Edmund, with no money to pay his men, could do little save stand and watch.

For many in England, the thirst for glory and the will to continue the wars had died out in the 1380s. Yet, when Henry V renewed the conflict in the 1410s, a new generation of gentry flocked to his banner with the same zeal as their fathers and grandfathers. Because of this, both Edward III and Henry V after him were capable of mustering and transporting substantial armies of 3,000 to 5,000 men to the Continent and to the discomfort of their French adversary.

In spite of this successful "militarization" of the gentry and the allure of profit in war to the lower orders of English society, the actual conduct of the war had little direct impact on the majority of the English population. The great campaigns and battles of the Hundred Years' War were all fought on French soil. It was the French who saw their towns destroyed, their countryside devastated, and their churches looted. It was the French who fled their homes, wandered the back roads of western France as refugees, and found themselves at the mercy of roving bands of militarized terrorists (some of them English) known as the Free Companies. It is a somewhat surprising paradox that most Englishmen knew little of the actual conduct and/or strategy of the wars and quite possibly cared even less. Yet, in spite of this ambivalent attitude, the vast majority of the English population endured heavy taxation to fund a series of costly military enterprises. The wars only directly touched the lives of those Englishmen who lived on the south coast or the northern marches and were unfortunate enough to fall victim to occasional French and Scottish raids, and, of course, the lives of those relatively few Englishmen who actually saw military service.

This generally ambivalent attitude toward the wars, coupled with the fact that so few Englishmen were directly impacted, demonstrates that the Hundred Years' War was not a total war. Although there are some examples of Englishmen and Frenchmen hating each other, the wars did not engender a broad base of deep seated and/or lasting animosities. Medieval battles, no matter how terrible, were tiny affairs and they did little (if anything) to fire the imaginations of Englishmen at home (in spite of what Shakespeare would have us believe). Trade and commerce between English and French merchants continued almost unhindered throughout the period. English literary figures such as Geoffrey Chaucer were as captivated and influenced by French literature as they were by Italian writings. French customs and Parisian fashions were often observed at the English king's court, and although not all Englishmen thought that good, this practice continued throughout the century of warfare. Even on the battlefield, English and French noblemen and knights who would fight each other one day would on another day work to marry into each other's family. If a combatant found himself a prisoner, he was treated with respect, often as an honored guest, until his family could raise a ransom that could make the captor very wealthy. No greater example of this exists than the treatment of the French king John II "the Good" (1340–1364), after his capture at the Battle of Poitiers in 1356. Edward III ordered his French counterpart brought to London where he was given a palace as his residence, complete with a household establishment. King John remained in England for much of the remainder of his life (he died in captivity in 1364) while the French kingdom worked to pay Edward III 3,000,000 gold florins (£ 500,000), literally a king's ransom, for John II's return.

In spite of the mixing of Anglo-French chivalry and politics, one of the most significant results of the wars was the growing feeling of Englishness as opposed to the universal ideal of all men being part of a greater Christian world. Disparities in language, lifestyle, and culture between the English and the French had been noticed well before 1337, and in some ways the wars further defined such distinctions and hardened those differences, but regional and local identity was more often stronger than any national feeling. Although Southampton merchants might have despised their French counterparts and preyed on their ships in the channel, the same Southampton merchants had little time for their English counterparts in Salisbury or Oxford. In addition, other forces could easily—if momentarily—override any nascent national feeling. For example, in the middle decades of the fourteenth century a number of French noblemen and ecclesiastics in southwestern France joined the Black Prince and many fought alongside him at Poitiers in 1356, just as they had fought alongside his father at Crécy ten years before. In part, this was because Prince Edward was a victorious, chivalric prince, and in part this was because the Frenchmen who joined him did not wish to be subject to what many perceived as the oppressive taxation and arbitrary government of the French Crown. Yet, by the late 1360s these same French subjects of the Black Prince in turn found his government arbitrary and his taxation oppressive. These two things were enhanced by the fact of Prince Edward's foreign origins, and one by one these French subjects withdrew their allegiance from him and offered their loyalties to the French king. Much the same was true for the French men and women who joined the victorious and chivalric King Henry V in the 1410s. A substantial Burgundian French element was key to both Henry V's and John, Duke of Bedford's, successes in northern France. Yet, even before the appearance of Joan of Arc in 1429 and the resurgence of French arms she signaled, the Anglo-Burgundian alliance was fraying at the edges and it was not long before England's erstwhile allies made peace with Charles VII "the Victorious" (1422–1461) and drove the English from northern France in the 1430s and 1440s.

The second major category of changes brought about by the wars includes those reforms in government, society, and religion that contemporaries were conscious of and those which they instituted. In terms of government, the English state in 1453 little resembled the small and, by comparison, relatively inefficient one of 1337. The fourteenth century saw a great leap in bureaucratic government and in centralization. Part of this was due directly to the fact that even when the king was on campaign in France he remained in close control of the government at home. In 1338 Edward III issued the Ordinances of Walton on the eve of his prolonged stay on the Continent prosecuting the war. Rather than leave a Justiciar in England with vice-regal powers as his Norman and Angevin predecessors had done, Edward III retained control of the government through the use of his private, or privy, seal. No major governmental function could therefore take place without his knowledge and consent.

In addition to close scrutiny of government at home when they were away in France, the English kings became more and more interested in controlling the existing county officials, such as sheriff, and in expanding the number of royally appointed officials in the counties. The most important of these new officials came in 1361 when the first Commissions of the Peace appeared in their recognizable form. These commissions were populated with justices drawn from the ranks of the nobility and the local gentry and supplemented with judicial officials from Westminster. Initially, these JPs were empowered to hear and adjudicate only select types of legal infractions. But as the fourteenth century continued, these JPs found their powers and the types of cases they could hear expanded until by 1400 they were the chief judicial instruments in the counties. In addition to JPs, other royally appointed officials such as escheators (tax collectors), coroners, and customs officials rose in stature and power as successive kings used them to further enhance control over county governance and bring more revenue into royal coffers. Some historians have interpreted this increased royal interest and control over local county officials as a move toward a "war state" as English kings harnessed virtually all available resources in order to realize more revenue so that they could then prosecute the war. Perhaps ironically, the creation of JPs and other local offices accelerated literacy within the English populace. To have access to governance, to hold one of the growing number of local offices, and even to have adequate access to justice, Englishmen from peasants to nobles had to have written documentation when dealing with the government. Not only did this result in a growing legal class, but it also increased basic literacy among all classes which allowed, in turn, for greater social mobility.

Although another chapter in this volume is dedicated to the growth of Parliament, it deserves some mention here. Parliament before the 1330s met only occasionally. Kings used Parliament in the early fourteenth century as a venue to ask for direct taxation in time of war. In these early days, the king would often demand a subsidy (tax) be voted to him before he would hear petitions from the Commons and give redress. The exigencies of war in the mid-fourteenth century meant that Parliament would need to meet much more frequently because Edward III desperately needed the Commons to vote massive amounts of money to fund his ongoing campaigns. Edward III had grown to rely so heavily on parliamentary taxation that even in the 1360s, a relatively peaceful decade following the Treaty of Bretigny in 1359, he found it necessary to call Parliament and ask for taxation to use in peacetime. Taxation was not only regular but could be heavy. Traditionally, parliamentary taxes were given in the form of tenths and fifteenths (that is, men were taxed on one-tenth or one-fifteenth of their movable goods), but there were occasions that the pressure for funding the wars led the government to create new forms of taxation. One of these new types of taxation was the poll tax that appeared in the reign of Richard II. The poll tax was a tax on everyone in the kingdom over the age of fourteen. It was first instituted in 1377, again in 1379, and for the third and last time in 1381. Although the tax was productive in terms of filling the royal coffers, it led directly to a series of revolts in 1381 known to historians as the Peasants' Revolt or Wat Tyler's Rebellion. Although the English government did not institute another poll tax until the time of Margaret Thatcher in the late twentieth century, such revolts did not stop kings from demanding and receiving new kinds of taxation from Parliament. In 1404 and again in 1411, Henry IV (1399–1413) negotiated new forms of taxation from his Parliaments, as did the Yorkist kings in the 1460s.

In addition to direct, parliamentary taxation, English kings also worked to increase their control over indirect taxation such as customs on wool and wool fells, wine, and other imports and exports. Here, too, kings generally succeeded in strengthening their control over their subjects and in dipping into their subjects' purses. For example, total revenue from indirect taxation on foreign trade in the early 1330s averaged a paltry £12,000 per annum. By the 1340s, however, increased duties on the importation of goods saw the total revenue from indirect taxation climb to nearly £110,000 per annum. Although this level was not sustainable, revenue from indirect taxation reached the substantial figure of between £30,000 and £70,000 per annum until the 1450s when it collapsed.

Whether new or traditional, direct or indirect, the taxation granted in the fourteenth century alone amounted to somewhere between £8.25 and £9.5 million. Although contemporaries did not know of the magnitude of their government's demands on them, they understood that what Edward III asked of them was even greater that what his grandfather, Edward I, had demanded of the political community for his conquests of Wales and Scotland roughly fifty years before. It is a telling comment on the robustness of the medieval English economy that it could sustain such a substantial and prolonged contribution of taxation into royal coffers in spite of a general economic downturn in the first half of the fifteenth century.

The exigencies of war that forced kings to call Parliament so often also elevated Parliament as an institution and made it a regular part of English governance. As kings came to rely on parliamentary subsidies, they found that they could not get what they wanted (that is, taxation) unless they first gave redress of grievances that the House of Commons might have. Thus, even a powerful king like Edward III was forced to sit in Parliament and adjudicate complaints brought by his subjects and give them redress *before* they, in turn, would vote him his subsidy to fight his wars. Sometimes King Edward listened with interest, sometimes he did not, but nonetheless he listened and answered the petitions. This "give and take" style of government was a different sort of government than any other in Europe and would be the foundation for the growing independence of Parliament in the centuries to come.

In addition to political and governmental growth and change, so too was there growth and change in the English church as opposed to the universal Catholic Church. Part of this resulted from the so-called Babylonian Captivity, when the pope departed Rome and took up residence at Avignon in southern France between 1305 and 1378, and part was the result of the Great Schism, when two and sometimes three prelates claimed the papacy between 1378 until 1417. The fourteenth-century English chronicler Adam Murimuth was not alone among Englishmen when he leveled harsh criticism at the papal curia in Avignon with its plethora of French cardinals and clerks. On their own, English churchmen began to settle disputes, debate, and decide over questions of doctrine rather than seek advice from Avignon or Rome. With increasing success, the Crown also sought greater levels of control over the church. For example, Edward III took control over so-called "alien houses"—those organs of the regular clergy (for example, monasteries and priories) in England who owed allegiance, and money, to their founding houses in France. King Edward also issued the Statute of Provisors (1351) and Statute of Praemunire (1353). The Statute of Provisors allowed the king to imprison churchmen appointed to various church positions by the pope and to appoint his own men to church offices usually under the purview of the Holy Father. The Statute of Praemunire forbade any churchman from taking any legal cases to Rome that could be tried in the king's courts.

Moreover, the plague rather than the wars themselves brought on a general questioning of religion from the mid-fourteenth century onwards. In the later fourteenth and fifteenth centuries, mystics such as Julian of Norwich and Margery Kempe represented an ultraorthodox, personal, highly emotional, and popular religious response to the societal problems they perceived. At the same time the Lollard heresy, which advocated such things as church divestment of all its worldly possessions (that is, giving all its wealth and lands to the poor, withdrawing from politics, and having clerics live in imitation of Christ), and the translation of the Bible into English so all could read and discuss it, struck at the church from below.

The mixed fortune of the wars not only brought great wealth to England and prestige to the monarchy, but on several occasions it also seemed as though England might end up dominating the western portion of the European continent. In the 1360s, after gaining a greatly expanded Aquitaine from John II at the Treaty of Bretigny, Edward III worked to marry his younger sons into two of the most powerful states on the Continent. The king's second son, Lionel of Antwerp, was married to the heiress of the Visconti dukes of Milan, while Edward sought the hand of Margaret de Male, heiress of the rich count of Flanders, for his fourth son, Edmund of Langley. Unfortunately for Edward III, the pope blocked the Flemish marriage because of consanguinity; Lionel died shortly after his marriage. An even greater success was the Treaty of Troyes in 1420 whereby Henry V gained the throne of France for his heirs. However, such stratagems proved ephemeral, and when the fortunes of war waned, England became politically divided and the century of warfare served as a backdrop for major political difficulties in the reigns of Richard II (1377–1399) and Henry VI (1422–1461). Both kings not only sought a truce with the French but also lasting peace as well. Such goals were unpopular with certain segments of the titled nobility, some of who were eager for military glory. The policy of peace nearly cost Richard II his throne in 1387, and it cost Henry VI his sanity in the 1440s.

In the end, the England of 1453 was much different from that of 1337. First, society itself had undergone a substantial transformation. The plague had carried off a large fraction of the entire population which, when combined with the opportunity for profits and social advancement that military and government service offered, transformed the face of English society. The needs for the war and several kings' ability to "sell" military service, completed the "militarization" of the English gentry that had begun under the reign of Edward I. Moreover, a greater number of Englishmen experienced a sense of national feeling. In the early fourteenth century, government rarely touched the daily lives of its subjects. By the mid-fifteenth century, this had changed. Large numbers of government officers appeared in this century that not only aided the Crown in gathering revenue but also aided the social advancement of those men who served in these offices. Direct taxation, which at the beginning of the period had been necessary only in wartime, was now regularly given by Parliament in times of peace. Indirect forms of taxation, such as customs duties—by 1450 more heavily controlled and regulated—directly affected most of the English king's subjects. Parliament grew as an institution, and the English king worked to control the various organs of the church within his borders. The final loathsome and anticlimactic collapse of

English arms at Castillion in July 1453 brought with it an end to the substantial English presence on the Continent that had existed since William the Conqueror crossed the narrow seas to contest for King Harold's throne nearly four centuries before. The defeat at Castillion ushered in an era of faction, civil disorder, and dynastic change, and brought to an end the Hundred Years' War—an era marked by reform and renewal, change and resilience, and teeming vitality.

SELECTED BIBLIOGRAPHY

Allmand, Christopher. *Henry V.* New Haven, CT: Yale University Press, 1996. The most recent, and extremely well-researched, biography of one of England's most famous kings, including a discussion of his Agincourt campaign.

_____. *The Hundred Years War.* Cambridge: Cambridge University Press, 1989. After a short chronological narrative, Allmand provides a fine general discussion of various facets of the war.

Barber, Richard. *Edward, Prince of Wales and Aquitaine: A Biography of the Black Prince.* Woodbridge, Suffolk: Boydell and Brewer, 1978. A fine study of the Black Prince.

_____. *The Life and Campaigns of the Black Prince.* Woodbridge, Suffolk: Boydell Press, 1986. The author edits and translates the contemporary life of Prince Edward by one of his heralds.

Bennett, Matthew. *Agincourt, 1415.* Oxford: Osprey Publishing, 1991. A popular history of the Agincourt campaign, loaded with pictures, color drawings, and color maps that supplement the lively text.

Curry, Anne, and Michael Hughes, eds. *Arms, Armies and Fortifications in the Hundred Years War.* Woodbridge, Suffolk: Boydell Press, 1994. A nice collection of essays ranging from the domestic response to the wars to a discussion of the evolution of battle tactics and to a chapter on the importance of the longbow.

DeVries, Kelly. *Infantry Warfare in the Early Fourteenth Century.* Woodbridge, Suffolk: Boydell Press, 1996. A fine discussion of infantry tactics in battles of the early fourteenth century by one of the leading military historians of his generation.

Fryde, E.B. *Peasants and Landlords in Later Medieval England.* Stroud: Sutton Publishing, 1996. A good study of the relationship between lords and peasants in the later medieval period detailing the effects of the plague and the economic downturn of the early fifteenth century.

Green, David. *The Black Prince.* Stroud: Tempus, 2002. A fine recent biography of Prince Edward.

Griffiths, Ralph, *The Reign of Henry VI.* Berkeley: University of California Press, 1981. A monumental study of the last Lancastrian king, who sought peace with the French but eventually lost the war in France and ultimately his throne.

Hewitt, H.J. *The Organization of War Under Edward III.* Manchester: Manchester University Press, 1966. One of the finest studies ever done on how armies were put together and used in the fourteenth century.

Kaeuper, Richard. *War, Justice and Public Order: England and France in the Later Middle Ages.* Oxford: Clarendon Press, 1988. A fine study arguing for the creation of the "war state."

Ormrod, W.M. *The Reign of Edward III.* New Haven, CT: Yale University Press, 1988. A good study of the reign by the current expert on Edward III.

Perroy, Edouard. *The Hundred Years War.* New York: Oxford University Press, 1951. One of the finest books on the subject, largely written by the author when he served in the French resistance during World War II trying to avoid capture by the Nazis.

Rogers, Clifford. *War Cruel and Sharp: English Strategy Under Edward III.* Woodbridge, Suffolk: Boydell Press, 2000. A fine modern account of the wars of Edward III and a new discussion of how the king employed his strategy.

_____, ed. *The Wars of Edward III.* Rochester, NY: Boydell Press, 1999. A fine collection of sources in translation including contemporary chroniclers' accounts of battles and the wars themselves along with eight classic articles by modern historians on various aspects of the wars.

Saul, Nigel. *Richard II.* New Haven, CT: Yale University Press, 1997. The most recent, and extremely well-researched, biography of Richard II who sought peace with the French in the 1380s and 1390s.

Seward, Desmond. *The Hundred Years War.* New York: Macmillan, 1978. A good general narrative of events with much information on the battles.

Sumption, J. *The Hundred Years War,* 2 vols. Philadelphia: University of Pennsylvania Press, 1991, 1999. This two-volume set provides a highly detailed narrative account of the entire Hundred Years' War; the work is as comprehensive as it is long, and even the smallest skirmishes and sieges are given extensive treatment.

Ziegler, Philip. *The Black Death.* New York: Harper and Row, 1969. This is a classic work on the plague and its effects on Europe and especially England.

The Wars of the Roses, 1455–1485

INTRODUCTION

The sanguinary Wars of the Roses represent the culmination of a long period of baronial strife and aristocratic unrest that unsettled England's fortunes and ultimately decimated its nobility. For generations prior to the conflict's outbreak, royal power in England had been on the decline as the country's restless nobility challenged a series of frequently weak or incapacitated monarchs. Of the eight men who ruled England between 1307 and 1485, a date often given for the end of the Wars of the Roses, three were deposed and subsequently murdered, one died on campaign in France, and one died in battle defending his throne. Of the remaining three who died a natural death, at one time or another each faced significant opposition from his lordly vassals.

The source of the problem is found in the confused succession to the English throne. With dynastic lines dying out, distant claimants seizing the crown, and royal infants being placed in the care of greedy and unscrupulous regents, chaos ensued. The resultant power vacuum emboldened powerful aristocrats and their retainers to act independently of the seriously weakened royal authority. These noblemen struggled against each other and against the crown for increased power, prestige, and wealth. By the middle of the fifteenth century, England was in turmoil as its most exalted families engaged in a seemingly endless competition for self-aggrandizement. Personal ambition ruled, and the nation be damned.

Baronial defiance of royal authority had characterized England from the time of William the Conqueror. This boldness reached something of a cli-

The Wars of the Roses saw England ruled by no less than five different kings in twenty-five tumultuous years. Richard III, the last Yorkist monarch and the subsequent object of William Shakespeare's venomous play of the same name, was killed at the Battle of Bosworth Field in 1485. (Reproduced from the Collections of the Library of Congress.)

max during the reigns of the despised King John (1199–1216) and his weak son, Henry III (1216–1272). However, the energetic Edward I (1272–1307) restored a good deal of royal authority. England unfortunately regressed under his heir, Edward II, whose high-handed behavior antagonized many nobles. In 1327 Edward II's wife, Isabella, and her lover, Roger Mortimer, led an ambitious court faction to depose and subsequently murder the king. Edward's son and successor, Edward III, brought a degree of stability to the crown upon reaching maturity in 1330. He executed Mortimer and sent Isabella away to a distant retirement.

Edward III's death in 1377 opened a Pandora's box. The crown went to his young grandson Richard, son of Edward, the Black Prince, Edward III's oldest son. Richard's uncles ruled in his minority, and they—along with other members of the high nobility—used their position to further their own selfish political and financial interests. In 1389 Richard, who ruled as Richard II, declared himself of age and ousted his corrupt and brawling uncles. Although not without ability, Richard managed to alienate most of England's powerful and influential families. He was deposed in 1399 and murdered a year later.

The specific act that precipitated Richard's overthrow was his seizure of his cousin's inheritance. When Richard's uncle, John of Gaunt, died in 1399, the king seized his estates rather than allowing them to pass to his cousin, Henry Bolingbroke, duke of Lancaster. In threatening the sanctity of property rights, Richard united his kingdom's landowning nobility against him. When Bolingbroke returned from exile to claim his lands, Richard found himself virtually without allies and abdicated under duress. Bolingbroke now claimed the throne as Henry IV.

The new king headed the House of Lancaster, which, according to William Shakespeare at least, carried on its escutcheon a red rose. Henry had triumphed through force of arms, although he was incomparably more popular than the deposed king. However, his hold on the throne was rather precarious; at least one other heir of Edward III had a stronger claim to the crown than he did. Moreover, Henry himself had set the precedent of seizing the throne by force. In fact, Henry spent much of his reign (1399–1413) warding off real and potential revolts.

Henry's son and successor, Henry V, the wild "Prince Hal" of Shakespearean fame, proved a competent king. However, fighting in France preoccupied him, and he died there in 1422. Although Henry V may have defeated various French forces, he made no real headway in reining in either his rebellious, lawless, conspiratorial, grasping, self-centered nobles or his equally unruly family.

The Wars of the Roses began in earnest during the reign of Henry VI, Henry V's only child. At the time of Henry V's unexpected death, Henry VI was an eight-month-old infant. Not unexpectedly, the regency that ruled England in this child's name consisted of important personages who were more intent on furthering their own selfish aims than they were in serving their king or advancing the interests of his realm. Among its other maladies, the English state now endured vicious in-fighting among the magnates and members of the extended royal family, private armies traipsing around the countryside, and diversions of wealth from the royal treasury to avaricious individuals.

This ruinous state of affairs continued long after the king reached maturity; he proved to be hopelessly incompetent. Kind, pious, gentle, and unassuming, Henry VI was the antithesis of the type of king that untamed, lawless, ungovernable England desperately required. Even worse, perhaps, as an adult Henry began to show signs of the insanity that had plagued his maternal grandfather, Charles VI of France. When Henry's insanity became more pronounced, surrogates whose personal interests frequently transcended those of the kingdom once again gained control of England's affairs.

By the middle of the fifteenth century, the duke of Somerset from the Beaufort family and Richard, duke of York, enjoyed primacy of place among handlers of the simple-minded and politically detached king. The Beauforts originated with Edward III's son John of Gaunt. His illicit liaison with Catherine Swynford produced children with the surname Beaufort. Although these children and subsequent offspring were legitimized, they were expressly barred from succession to the throne. The Beauforts, including the duke of Somerset, staunchly supported the king and buttressed the Lancaster faction at court.

Richard, duke of York, whose family symbol was the white rose, actually had a stronger claim to the English throne than Henry VI. As Henry V's brothers had died without children, and Henry VI himself proved childless, the Lancaster line neared extinction. Richard was the heir apparent to the crown of England. On his maternal side he was a direct heir of Lionel, duke of Clarence, Edward III's third son; on his paternal side he was a direct heir of Edmund, duke of York, Edward III's fifth son. This left only the Beauforts, with their most tenuous claim to the throne, to challenge Richard.

One other player of great importance was the queen, Margaret of Anjou, niece of the French king. Unlike her husband, Margaret was strong, forceful, and deeply involved in the political intrigues of the day. She allied herself with the Beauforts and opposed the Yorkists.

In 1453 three events of great significance occurred. The seemingly eternal Hundred Years' War came to an unhappy end with England's defeat. As a result, the mood in England—which had not been bright to begin with—turned positively sour as the English began to seek scapegoats for their defeat and to contemplate the lost millions of pounds sterling that had been poured down the French rat hole. Moreover, the end of the war meant the return to England of hundreds if not thousands of English soldiers—rude and crude battle-tested veterans who knew nothing except the arts of killing, plundering, raping, and looting, and who would now freely practice their skills at home. Moreover, in that year Margaret gave birth to an heir to the throne, Edward, Prince of Wales and Richard of York lost his place as heir apparent. Finally, Henry VI went insane (temporarily, as it turned out) and Richard was designated Protector of the Realm, much to Margaret and the Beauforts' distress. However, a mere eighteen months later Henry regained his sanity, and the Lancastrians prevailed upon him to dismiss Richard and all the Yorkists from his household. The duke of Somerset now replaced Richard as the most powerful man in England.

Frightened by the possibility that the Lancastrians would wreak vengeance on the Yorkists, and eager to regain their place at the national trough, Richard and his allies took up arms. Although they cited the need to rid the king of evil counselors as reason for their aggressive behavior, in fact they were pursuing their own selfish interests. The first clash between the white rose and the red rose occurred in 1455 at the Battle of St. Albans. Richard triumphed, and the duke of Somerset was killed in an exceptionally bloody skirmish that came to characterize almost all engagements during the Wars of the Roses. Richard now regained his position of preeminence at court as Henry once again descended into insanity; but neither the Lancastrians nor Queen Margaret was vanquished.

In a short time, Henry regained his sanity and Margaret replaced Richard as the power behind the throne. For several years both Yorkists and Lancastrians bided their time as they prepared for a renewal of hostilities. In 1459 the Lancastrians inflicted several small defeats on the Yorkists, and the leaders of that faction fled the country. However, in 1460 they returned and the war resumed in earnest as Richard, duke of York, claimed the throne by right of birth.

Although the Lancastrians achieved victory at Wakefield—killing Richard in the process—and bested the Yorkists at a second Battle of St. Albans, the York faction triumphed at Northhampton. In March 1461 the Yorkists, now led by Richard's son Edward and his cousin, Richard Neville, earl of Warwick, crushed the Lancastrians at the Battle of Towton

Moor. Fought in a driving snow storm, the battle lasted for most of the day and killed approximately 10,000 men, most of them Lancastrians, in what is generally acknowledged to have been the bloodiest battle ever fought on English soil. After the battle, Edward, duke of York, was crowned king as Edward IV; but Margaret and her son, the Lancastrian heir, escaped to France while the disengaged Henry VI took up a rather comfortable imprisonment at the Tower of London.

The Yorkist triumph did not, however, end the bloodshed. Both Edward and his ally and cousin, the earl of Warwick, proved to be ambitious, strong-willed men. Warwick, nicknamed the "kingmaker," saw himself as the power behind the throne; Edward was just as intent on ruling independently. Eventually these powerful personalities quarreled. Not only was Warwick disappointed at his lack of control over England's affairs, but he and his family were also outraged that King Edward was bestowing great honors, wealth, and land on the family of his new wife, Lady Elizabeth Woodville. Although the Woodvilles were obscure nobility, a fact that greatly offended England's most powerful families, their avarice and greed were insatiable. An angry and humiliated Warwick now turned to his former enemies, the Lancastrians.

Margaret and the remnants of the Lancastrian faction had been nursing their grievances and planning a comeback. Even though they despised Warwick, they realized his usefulness for their schemes to regain the throne. In 1470 the Lancastrians, now led by Warwick, invaded England and forced Edward IV to flee abroad. He returned to England a year later at the head of an army, and on Easter Sunday he defeated and killed Warwick at the Battle of Barnet. A few weeks later, at the Battle of Tewkesbury, Edward routed Margaret's forces, capturing the queen and killing her son, the Lancastrian heir to the throne. Shortly thereafter he murdered the imprisoned Henry VI. Edward IV now stood alone as king of England, and the Lancastrians appeared finished.

Although some historians conclude that Edward's triumphs in 1471 and the extinction of the Lancaster line marked the end of the Wars of the Roses, the game of royal musical chairs continued until 1485. Tall, handsome, and intelligent Edward proved an able king when the spirit moved him. He restored the monarchy's prestige and to some extent tamed the rebellious barons. He brought a degree of stability that England had not seen for decades, and he lived within his means, thereby freeing the Crown from an overdependence on Parliament for its revenues. However, Edward was a "party animal" of the first magnitude, and he died unexpectedly in 1483 at age forty, exhausted by his corporal excesses.

At Edward IV's death, the crown passed to his twelve-year-old son Edward, who became King Edward V. Edward V was a minor, and his father's younger brother, Richard, duke of Gloucester, was selected as regent. Talented, ambitious, and unscrupulous, Richard soon had the king and his younger brother declared illegitimate and took the throne for himself as the infamous Richard III. The "little princes" were housed in the Tower of London and subsequently disappeared; the presumption—greatly reinforced by Shakespeare's play about Richard's reign—was that the new king had them killed.

It is indisputable that Richard was certainly not the ogre that Shakespeare portrayed him to be, although he clearly overreached himself. The disappearance of the princes, executions (not entirely unjustified) of foes and former friends, and costly preparations for a renewed struggle with France that never materialized made Richard increasingly unpopular.

Waiting in the wings was Henry Tudor, earl of Richmond. A member of the Lancastrian faction, Henry had scant claim to the English throne. On his maternal side he was of the Beaufort family and thus barred from inheriting the crown. His grandfather was Owen Tudor, a minor Welsh nobleman whose liaison with Catherine, widow of Henry V, which produced Henry's father, may or may not have been out of wedlock.

Henry Tudor invaded England with a small force from his French exile in the summer of 1485 and gathered momentum as he made his way toward a showdown with Richard at Bosworth Field in the heart of the country. Although Richard's force was larger, his lieutenants were untrustworthy; several either refused to fight or defected to Henry. The result was a crushing defeat for Richard who was left dead on the battlefield. The victorious Henry now claimed the crown as Henry VII, and his Tudor family held the throne of England until 1603.

INTERPRETIVE ESSAY
Kristen Post Walton

Richard Plantagenet	Let him that is a true-born gentleman
	And stands upon the honor of his birth,
	If he supposes I have pleaded truth,
	From off this briar pluck a white rose with me.
Earl of Somerset	Let him that is no coward nor no flatterer,
	But dare maintain the party of the truth,

	Pluck a red rose from off this thorn with me.
Earl of Warwick	I love no colors; and without all color
	Of base insinuating flattery,
	I pluck this white rose with Plantagenet.
Earl of Suffolk	I pluck this red rose with young Somerset,
	And say withal, I think he held the right.
Vernon	Stay lords and gentleman, and pluck no more,
	Till you conclude that he upon whose side
	The fewest roses are cropp'd from the tree
	Shall yield the other in the right opinion.
Somerset	Good Master Vernon, it is well objected;
	If I have fewest, I subscribe in silence.
Plantagenet	And I.
Vernon	Then for the truth and plainness of the case,
	I pluck this pale and maiden blossom here,
	Giving my verdict on the white rose side.
Somerset	Prick not your finger as you pluck it off,
	Lest bleeding, you do paint the white rose red,
	And fall on my side against your will.

William Shakespeare, *1 Henry VI*, Act II, scene iv

Readers have traditionally looked at the Wars of the Roses through the eyes of the Tudor dynasty. The history one studies is often the history of the victors, and the most accepted version of the Wars of the Roses is the one propagated by the descendants of the victorious Henry VII and the writers of the sixteenth century, particularly William Shakespeare. Shakespeare has vividly brought to us the great image from that time—the evil Richard III, hunchbacked, hobbling through the darkest days of the Middle Ages, and cruelly murdering his two nephews, the princes in the Tower. Although less well known, the scene in *Henry VI, Part I* in which the Yorkists and Lancastrians pluck their roses demonstrates how the Tudors perceived (or at least wanted their subjects to perceive) the commencement of the wars that led to strife, disorder, and, ultimately, the Tudor dynasty. The Tudor monarchs wanted to ensure that the crown remained stable on their heads, and as a result, they portrayed the wars of the late fifteenth century as a constant disturbance of the peace that harmed the English people. In actuality, the Tudors' version rested in part on fact, but often the new dynasty exaggerated or embellished the facts in order to gain its own ends. By lifting the curtain that Henry VII lowered in the 1480s, one can learn what these chivalrously named Wars of the Roses truly encompassed.

The Wars of the Roses lasted from 1455 to 1485, though the infamous royal roulette, in which four kings occupied the throne (two of them held the crown twice), was shorter in duration, from 1461 to 1485. The wars were not continuous during this time, and from 1471 to 1483, a period of stability occurred under Edward IV. Why did the Wars of the Roses occur? What were their effects on the people, society, and political traditions within England? Historians regularly debate these questions, but looking at English history in the second half of the fifteenth century can offer insight into the answers. The nobility were the movers and shakers of fifteenth-century England, and they were the ones who most greatly influenced the conflict and whom the wars affected the most as well.

The infant Henry VI inherited the English throne in 1422. He was the first English monarch who was too young even to speak his coronation oath. His father, Henry V, had been a vibrant man, engaging in almost continual (and successful) warfare against the French monarch. Henry VI was the polar opposite of his father. The first king in English history not to lead an army in battle, Henry was a pious man more concerned with education and his personal life than with actively running the kingdom. His lack of military ability (or at least desire) weakened his position from the start; the English nobles, at least, yearned for a strong king such as Henry V who could triumph in battle for the economic benefit of his subjects and the pride of the land. Henry VI also governed poorly, committing the English mortal sin of relying too heavily on favorites such as the dukes of Suffolk and Somerset, who gained great control over the government. As a small number of favorites increased their power, the other nobles of the realm, particularly Richard, duke of York, felt that Henry VI unfairly excluded them from their rightful position as councillors to the king. Factions developed, and in 1453, when Henry VI began his long battle with insanity, the tensions between these factions increased significantly, resulting in the following wars. Henry VI's weakness as a king allowed other problems to develop during his reign, and a complex mixture of events and fate caused the Wars of the Roses and the instability they created.

During the long minority of Henry VI, which he ended in 1437 at the age of fifteen, a council ruled the kingdom. Although there was a protector of the realm, the council did not appoint a regent, and as a result a group of nobles governed the land. The minority government allowed for the social system now known as "bastard feudalism" to grow out of control. Bastard feudalism (the term was coined in 1885) was a mutation of the original landed feudalism of the earlier Middle Ages. The earlier tenu-rial bonds between a lord and his man began to be replaced by a personal bond, usually based on a monetary as opposed to a land grant system. Bastard feudalism did not begin under Henry VI, nor did it die with the commencement of the Tudor dynasty. Usually, the king manipulated the system in order to maintain order and to control the kingdom; however, the long minority of Henry VI, combined with his weakness as a ruler when he matured to allow his noble subjects to increase their own follow-ings and to become almost kings in their own right. The martial and eco-nomic strength of some of these nobles grew to such an extent that they challenged the king, first by becoming his equal in arms and finance, and later on the battlefield.

In general, the king should be at least two times as wealthy as his most wealthy subject; under Henry VI, that was not the case. The minority council allowed for a policy of noninterference between the nobles, and Henry did nothing to reverse that policy. In addition, Henry was a simple man and has been called "generous to the point of idiocy." He spent money and handed out favors without thought to the well-being of the crown and the kingdom. As a result, men such as Richard of York and Richard Neville, earl of Warwick, grew strong enough to defeat the king and his supporters in 1461. Warwick's strength was so great that he has been called the "kingmaker," for his support in the wars was twice deci-sive in the game of royal roulette.

The growth of noble strength and the minority council of government also affected both Parliament and the law of the land. For example, in the 1430s legislation passed that prevented men of "small substance and no worth" from voting, allowing only those with at least 60 acres to be involved in the political process. Those who were involved in Parliament enacted legislation, but bastard feudalism made the enforcement of laws extremely difficult, as lords would often pressure the courts, justices, and juries in order to protect their men. A strong king could enforce laws, but a weak one such as Henry VI allowed for instability across the land. Most lords, through the system of bastard feudalism, created their own armies, controlled the justice in their localities, and increased their financial worth during the minority of Henry VI. In 1450 a common man by the name of Jack Cade led a rebellion in Kent and London. Cade reacted to what he and his supporters saw as instability within the realm. Moreover, mount-ing losses in France and the weakening economic situation in England helped to spur Cade to action.

The question of royal succession also played an important role. The fact that Henry's queen, Margaret of Anjou, had not yet produced an heir meant that the succession was not settled, a condition that could lead to even more troubles. As problems in the kingdom increased, the dynastic question began to play a larger role in the growing tension throughout the realm. From the death of Henry's uncle, Duke Humphrey of Gloucester, until 1453, when Margaret finally bore a son, Prince Edward, the question of succession was in people's minds. An additional source of misfortune was the "curse" left on the royals by Edward III: the curse of too many sons and not enough thrones to go around. By 1450 the possible succession realistically could lie in two quite different directions. The first claimant was Richard, duke of York. Based on the principle of primogeniture, Richard had the best claim to the throne, being descended on his mother's side from Edward III's second surviving son, the duke of Clarence, and through his father's side from the duke of York, the fourth surviving son of the former king. In fact, by the usual laws of inheritance, Richard's claim to the throne was even better than that of King Henry. Henry VI claimed the throne through right of descent from his grandfather, Henry IV, son of John of Gaunt, Edward III's third surviving son. Although Henry IV gained the throne only by deposing Richard II in 1399, Parliament had confirmed his crown and no one seriously challenged the sitting king until 1460.

Until his son was born in 1453, Henry appeared to favor someone other than Richard, duke of York, as his successor. Evidence indicates that Henry was preparing his cousin, Margaret Beaufort (married at the age of twelve to Henry's half-brother Edmund Tudor), to succeed him if he died without a direct heir. Margaret was also a descendant of John of Gaunt, but through the line of Gaunt's one-time mistress, Catherine Swynford, whose children were only legitimized well after their birth by Henry IV and an act of Parliament. In addition, Henry IV had also ordered that with their legitimization the line from Swynford should be excluded from inheritance of the crown. Despite the support given to Henry IV through the 1450s, the question of who should counsel him remained important, as did the question of who should succeed to the throne. The fog and confusion surrounding the succession led men such as Jack Cade to argue that York should be next in line to the throne and should maintain a role in the government. York, at one point practically banished from England as the deputy of Ireland, returned to the kingdom and pressed his position as heir apparent in order to be named regent when Henry VI entered his first bout of madness in 1453.

The year 1453 was extremely significant for the growing tensions that led to battle in 1455. In addition to Henry's inability to rule as a result of his madness, his son, Edward, Prince of Wales, was born (though the king did not even react to the news of the birth). Richard of York suddenly found himself a long step away from the throne. More importantly, England lost its war with France and Henry was left with only Calais, a mere thirty-three years after his father, Henry V, had won the French crown. The losses were important psychologically for the English, who blamed Somerset and Henry's other advisers for the loss. The defeat also affected England's economy. The English merchants were accustomed to exploiting the French lands for commercial gain, and the English people expected to consume French goods, such as wine. Though the end of the war would have benefited trade in some ways, the loss of France meant that the import of French goods into England would be subject to French tariffs and French business practices. The change was clearly reflected in the drastic reduction in the importation of wine in the early years of the 1450s.

These losses encouraged many merchants to desire a change in the governmental council and to support Richard, duke of York. Few, if any, argued that York should sit on the throne in Henry's place at this point, but many merchants and artisans, particularly in London, wanted York to increase his role in the government. In the countryside, the Yorkists and Lancastrians began to split into parties. Nobles would choose a side to support and their men, sworn to them under the system of bastard feudalism, would follow. The nobles, though, did not always (or even often) choose sides based on their support of Henry's government or York's, but usually made their selections based on personal feuds or the possibility of personal gain. For example, when the Nevilles entered the turmoil supporting York, their long-standing rivals the Percys immediately decided to support Lancaster. Despite the question of succession and the weakness of the economy and law enforcement, the Wars of the Roses were fought more for self-aggrandizement than for any constitutional principles. In 1453, though, the decision of whom to support was made temporarily moot when York became lord protector. Once Henry VI recovered his senses and replaced York with his own counselors, the tensions increased dramatically and the violent side of the wars began.

At Christmas time in 1454, Henry VI suddenly recovered his wits, and early in 1455 he regained control of the government. One of his first actions was to restore Somerset, another Beaufort cousin, to control of the government. York resisted being replaced so abruptly by the man that he and many others believed responsible for the loss of the French war and the cause of most of the kingdom's problems. As a result, in May 1455 the Neville family (Salisbury and Warwick) joined arms with Richard, duke of York, and marched on London. Somerset and Henry met the Yorkist forces at St. Albans, where they fought the first battle of the war. Henry sustained a slight injury and immediately fled the battlefield. The Yorkists routed the Lancastrians and slew Somerset in battle at a pub in the town.

After his victory, Richard of York did not claim the crown; instead, he was content with the elimination of Somerset as a contender for the king's ear. For a brief period of time following the first Battle of St. Albans, the two sides attempted reconciliation, but the lines had been drawn and the enmity between the two sides had grown too intense. In November, York again became the lord protector of the land, until once more Henry relieved him of his duties the following year. Meanwhile, Henry's wife, Margaret of Anjou, worried for the future of her young son, created a queen's party and worked more to ensure the continuation of the Lancastrian dynasty than for the peace and order of the realm. The situation in England continued to grow more and more desperate as York's followers settled increasingly on the idea that he should succeed to the throne despite the existence of the young Prince of Wales and Margaret's determination to stop him. By 1459, the parties realized they could not reach a peaceful conclusion and war broke out once more.

The period from 1459 to 1461 was the most militarily intense of the wars. From the Yorkist victory at the opening Battle of Blore Heath, to the Battle of Wakefield in which Richard of York was killed and his opponents placed a paper crown upon his battered head, to the blizzard that accompanied the final Yorkist victory at Towton Moor, the wars were bloody affairs and many nobles died. Margaret led the Lancastrian forces and was savage in her reprisals against any who fought against the anointed king. In 1459 Margaret encouraged Parliament (the so-called "Parliament of Devils") to accuse York and his followers of treason and to attaint them. The queen's severe actions resulted in growing sympathy for the Yorkist cause. In 1460 Warwick successfully entered England from France and captured Henry VI at the Battle of Northampton. This allowed the Yorkists to reply in kind to Margaret by passing the Act of Accord, which allowed Henry VI to retain the crown until his death but stipulated that it would then pass to York, thereby setting aside the claim of Margaret's son, the Prince of Wales.

Following the death of Richard of York on December 30, 1460, his handsome nineteen-year-old son Edward inherited not only his dukedom but also his claim to the throne. Following a success at the Battle of Mortimer's Cross, Edward reached London (where he had great support) and seated himself on the throne at Westminster on March 4, 1461. The game of royal roulette had begun in earnest. When Edward defeated Margaret and forced her into exile at the Battle of Towton Moor, he asserted himself as the new king and immediately called a Parliament in order to depose and attaint Henry VI.

Overall, these battles, like most of the war, involved largely the nobles and their retainers. Merchants, though rarely fighting, usually supported York, but most Englishmen were not personally involved in the wars. Unless part of a lord's retinue and forced into fighting, such as at the Battle of Towton Moor where up to 28,000 men died, the wars affected the average man only on the rare occasions when the armies turned free upon the countryside, such as Margaret allowed her soldiers to do following her victory at Wakefield. The battles fought in 1459 to 1461 demonstrate clearly that this was not an ideological war of the people, such as the seventeenth century's civil wars. Rather, this was a war of the nobility, and it was fought more for personal reasons than for idealistic ones.

The wars did not end with Edward's ascension to the throne. In fact, small skirmishes continued throughout the first half of the 1460s until Henry VI left his Scottish haven and was captured again by the Yorkists. From 1461 to 1470, Edward IV ruled, but he did not necessarily rule well. The old king, a man anointed to wear the crown, still lived; his wife and son, exiled in France, continued to plot to regain the throne; and the succession was not secure. Edward himself made a major error in governance when he ignored Warwick and his attempts to arrange a French marriage to gain the friendship of the French king. Instead, Edward secretly married the young, widowed Elizabeth Woodville. Not only did this marriage ruin the international agreements that Warwick had proposed, thereby demonstrating Edward's desire to place his own happiness above the welfare of the state, it also opened the door for the large Woodville family to gain precedence in the kingdom. Elizabeth had many sisters, who were quickly married off to the greatest men in the land, and her father and brothers soon gained the new king's ear. Warwick, previously Edward's right-hand man, was made a fool by the rejection of the French negotiations, was ignored as counselor to the king, and (perhaps most importantly) was left with two daughters for whom he suddenly found it nearly impossible to find husbands. As a result of Edward's marriage, Warwick, joined by Edward's younger brother, George, duke of Clarence, abandoned the Yorkist cause and departed for France. Marrying one daughter to the duke of Clarence and the other to Edward, Prince of Wales, Warwick soon established himself as "The Kingmaker," by successfully leading the Lancastrian forces against Edward in 1470 in order to regain the throne for Henry VI. Edward IV found he did not rule by grace of God, but instead by grace of Warwick, the kingmaker.

In 1470, the exiles declared Henry VI king once more, and the next year the duke of Clarence, Margaret, and Warwick invaded England, forcing Edward IV to flee to the Burgundians. The wars recommenced and a confused and uncomprehending Henry returned to the throne. The victory was astonishing, but also it was brief. Most of the Lancastrian lords resented the realignment with Warwick as an ally, and the populace craved peace and strong royal authority, not a return to the factions of the previous decade. In March 1471 Edward returned to England with a miniscule army, but he gathered much support from friends and former enemies. During the spring, the two sides fought two major battles, at Barnet and Tewkesbury. At Barnet, a fog had settled in across the battlefield and friend and foe were indistinguishable. Warwick died trying to escape and Edward IV was victorious. The next month, at Tewkesbury, Margaret was captured and her son Edward was killed. York had won. Following the Battle of Tewkesbury, on May 23, 1471, Henry VI died at the age of fifty in the Tower of London. Officially, his death was attributed to "melancholy and displeasure." Edward IV, previously duke of York, had retained his crown, and it appeared that the wars had ended. The direct line of Lancaster had been extinguished, and Edward could concentrate on ruling the kingdom. The next twelve years showed the new king's strengths as a monarch and administrator, although his personal habits and his reliance on court favorites raised eyebrows. As long as Edward remained on the throne, England appeared to have finished with the violence and civil disorder of the Wars of the Roses. A generally stable government ruled the land.

On April 9, 1483, tragedy struck. Only in his early forties, Edward IV breathed his last, leaving a twelve-year-old boy, Edward V, to rule as king. Consequently, another minority government appeared, and again the factions quickly developed. The new king's royal uncle, Richard, duke of Gloucester, became the protector of the king and of the realm. By early July Richard had executed the young king's maternal grandfather and uncle, and had imprisoned Edward and his little brother, claiming that they were illegitimate. Richard was stealing the throne for himself. The princes vanished in the Tower of London, leading many people both then and now to believe that Richard had secretly murdered his two nephews. The foundation of the Shakespearean Richard III had been laid, probably by the new king's own actions. Again, the succession was in doubt, and again, factions could grow and men could see ways to gain new lands and power for themselves. In addition, Richard's usurpation split the Yorkist party, as many who had supported Edward IV resented the deposition of his son. In October 1483 Richard's former supporter, the duke of Buckingham, rebelled; Richard defeated and executed him, but the door to war had been opened once more. In August 1485 the young Lancastrian heir, Henry Tudor, son of Margaret Beaufort and Edmund Tudor, left France and landed in Wales where he gained support against Richard III. The twenty-eight-year-old marched to the Midlands, where his forces met those of the king at Bosworth in Leicestershire. A last minute realignment of supporters occurred when Lord Stanley switched to Henry's side, an act that allowed for the Tudor victory. Richard III died on the battlefield.

Following Henry Tudor's victory at Bosworth Field, he took the crown as Henry VII. With this, the royal roulette of the Wars of the Roses ended. In 1487 Henry fought a final battle to secure his throne, but his dynasty would not fail for more than one hundred years and his descendants remain on the throne today. Henry claimed the throne by right of conquest and justified his claim through both his mother and the Beauforts, and his father as the son of Princess Catherine of France, the widow of Henry V. In addition, to secure the throne further and to end all doubts about succession, Henry VII married Elizabeth of York, the eldest daughter of Edward IV. Throughout his reign, Henry worked to strengthen the monarchy, not only by disposing of many of the remaining descendants of Edward III who might challenge his rule, but also by increasing the royal coffers and working to maintain international peace through agreements with France and Scotland. Perhaps it was knowledge of the disastrous effects of the precarious economic situation during the reign of Henry VI that convinced Henry VII to concentrate so effectively on financial issues, leading to a desire for peace over conflict. Henry and his heirs worked hard to create a strong, stable, and largely centralized government, and as a result, the Wars of the Roses have been seen as a momentous watershed in English history: the end of the Middle Ages and the beginning of the modern era. Did the Wars of the Roses have such a great effect on English society? According to the Tudors, the answer would be yes, as the wars allowed the Tudor dynasty to gain the throne and to establish a newly ordered kingdom.

The fifteenth century was one of the most turbulent in English history. From the deposition and murder of Richard II in 1399 to the end of the Wars of the Roses, England had seven kings, two of them placed on the throne twice. Underlying the monarchy's weakness was the social structure of bastard feudalism that by the middle of the century allowed for the growth of overmighty subjects. During the Wars of the Roses, almost half of the noble houses in England were exterminated, though elimination of only five of those (besides the royal houses) were due directly to the wars. From 1455 to 1487, the English faced periods of sporadic warfare, but it is important to remember that it was only sporadic. Although the fifteenth century resulted in problems for the royals and the nobility, in general the situation was not as dramatically unstable as it appears from looking only at the moments of fighting or at the upper classes. Between the battles, England was not in bad shape. Edward IV's second reign was amazingly stable, and he increased the royal treasury. Art and architecture continued during the period, and many of the houses built showed signs of being made for a less violent age. The landed classes regularly began to build houses that were made more for living than for operation as fortresses in private wars. Edward IV also anticipated Henry VII by moving to a system that utilized more lawyers and fewer nobles to run the governmental machine.

The Wars of the Roses did not signify an "end" of an era by themselves, but the later interpretation of the wars by Henry VII and his progeny have established them as the event that ended the instabilities of the Middle Ages in England. No transformation, though, occurred overnight at the moment of Henry VII's victory at Bosworth Field. Henry wanted to secure his government, his kingdom, and his seat on the throne, and therefore looked back at the fifteenth century in order to discover what worked and what went wrong. He continued many of the policies initiated by Edward IV, but he had one advantage that the Yorkist king never realized: a child who was able to gain and keep the throne upon his own death. Between 1485 and 1547, England benefited from two strong kings, who worked hard to maintain the stability of the land (even when, in the case of Henry VIII, that stability required a male heir and a subsequent break from the Roman church), and largely succeeded in achieving their goals, although the English people did not always support them wholeheartedly. The Tudors took advantage of the civil disorder of the Wars of the Roses to secure their grip on the throne, but their actions were not significantly new. They downplayed the successes of Edward IV, rejected any worth of Richard III and utilized the conclusion of the wars to create a symbol of unification. The white rose and the red rose joined together in order to end the strife. The roses, more symbolic of the wars after their conclusion, together became an emblem of the Tudor house and what through hindsight became a new era.

SELECTED BIBLIOGRAPHY

Bellamy, J.G. *Bastard Feudalism and the Law.* Oxford: Clarendon Press, 1989. This work discusses bastard feudalism and its impact on legal matters and the English courts.

Britnell, R. H. *The Closing of the Middle Ages?: England, 1471–1529*. Oxford: Basil Blackwell, 1997. A general introduction to the period by a thoughtful economic and social historian.

Carpenter, Christine. *The Wars of the Roses: Politics and the Constitution in England, c. 1437–1509*. Cambridge: Cambridge University Press, 1997. A solid overview that looks at localities and the court to gain greater insight into the wars and the perceptions of the king's role in the fifteenth century.

Chrimes, S. B. *Lancastrians, Yorkists and Henry VII*. London: Macmillan, 1965. This classic work argues that the wars were the result of Lancaster's bad governance and that hereditary right meant little.

Chrimes, S. B., C. D. Ross, and R. A. Griffiths, eds. *Fifteenth-Century England*. Manchester: Manchester University Press, 1972. An older but still important collection of essays that introduces students to issues at stake in the wars.

Cook, D. R. *Lancastrians and the Yorkists: The Wars of the Roses*. London: Longman, 1984. This well-written book touches on the strengthening of bastard feudalism during the minority of Henry VI.

Davies, C. S. L. *Peace, Print, and Protestantism, 1450–1558*. London: Hart-Davis, MacGibbon, 1976. Though older, this volume remains an indispensable overview of the period as it examines the various factors involved in causing the wars.

Dockeray, Keith. *Henry VI, Margaret of Anjou and the Wars of the Roses: A Source Book*. Stroud, UK: Sutton Publishing, 2000. This book allows the reader to gain further insight into the period through a presentation of original material.

Gillingham, John. *The War of the Roses*. Baton Rouge: Louisiana State University Press, 1981. An important book from one of the most important historians in the field. Looking more at the military than the political side of the wars, Gillingham sees them as three distinct conflicts and emphasizes that the wars do not equate with the decline of the Middle Ages.

Goodman, Anthony. *The Wars of the Roses*. London: Routledge and Kegan Paul, 1981. This focuses on the strategic, technical, and logistic aspects of the wars with regard to developing English military skills.

Griffiths, R. A. *The Reign of King Henry VI: The Exercise of Royal Authority, 1422–1461*. Berkeley: University of California Press, 1981. Concentrates on the role of the court and patronage during the reign of Henry VI. Griffiths' other royal biographies are also excellent.

Harvey, I. M. W. *Jack Cade's Rebellion of 1450*. Oxford: Clarendon Press, 1991. An important historical study based on manuscript sources that examines the reasons for Cade's rebellion in 1450.

Hicks, M. *Warwick the Kingmaker*. Oxford: Basil Blackwell, 1998. A masterful biography of the kingmaker, though a bit complex for younger students.

Keen, Maurice H. *England in the Later Middle Ages*, 2nd ed. London: Routledge, 2000. A good introduction to the period; Keen takes the position that the wars were less due to overmighty subjects than to an undermighty king.

Lander, J. R. *Government and Community: England 1450–1509*. Cambridge, MA: Harvard University Press, 1980. An in-depth look at the period and the relations between king and lords; notes the importance of bastard feudalism for maintaining order in the country.

Pollard, A. J. *The Wars of the Roses,* 2nd ed. New York: St. Martin's Press, 1997. A narrative account of the wars emphasizing constitutional history, this volume comments on both traditional historiography and problems with the interpretations of the wars.

Ross, Charles and R. A. Griffiths. *Edward IV.* New Haven, CT: Yale University Press, 1998. This reissue of a classic study looks at the manner in which Edward IV retained power and his crown.

Seward, Desmond. *The War of the Roses: Through the Lives of Five Men and Women of the Fifteenth Century.* New York: Viking, 1995. A popular but interesting history of the wars for the novice.

Storey, R. L. *The End of the House of Lancaster.* London: Barrie & Rockliff, 1966. Another older classic, this volume cites the growth of factions and the lords' scramble for power.

Thompson, J. A. F. *The Transformation of Medieval England, 1370–1529.* London: Longman, 1983. This work develops a comprehensive overview of the period.

Wolffe, B. P. *Henry VI.* London: Eyre Methuen, 1981. Wolffe blames the wars on the weakness of Henry VI and the loss of France.

6

The English Reformation, 1529–1536

INTRODUCTION

The Protestant Reformation, of which the English Reformation is an important part, may be said to have begun in 1517, following more than a century of growing problems with the Roman Catholic Church. As early as the fourteenth century, religious and secular leaders believed church reform necessary to deal with immoral and ignorant priests and corrupt popes. Despite this, the vast majority of European people clung to their faith in the fifteenth century and continued to give the church their loyalty and financial support. Yet problems persisted, and in 1512, Pope Julius II convened a churchwide council to discuss possible reforms. The meeting, however, produced nothing of consequence, however, and it was left to Martin Luther, a German cleric to launching the reformation. Luther, born in 1483, and the son of a German copper miner, trained to be a lawyer but instead entered a monastery in 1505 and became a priest two years later. He continued his theological studies, earned a doctorate, and became a professor at the University of Wittenberg.

During the course of his studies, Luther became convinced that salvation came to the believer not through devotion to the rituals of the organized church but by a simple and direct faith in God. In a more practical sense, his dispute focused on the church's practice of raising money through the sale of indulgences, or exemptions from the penalties associated with a sin. This practice had been going on since the Crusades in the twelfth century, and by Luther's time, one could purchase an indulgence to buy oneself out of almost any transgression. Luther considered this a betrayal of faith. He spoke out on the issues and won adherents to his

King Henry VIII is shown here wooing his lover, Anne Boleyn, at the residence of his adviser, Cardinal Wolsey. As the king aged, he became increasingly worried about the succession to the throne. Concluding that his wife, Catherine of Aragon, would not produce the much-desired male heir, Henry sought an annulment in order to marry Anne Boleyn. When the pope refused Henry's request, the king initiated the English Reformation. (Reproduced from the Collections of the Library of Congress.)

point of view, and the Protestant Reformation was born. Its success created Protestant denominations that rejected the hierarchical and authoritarian governance of the Vatican and persuaded followers that salvation could indeed be theirs by virtue of a genuine faith in God.

The Protestant Reformation in England took a much different course from that in Germany. Ever since the late thirteenth century, the crown and the church rivaled each other over such matters as taxes, the judicial authority of Rome, and clerical property rights. In the fourteenth and fifteenth centuries, the rise of humanism further heightened the conflict. Luther's ideas were circulating in England by the 1520s, and William Tyndale translated the New Testament into English much as Luther had translated it into German. Sir Thomas More, also a humanist, and Cardinal Thomas Wolsey defended the church against the increasing demands for reform, and King Henry VIII personally defended Catholic sacraments against Luther's criticism in a document titled *Defense of the Seven Sacraments*. For this, a grateful pope gave him the title Defender of the Faith.

Henry, who became king in 1509, was an unlikely figure in the religious conflict. When he became king, he was not particularly religious but was more interested in chivalric traditions, military matters, and the arts. Six weeks after his accession to the throne, he married Catherine of Aragon, the widow of his older brother Arthur, who had died in 1502, less than a year after his marriage to Catherine.

Despite his spirited defense of Catholicism in 1521, Henry's devotion to the church began to falter in 1527. After eighteen years of marriage, he and Catherine had produced no male heirs, and he, moreover, had become strongly attracted to Anne Boleyn, daughter of the earl of Wiltshire. In order to marry Anne (who might produce a male heir), Henry sought to have his marriage to Catherine annulled, based on a biblical mandate in the book of Leviticus that forbade one to marry his brother's widow. He argued, furthermore, that the pope lacked jurisdiction over religious matters in England, and that the monarch court not be summoned before any foreign court, including that of the church. Cardinal Wolsey argued Henry's case for annulment, and his failure to win the pope's assent brought about his fall from his powerful position as lord chancellor, the king's most powerful adviser. Sir Thomas More replaced Wolsey, despite the fact that he had never supported the annulment, although most of Wolsey's secular duties were assumed by Thomas Cranmer.

Cranmer and Thomas Cromwell, another of Henry's close confidants, developed the doctrine that the monarch was not only the secular head of state but also the spiritual head of state. Other statutes sent to the Parliament that sat between 1529 and 1536 declared that the pope no longer had any authority in England and that all monasteries should be closed. In addition, Parliament approved the Act of Supremacy, acknowledging Henry's spiritual authority in England, an act of succession, confirming that Elizabeth (the child of Henry and Anne) was in line to succeed Henry in the absence of a male heir, and a treason act, providing the death penalty for anyone denying Henry's authority as England's spiritual leader.

Monasteries were seized without compensation, although monks received state pensions for life. Much of the land was sold to local families of wealth and strengthened their attachment to the new Protestant church, since a return to Catholicism would mean the restoration of the monasteries. In addition, shrines containing priceless Catholic relics and sites where miracles were performed were shut down, and the relics destroyed or carted off to the royal vaults in London.

Parliament also passed laws forbidding the use of the term "pope," and compelling people to attend church where they listened to sermons that repeatedly endorsed the king as the spiritual leader of England. Another parliamentary act provided the death penalty for anyone arguing otherwise, and church officials had to swear an oath affirming Henry's spiritual authority; Sir Thomas More's refusal to do so led to his execution in 1535.

Despite the split with Rome, England was no paradise for many Protestants. Those who advocated more radical doctrines were routinely burned at the stake, and sympathetic church leaders such as Cranmer had to be quite careful in their words and deeds.

Cromwell tried to align the new church in England with the Lutherans in Germany and to introduce more radically Protestant practices into English church life, but Henry was reluctant to push the movement that far. He struck hard at the Pilgrimage of Grace, a quasi-religious movement that had social and economic aspects as well. The pilgrimage was in fact more a series of revolts in the northern part of England in the winter of 1536–1537 that the monarchy suppressed.

In 1538, Henry issued a royal proclamation cracking down on more radical forms of Protestantism in England. This move undercut Cromwell's authority soon after he had directed the publication and placing in every church an English-language version of the Bible. By this time, Henry had become convinced that the Reformation had gone too far and was worried that a Catholic alliance on the continent might launch an invasion of England. Henry no longer trusted Cromwell and had him tried, convicted, and executed in the summer of 1540. Henry also enforced an older law that called for the death penalty for those convicted of questioning traditional Catholic doctrine. In the final years of his reign, more Protestants than Catholics were executed.

Thomas Cranmer was more successful in maintaining the king's favor. Made archbishop of Canterbury in 1532, Cranmer quickly authorized the annulment of Henry's marriage to Catherine and his subsequent marriage to Anne Boleyn. Cranmer was also instrumental in writing or editing early documents on the principles of faith in what soon became known as the Church of England—*The Ten Articles* (1536) and *The Bishop's Book* (1537). Later, in 1549, he authorized the spiritually moderate *Book of Common Prayer*.

The English Reformation continued long after Henry's death in January 1547. His successor, Edward VI (1547–1553), was only a boy, and the royal authority was exercised by adult councillors such as Edward Seymour and John Dudley. Edward and his advisers did maintain the reforms engineered under Henry, but that would change under the rule of his half-sister, Mary, who succeeded him in 1553.

Mary, more than twenty years older than Edward and queen in her own right, was the daughter of Henry and Catherine of Aragon and was always closer to her mother and her Catholic friends, such as the Emperor Charles V, than to her father and his Protestant entourage. Her marriage to Charles's son Philip only confirmed her Catholicism, and as queen, she tried to restore the trappings of Catholic practices and papal authority. While the first found welcome with many who missed the often elegant rituals of the Catholic mass, attempts to restore papal authority did not. One consequence was an unprecedented period of religious persecution in England, during which some 300 people were killed and 800 driven into exile, all to no avail, as Protestant zeal continued unabated. Mary's premature death in 1558 led to the peaceful accession of her younger half-sister Elizabeth, who was as staunchly Protestant as Mary had been Catholic.

Upon Elizabeth's accession, Protestants exiled under Queen Mary returned to England, and many entered Parliament, where in 1559, new Acts of Supremacy were passed. These made it a criminal offense to hold a Catholic mass and provided for fines for those who failed to attend Church of England services. Although these acts and Elizabeth's long reign would seem to have made Protestantism safe in England, her failure to produce an heir kept the succession question open, and with it, the religious question. Her closest relative was her Catholic cousin, Mary, Queen of Scots. Mary, who had been forced to abdicate from her Scottish throne, lived in exile (and house arrest) in England for nearly twenty years until Elizabeth signed orders for her execution in 1587 for her involvement in one Catholic plot too many.

The key to the lasting institutionalization of Protestantism in England was imbedded in the Act of Supremacy and the Act of Uniformity, both passed in 1559. In 1563, a doctrinal statement known as the Thirty-Nine Articles was approved by a convocation, a gathering of clergy. The Act of Uniformity brought back the *Book of Common Prayer* authorized in 1552 under Edward and directed its use throughout England. While other controversies arose from time to time, such as the Vestarian Controversy about what clergy should wear, the acts of 1559 provided the means for gradual change through the monarch and Parliament working together.

INTERPRETIVE ESSAY
Kenneth L. Campbell

Any attempt to offer an interpretation of the English Reformation requires an answer to several fundamental questions. Was the English Reformation a political movement in which King Henry VIII decided to break with Rome and establish royal control over the English Church? Was it a religious movement, in which the new reform ideas created a groundswell of support for a change in the national religion? Was it a combination of the two? Was it imposed from above by the English government on an unwilling population? Was the English Reformation a single process by which England converted from a Catholic to a Protestant nation? Or were there four separate Reformations of Henry VIII, Edward VI, Elizabeth, and the Puritans? This essay will attempt to provide answers to these and other questions about the political, diplomatic, cultural, and social repercussions of the English Reformation.

At first, Henry VIII (1509–1547) did not respond enthusiastically to the budding Reformation Martin Luther spurred on the Continent. Henry composed a treatise on "The Defense of the Seven Sacraments," for which Pope Leo X dubbed him "Defender of the Faith." Henry was interested in religious matters and gave no indication prior to 1529 that he had any reservations about his Catholic faith or his allegiance to Rome. He attended mass regularly, sometimes several times a day. Henry's chancellor and chief minister during the 1520s was Cardinal Thomas Wolsey, a prominent cleric who held special authority to act as a papal representative in England. When Wolsey fell from grace because of his failure to obtain a divorce for the king from his wife, Catherine of Aragon, Henry appointed in his stead a layman, Thomas More. More also was an ardent defender of Catholicism, an advocate of religious persecution of non-Catholics, and eventually became an opponent of Henry's divorce.

More's appointment, however, coincided with a division within the upper echelons of the English government. Religious conservatives, such as Thomas Howard, duke of Norfolk, and Stephen Gardiner, bishop of Winchester, tried to convince Henry to work out his problems with the pope. Those inclined toward the new religious ideas believed that the divorce issue presented a golden opportunity to break with Rome and reform the English Church. The latter group included Thomas Cranmer, who became Henry's archbishop of Canterbury; Thomas Cromwell, who became chancellor; Anne Boleyn, who became Henry's second wife; and the duke of Somerset, Edward Seymour, whose niece Jane became Henry's third wife and who himself became lord protector after Henry's death. The reformers won out because Henry had thoroughly convinced himself that Catherine of Aragon's inability to produce a surviving male heir indicated God's displeasure with the marriage and because he wanted his divorce so badly.

When Henry initially considered breaking with Rome it was not because he was favorably disposed toward Luther's ideas. However, he was motivated by more than just his desire to divorce Catherine and marry Anne. Once Henry began to encounter obstacles from the papacy, he began to realize that historical arguments could be made for royal supremacy over the church. Both the kings of France and Spain had acquired a wide power over their national churches. Arguments for the power of the king over the clergy within his realm had been constructed by a series of thinkers in the fourteenth century, including the Englishman, John Wycliffe. Henry decided to call Parliament and have it gradually assert the independence of the English Church in order to put pressure on Rome to concede him the same rights as other monarchs. It is unclear that these rights would have covered the divorce, since Henry had been allowed to marry Catherine, his brother's widow, only by papal dispensation. Presumably only the pope could overturn a decision made by a previous pope. Even so, Parliament passed legislation that was quite radical in its approach to papal authority.

When More resigned and was succeeded by Cromwell, the movement toward reform proceeded apace. Cromwell began to make his plans for the dissolution of the monasteries and to justify Henry's position as head of the Church. Henry appointed the reformer Cranmer to the see of Canterbury, though largely because of Cranmer's willingness to grant the divorce and support royal supremacy over the Church. By 1536, Henry had appointed other reformers such as Edward Fox and Hugh Latimer to important positions within his church. Meanwhile, reformers such as William Tyndale took advantage of the printing press to continue the spread of Lutheran ideas in England.

Assessing the English Reformation of Henry VIII is a complicated matter because Henry himself embodied so many contradictory tendencies. On the one hand, Henry approved the Ten Articles in 1536, which were Lutheran in tone and content; he approved the dissolution of the monasteries, a bulwark of medieval Catholicism that many regarded as outdated and superfluous in sixteenth-century society; he approved the publication of the *Great Bible,* a new English translation, which was one of the main goals of the Protestant reformers; and he appropriated to the crown revenues from chantries, which had been designed to support prayers for the dead, but which were no longer deemed necessary by Protestants who believed in justification (or salvation) by faith alone.

On the other hand, Henry approved the Six Articles in 1539, which affirmed Catholic doctrines on several key points, including masses for the dead and the need for confession, prescribing the death penalty for those who would deny them; he dissolved monasteries without challenging the principles behind monasticism (some remained open); he affirmed the doctrine of purgatory that seemed to justify prayers for the dead; and in 1543 he authorized and gained Parliament's support for the King's Book (*A Necessary Doctrine and Erudition for any Christian Man*), which continued to defend the seven Catholic sacraments and contained the Catholic position on communion and free will in matters of salvation. Henry believed in clerical celibacy, upheld by the Six Articles, but he allowed his own archbishop of Canterbury, Thomas Cranmer, to marry. He refused to allow further reform in the 1540s, but his last wife, Catherine Parr, had Protestant sympathies, as did the men placed in charge of raising his son, Edward. Even those closest to him must have wondered where Henry really stood on matters of religion, not to mention the common people who had to decipher the significance of the various and often contradictory tendencies displayed by the king.

Therefore, was the Reformation of Henry VIII then a legitimate religious movement or merely a political power play that involved breaking ties with Rome and asserting the authority of the king and the state over the church? First, the Reformation under Henry VIII possessed an undeniable political significance in that it did make Henry the supreme head of the Church of England (Act of Supremacy, 1534). Henry eliminated papal authority in England and by appropriating that authority for himself he greatly enhanced the power of the monarchy. Clerics now served solely at the will of the monarch who had eliminated any notion of a dual allegiance to pope and king. At the same time, the religious and ecclesiastical changes under Henry had all been ratified by parliamentary legislation, thus elevating the status of Parliament as an indispensable institution for changes of this magnitude. But to view Henry's Reformation as exclusively political in nature would be a mistake, although even some contemporary Protestants viewed it as such. Henry maintained some Catholic doctrines and did not carry reform as far as he might have, but momentum toward transforming England into a Protestant nation had been established. Cranmer's position as the highest ecclesiastical official under the king was particularly significant for the future direction of the English church.

However, another important issue involves the extent to which the English people were receptive of these religious changes and how far they supported the Reformation. This issue centers on a debate about the strength and popularity of pre-Reformation Catholicism. If, the argument runs, Catholicism in England represented a living, vibrant faith to which the people retained a high level of devotion and attachment prior to the Reformation, then the English Reformation could not have been a popularly inspired movement that produced a population naturally inclined to support the religious changes brought about by Henry VIII and his son, Edward VI. Therefore, the Reformation must have succeeded only because it was sustained by the awesome power of the state, which forced people to accept reforms to which they were not otherwise inclined.

Several arguments can be offered in support of this position. The Church had made attempts to improve the quality of its service to the lay population and exhibited signs of vigor and strength prior to the Reformation. The clergy had become better educated on the whole and the strongest advocates for reform came from within the church. Even Martin Luther, a professor of theology and previously a monk, was a product of the early sixteenth-century Church. John Fisher, the bishop of Rochester, and John Colet, the dean of St. Paul's Cathedral, were among the English clerics who favored a more humanistic approach to religion.

Secondly, wills from the first decade of the sixteenth century generally demonstrate that a significant proportion of the people who left them bequeathed money and gifts to the Church. Whether these gifts indicate the popularity of the Church or additional insurance for the afterlife is open to debate. But the vast majority of wills prior to the Reformation also provided money for prayers to be said for the deceased's soul to lessen the time spent in Purgatory. Most wills also made reference to the expected intercessory role to be played by the saints and the Virgin Mary. No one denied the importance of Christ's sacrificial role or the necessity of grace for salvation, but wills do provide evidence that most people felt comfortable with the Catholic emphasis on the need for both faith and works.

Thirdly, many Catholic practices remained popular in England at the time of the Reformation. Prayer to saints and devotion to the mass were reflected in both popular and devotional literature from the period. Thomas Cromwell received information in 1538 that five or six hundred people a day were making pilgrimages to an image, illustrating the persistence of medieval forms of popular piety. Fewer men entered the priesthood in the years immediately after 1536, perhaps indicating a lack of support for Henry's religious changes. Long after the beginning of the Reformation, people continued to engage in special activities no longer practiced in church, such as prayers for the dead, special blessings, and the use of religious objects associated with specific religious holidays.

Proponents of this sympathetic interpretation of English Catholicism have made a strong case for their position and done much to challenge the notion of the English Reformation as a popular reform movement. Ever since the reign of Henry, Catholics have tended to view the royal divorce as the "cause" of the English Reformation, while Protestants point to genuine religious and social factors. Can the two views be successfully reconciled? There is much evidence to suggest that people in many parts of England retained a positive attachment to religious practices and beliefs associated with Catholicism that became altered or eradicated under the influence of the Reformation. However, in other parts of England positive attitudes toward reform clearly existed.

Proponents of viewing the Reformation as a popular religious movement point to the strong tradition of anticlericalism that existed in England on the eve of Henry's decision to break with Rome. Anticlerical attitudes in the 1520s found a natural target in Cardinal Wolsey, who had attained vast amounts of wealth and had reached the pinnacle of political power in England in addition to holding more than a dozen ecclesiastical positions, including archbishop of York, bishop of Winchester, and abbot of St. Alban's monastery. Wolsey embodied the clerical abuses of pluralism (holding more than one office) and absenteeism. Parliament took steps to address such abuses in its legislation in 1529 during the opening stages of the English Reformation. As for the lower clergy, even if educational standards had improved, the chorus of complaints against clerical ignorance and immorality had not died down significantly. Simon Fish, in his 1529 pamphlet "The Supplication of Beggars," criticized the morals of clergy who paid women (and men) to sleep with them. Finally, regarding the monastic houses that came under attack in the 1530s, even Wolsey seemed to acknowledge their flaws when he eliminated some of the smaller monastic communities prior to the Reformation. The English Reformation drew support as well from the emerging humanist thinking at Oxford and Cambridge, though the Dutch writer Desiderius Erasmus, Fisher, and other humanists proved that humanism was not incompatible with a continued allegiance to Catholicism.

It is highly doubtful that Henry could have succeeded in even his modest strides toward reform had the vast majority of his people been implacably opposed. Henry did in fact face some opposition: John Fisher and Thomas More both were executed for their failure to support the royal divorce and Henry's new position as the supreme head of the Church of England. The Pilgrimage of Grace, a rebellion in northern England in 1536 triggered by the dissolution of the monasteries, represented Henry's most serious challenge during his reign. Support from individuals of all social classes rendered the revolt particularly dangerous. The Pilgrimage of Grace represented a combination of social, economic, and religious grievances combined under the banner of the Five Wounds of Christ. It drew much of its support and leadership in northern England from the yeomen farmers, lower clergy, and skilled artisans. Henry's crushing of the rebellion did not eliminate popular opposition in Yorkshire and may have added to it. But the rebellion did not spread throughout the country and the vast majority of the populace remained loyal. Most of Henry's clergy passively acquiesced; even if economic considerations militated against resignation or opposition, they must not have found the changes too objectionable.

In the end, on the matter of causation, it can be argued that early sixteenth-century English Catholicism had enough problems and reform ideas had sufficient popular appeal that an English Reform movement would have occurred independently of Henry's desire to divorce Catherine of Aragon, his desire for a male heir, or his desire for Anne Boleyn. Without Henry's leadership, the English Reformation would have taken more of the form of the Scottish Reformation, growing as an underground movement under a Catholic government until such time as it became strong enough to force the monarchy to acquiesce in ecclesiastical reform. Some at the time would have even preferred it that way; the reformer William Tyndale distrusted the king's motivations and suggested that the Church could only be reformed by the actions of the people. By taking the initiative, Henry had asserted royal control over the process of reform and by the end of his reign had slowed the pace far beyond that desired by reformers such as Cranmer and Tyndale. Even without Henry, an English Reformation of some sort would have occurred.

Still, it is entirely possible to argue that the Reformation had not yet been solidly established in the hearts of the majority of the English people when Edward VI ascended the throne in 1547, at Mary's accession six years later, or even when Elizabeth became queen in 1558. In the last years of Henry's reign, the Church of England remained divided, Cranmer serving as the leading proponent of reform and Gardiner still the leading conservative. Popular uprisings in 1547 and 1548 opposed the extension of reformed practices and the imposition of a new prayer book. Even among towns that quietly or passively acquiesced to the religious changes under Henry or Edward, some towns must have conformed outwardly without altering the hearts and minds of the inhabitants. Especially under Henry's reign, the mere elimination of papal authority would have done little to alter outward forms of behavior or inner forms of belief. Evidence indicates little change in these forms until late in Elizabeth's reign. To carry out the religious changes of Edward's reign at the parish level required the careful oversight of church officials, indicating that in many places the Reformation was established only by a top-down approach. Local parishioners sometimes hid venerated crucifixes, images, or religious objects from Protestant officials or removed them only under pressure from above.

Catholicism did retain its strength and appeal in some regions, particularly in the north and west. Queen Mary believed that most people who had acquiesced in the religious changes of the preceding reigns would return penitently to the Catholic faith under her guidance and leadership. Parliament acquiesced with Mary's plans to repeal the Protestant legislation of Edward VI, though it did not formally restore the authority of the pope or rescind the confiscation of monastic lands. Mary attempted to address some of the complaints of reformers by placing a greater emphasis on churchmen fulfilling their pastoral obligations and on preaching, but she also had Protestants burned at the stake because of her belief that they represented only a tiny minority. She had no tolerance for those whom she regarded as heretics and minions of the devil. In her eyes, Protestant leaders, including Cranmer, had deceived the people and deserved their horrid fate.

But even if the majority of people continued to hold to Catholic practices in the mid-sixteenth century, it is difficult to prove that they did so out of positive devotion as opposed to ingrained tradition or force of habit. It is undeniable that some still found their spiritual needs met in the traditional faith but equally undeniable that others did not and found those needs met in the new faith. Uprisings in London and the southeast at the beginning of Edward's reign put pressure on the government to enact further reform, countering opponents in other parts of the country. While some people in the country hid crosses to preserve them from destruction, others in London forcefully removed crosses even before they had received orders to do so. Meanwhile, the majority of the people may well have been sufficiently flexible (or apathetic) to bend to the shifting religious winds in whatever direction they blew. Both Protestants and Catholics in the sixteenth century expressed concern that this was in fact the case.

In many respects, it makes sense to consider the religious changes of Edward and Elizabeth together as a continuation of the Reformation started under Henry, with Mary's reign as a brief and temporary attempt to reverse that process. Under Edward, who was only nine years old when he became king, Parliament passed laws repealing the Six Articles and steering England more in the direction of Protestantism while Thomas Cranmer reformed the religious service itself in his *Book of Common Prayer.* The first *Book of Common Prayer* in 1549 provided the people of England a worship service that they could fully understand for the first time. The reform occurred under Edward, but Cranmer had prepared materials for the prayer book in the later years of Henry's reign. The duke of Somerset presided over the government in the early stages of Edward's reign and carried through a thoroughgoing program of religious reform. Edward was likened to a new Josiah, an Old Testament king who ascended the throne at an early age and took a particularly strong stand against idolatry. The clergy received permission to marry in 1549, and many among them took advantage of the new legislation in a highly visible expression of support for the religious changes taking place. Mary reintroduced the prohibition on clerical marriages in 1554 and mandated the separation of married clergy and their wives, but those who separated did so under compulsion while others chose to relinquish their clerical positions. Those who had married under Edward did so entirely voluntarily.

Elizabeth ascended the throne amidst a great deal of religious anxiety and gloom created by Mary's persecutions. In Elizabeth's case, the religious uncertainty worked in her favor since she managed to retain the allegiance of the vast majority of her subjects by not taking a firm stand at the beginning of her reign. By the late 1660s, however, Elizabeth, her ministers, and Parliament had reestablished the Protestant Church of England, with Elizabeth as supreme governor of the Church, and had further sustained the English Reformation. Elizabeth adopted the more moderate of the two editions of the *Book of Common Prayer* and approved the Thirty-Nine Articles as a creed, which were more moderate than the Forty-Two Articles approved by Edward. She supported the Scottish Reformation. By the time that she was excommunicated by the pope in 1570, the vast majority of people had accommodated themselves to her rule, although she continued to face dangers from Catholic plotters, who were, however, much in the minority in wanting her dead. England had become, for better or worse, a Protestant nation, although it is only with hindsight that we know that it would remain so.

The most obvious domestic consequence of the English Reformation was that the country became religiously divided between those who accepted the authority of the state in matters of religion and those who did not. The latter group fell into two main categories: Roman Catholics, known in England as "papists," and Protestant separatists, sometimes known as "Congregationalists." While there are divisions within both of these main groups, both groups made the political argument that the monarch, even with the support of Parliament, simply had no authority over spiritual matters. Catholics believed that religious authority belonged with the Church, not the state. Protestants who regarded scripture as the sole authority rejected the establishment of another church hierarchy with the monarch replacing the pope at the top of it. Protestant separatists also objected to worshiping in a church that contained all manners of people, including the ungodly who came to church unwillingly.

Henry regarded himself as a member of the clergy and appropriated to the monarchy the right to judge heresy. Nonconformists legitimately argued that to give a monarch this right meant that definitions of orthodoxy and heresy changed depending on the individual who happened to inherit the throne, an intolerable situation for those who believed in the concept of religious truth.

Many Puritans who chose to remain within the established Church of England shared the same religious views as many of the separatists, but differed with them by defending the legitimacy of a state church and the power of the government to enforce conformity. Puritans generally adhered to Calvinist theology with its emphasis on predestination, the doctrine that God had predestined select individuals for salvation or damnation. Puritans tried to work within the established Church to promote their religious views, beginning in the reign of Elizabeth. Puritans sought to make religious concerns the primary force in directing the future history of the English Reformation. They did not regard the Reformation as complete and under Elizabeth began to advocate for further reforms on a fairly consistent basis. In a 1572 petition, *The Admonition to Parliament*, Puritans criticized the continued use of such Catholic remnants as making the sign of the cross, the wearing of elaborate vestments by the clergy, and private baptism.

The growth of Calvinism during the reign of Elizabeth represents perhaps the most significant religious development associated with the English Reformation. Elizabeth had no interest in promoting Calvinism in its strict sense but faced a rising tide that persisted until the end of her reign. In fact, Elizabeth had no interest in further reform at all and she and her advisers primarily concerned themselves with opposing separatism or nonconformity in any form. Elizabeth demanded outward conformity as an indication of political allegiance, while not feeling the need to "make windows into men's souls." Elizabeth thus had no particular objection to the Church-papists, Catholic sympathizers who attended Anglican services to stay within the law. The Calvinist Puritans found such an attitude lacking in sufficient religious zeal. They also sought to refine the broad and flexible statements on doctrine contained in the Thirty-Nine Articles. Elizabeth refused to recognize the validity of the Lambeth Articles, which a group of clerics had approved in 1595. Those articles provided a strict Calvinist interpretation of the doctrine of predestination, that "those who are not predestinated to salvation shall be necessarily damned for their sins." Elizabeth's attitude left the Puritans in a position of deploring what they viewed as a continuation of church abuses and looking to a future monarch to promote a further reformation of the Church of England, even as most of them remained within the national church.

The English Reformation had other political consequences. The English followed the general European principle that the religion of the ruler would be the religion of the state. The adoption of a state religion, therefore, raised questions about the relationship between the individual and the state, inextricably linking religious concerns with political theory. Richard Hooker's *Laws of Ecclesiastical Polity* became the central work justifying the authority, organization, and worship service of the Church of England. Hooker also defended the Calvinist position on justification, but dealt with general political theory as well. Hooker constructed the important argument that membership in the commonwealth and membership in the state Church were inextricably connected. He based his argument on the concept of the distinction between the visible church, to which, like the commonwealth everyone belonged, as opposed to the invisible church, whose membership could only truly be known by God.

From its inception, the English Reformation carried with it enormous international ramifications as well. Prior to the Reformation, England's main political rival had been France, particularly during the Hundred Years' War, which lasted from 1337 to 1453. Henry VIII had revived the French wars and even staked his claim as king of France. Henry's marriage to Catherine of Aragon had created diplomatic ties between England and the Spanish crown. However, when Henry decided to divorce Catherine, he threatened to undermine his relationship with King Charles I of Spain, who in 1519 had become Holy Roman Emperor, extending his authority over German lands. Charles, Catherine's nephew, had his own problems with the pope and even sacked Rome in 1527, but he was not about to support Henry's desire to divorce his aunt. Furthermore, Pope Clement VII, under intense pressure from Charles, had no wish to alienate the emperor further, leading to a series of stalling tactics to avoid granting Henry's request.

Henry's break with Rome alienated the major Catholic powers of Europe (Spain, France, and the Holy Roman Empire, not to mention the papacy) and shaped England's diplomacy until Henry's Catholic daughter Mary inherited the throne in 1553. Henry's divorce from Catherine raised the specter of an invasion by Catherine's nephew, Emperor Charles V. The threat of invasion by Catholic powers might have inhibited the extent of reform that occurred under Henry, especially since his attitudes toward reform seemed to soften as the threat started to wane late in his reign. But the threat still influenced diplomacy during Edward's reign, especially since Mary, Henry's Catholic daughter with Catherine of Aragon, waited in the wings.

The English Reformation greatly affected the government's concern with Ireland, which remained Catholic and, therefore, represented a potential threat from which a hostile foreign power could launch an invasion of England. Tudor governments under Henry and Elizabeth accelerated efforts to establish English control there. Almost immediately after Henry's Reformation, Irish priests began preaching in favor of resistance to royal authority, even promising salvation for those who resisted. Unlike Ireland, Wales had already fallen firmly under English control and yet had no voice in the religious changes imposed upon them. No previous reform tradition existed in Wales, which shared a basic religious conservatism with northern and western England. Wales, however, did not revolt against the religious changes, perhaps because the Welsh recognized from the start that it would have been a losing proposition.

Scotland had a long history of a political alliance with France, which now carried religious overtones as well. If Scotland remained a Catholic nation like Ireland, it could have proven a haven for England's enemies. Henry VIII had fought two wars with Scotland during his long reign. The Scottish reformer John Knox preached in England during Edward's reign, led a congregation of English refugees on the Continent during Mary's, and returned to Scotland to push for Reformation in the early years of Elizabeth's reign. Elizabeth supported the Reformation in Scotland and then kept her Catholic cousin, Mary Queen of Scots, under house arrest in England from 1568 to 1587 because of her desire to prevent a Catholic Scotland from realigning itself with France. Mary's execution in 1587 after being implicated in a treasonous plot to overthrow Elizabeth was one of the immediate causes for King Philip II of Spain to declare war on England and launch the famous Spanish Armada in 1588.

Puritans especially supported the war with Spain that lasted from 1587 to 1604 because they viewed religion in international terms, both as a result of their professed connection with reformed churches of a Calvinist persuasion on the Continent and their vehement anti-Catholicism. To them, Spain was an "evil empire" representing the forces of the devil against the godly. Elizabeth's informal support for the French Calvinists, known as the Huguenots, and the Protestant Dutch in their struggle for independence from Spain also met with popular acclaim and formed important components of Elizabeth's pro-Protestant foreign policy.

The English Reformation had a number of social and cultural ramifications as well, which can only be touched on briefly here. Most importantly, the Reformation challenged people's attitudes and beliefs, not just about religion but also about the world in general. Protestants denied many of the magical and miraculous elements of medieval Catholicism and called on people to put their trust entirely in the will and power of God. Many people failed to live up to this ideal, consulting local astrologers and men and women reputed to have special psychic or healing powers to assist them with their mortal lives, with the church now reserved for the needs of their immortal souls. By placing an emphasis on Scripture, many people in Reformation England took the power of the devil quite seriously, leading to new laws against witchcraft and opening the door for numerous such accusations. England, however, generally avoided the massive witch-hunts and hysteria that occurred on the Continent during the same period. Furthermore, belief in witchcraft was widespread at the time and not associated with any particular shade of religious sentiment. In the long run, the Reformation may have helped to undermine belief in witchcraft by fostering a less magical view of the world.

Anti-Catholicism became a prominent attitude throughout English society from the late sixteenth century, reinforced in the minds of Protestants by the legends of the Spanish Inquisition, the Marian persecutions and the treatment of them in John Foxe's extremely popular book *The Acts and Monuments of the Christian Martyrs*; the St. Bartholomew's Day Massacre in 1572 in France; the treasonous activities of Mary, Queen of Scots; the war with Spain; and culminating in the Gunpowder Plot of 1605, in which a small group of Catholic terrorists attempted to blow up the assembled houses of Parliament with King James I in attendance. But the English Reformation also contributed in the long run to ideas of religious toleration and skepticism about the absolute nature of religious truth, since people held so many different opinions, even those claiming to use the Bible as their authority.

Puritans attempted to enforce in society an atmosphere conducive to moral righteousness, including opposition to such activities as gambling, drinking, dancing, blasphemy and cursing, and playing sports on the Sabbath. These attempts did not succeed in fundamentally altering English society or transforming England into a Christian utopia, but they did create divisions and tensions within society. In places where Puritans had the support of local constables or control of church courts, which operated independently of the secular authorities, ordinary people could find themselves humiliated or disgraced for moral offenses. Reformed preachers could exercise a great deal of influence over their congregations.

The Reformation involved a different attitude toward poverty, since under Catholicism giving alms represented the kind of good work that could help one attain salvation. With the Protestant doctrine of justification by faith alone, relief for the poor became more of a voluntary act related to Christ's command to love one's neighbor. This change did not necessarily make Protestants less charitable than Catholics, but the Reformation happened to coincide with economic changes in the sixteenth century, including population growth, inflation, and an increase in poverty, unemployment, and homelessness that made charitable giving less appealing. The dissolution of the monasteries had contributed to economic change by producing a more capitalist-minded landlord class. Protestantism could at times contribute to a hostile attitude toward the poor as undeserving or lacking God's favor. In the lurch, the English government began to pass the first welfare laws in which the state began to provide poor relief for those registered at the parish level.

Examined as a whole, the English Reformation was not so much an event as a process by which England became gradually transformed into a Protestant nation. This was not accomplished at one fell swoop and involved several religious changes that have led some historians to speak about English *Reformations*. Even as the Reformation became transformed, Protestant ways frequently became assimilated with older traditions, despite the best efforts of Puritans to eliminate everything from clerical vestments to Christmas celebrations. Protestantism emphasized justification by faith alone, but still retained the sacraments of baptism and communion. Protestants provided different interpretations of these sacraments, but had to walk a fine line in those interpretations to ensure that people took them seriously, although not as seriously as Catholics did. Catholics believed that infants who died would not go to heaven unless they were baptized; Anglicans denied this while still emphasizing how important infant baptism was. Anglicans treaded carefully in the language used at funerals, lest their prayers for the dead smack of Catholic prayers offered to assist souls in purgatory. The Church of England retained ritual, but simultaneously condemned the Catholic mass for its magical elements.

As a process, the Reformation continued through the seventeenth and into the eighteenth century, if John Wesley's Methodist movement is included. John Smith and Thomas Helwys helped found the English General Baptists in the early seventeenth century. The Quakers and other radical religious sects emerged in the radical atmosphere of the English Civil War in the mid-seventeenth century. Puritanism continued to evolve in the late seventeenth century as a more politically quiescent movement inspired by people such as John Bunyan, who wrote the religious classic, *Pilgrim's Progress.* Thus, religious-minded people continued to assess their relationship with God, the church, and human society. Perhaps the continued struggle to address such fundamental issues that still concern us today represents the greatest legacy of the English Reformation.

SELECTED BIBLIOGRAPHY

Aston, Margaret. *The King's Bedpost: Reformation and Iconography in a Tudor Group Portrait.* Cambridge: Cambridge University Press, 1993. A fascinating and in-depth of one sixteenth-century painting, *Edward VI and the Pope,* through which the author provides much insight into the thoughts associated with the reforming process.

Brigden, Susan. *London and the Reformation.* Oxford: Clarendon Press, 1989. London played an extremely important role in the English Reformation and Brigden's study complements those dealing with other local regions.

Carleton, Kenneth. *Bishops and Reform in the English Church, 1520–1559.* Woodbridge, Suffolk, UK: Boydell Press, 2001. Carleton examines the importance of the selection of bishops appointed to lead the Church after Henry VIII initiated his break with Rome and the role that bishops played through the first year of Elizabeth's reign.

Collinson, Patrick. *Godly People: Essays on English Protestantism and Puritanism.* London: Hambledon Press, 1983. Collinson, a prominent historian of English religion in the early modern period, focuses on the lives of the people who, he argues, used their own minds and wills to shape the evolution of Protestantism during Elizabeth's reign.

Collinson, Patrick. *The Religion of Protestants: The Church in English Society, 1559–1625.* Oxford, UK: Clarendon Press, 1982. Collinson helps to demonstrate why most Puritans chose to remain within the Church of England and their ability to help shape the religious consciousness of their age.

Cressy, David. *Birth, Marriage, and Death: Ritual, Religion, and the Life-Cycle in Tudor and Stuart England.* Oxford: Oxford University Press, 1997. In this impressive and comprehensive work, Cressy examines the different stages of the life cycle and their relationship to the religious and cultural beliefs that gave meaning to people's common experiences.

Dickens, A.G. *The English Reformation.* University Park: Pennsylvania State University Press, 1991. This important and largely sympathetic treatment of the English Reformation treats the Reformation as a popular movement while also providing an overview of the religious history of sixteenth-century England.

Duffy, Eamon. *The Stripping of the Altars: Traditional Religion in England, 1400–1580.* New Haven, CT: Yale University Press, 1992. Duffy has contributed a monumental work to the scholarship on the English Reformation, showing in detail the important role that traditional religion played in people's lives prior to and during the English Reformation.

———. *The Voices of Morebath: Reformation and Rebellion in an English Village.* New Haven, CT: Yale University Press, 2001. Here Duffy uses the experience of one village to tell the story of how and why some people reluctantly accepted the Reformation, in spite of their previous devotion to traditional Catholicism.

Haigh, Christopher. *English Reformations: Religion, Politics, and Society under the Tudors.* Oxford, UK: Clarendon Press, 1993. Along with Duffy, Haigh supports the view that the English Reformation was largely imposed by the state on an unreceptive people in this important and in-depth survey of the Reformation period in England.

Higgs, Laquita M. *Godliness and Governance in Tudor Colchester.* Ann Arbor: University of Michigan Press, 1998. An important local study, Higgs's book examines the conditions that led to Colchester's speedy embrace of the Reformation before tracing the history and impact of the Reformation there during the remainder of the sixteenth century.

Jones, Norman. *The Birth of the Elizabethan Age: England in the 1560s.* Oxford, UK: Blackwell, 1993. Jones's important book on the political culture of early Elizabethan England provides an excellent understanding of the religious conditions and concerns that prevailed at that time.

Litzenberger, Caroline. *The English Reformation and the Laity: Gloucestershire, 1540–1580.* Cambridge, UK: Cambridge University Press, 1997. Litzenberger emphasizes how slow many lay people in Gloucestershire were to abandon traditional lay piety in the last years of Henry's reign and the responses of such individuals to the various religious changes that followed.

MacCulloch, Diarmaid. *Thomas Cranmer: A Life.* New Haven, CT: Yale University Press, 1996. MacCulloch's landmark biography details the important role of Cranmer in the English Reformation and the gradual triumph of Protestantism in England from the reign of Henry forward.

O'Day, Rosemary. *The Debate on the English Reformation.* London: Methuen, 1986. Though published before much intervening important scholarly debate and now a bit dated, this book provides an excellent survey of the history of historical writing on the English Reformation from the sixteenth to the twentieth century.

Parish, Helen L. *Clerical Marriage and the English Reformation: Precedent, Policy, and Practice.* Aldershot, UK: Ashgate, 2000. Parish deals with one of the most important issues associated with the English Reformation and the relationship between clerical marriage and the Reformation as a whole.

Scarisbrick, J. J. *The Reformation and the English People.* New York: Basil Blackwell, 1984. Scarisbrick provides a counter-argument to Dickens and anticipates the work of Duffy and Haigh in a treatment that is sympathetic to the appeal of late medieval Catholicism.

Thomas, Keith. *Religion and the Decline of Magic.* New York: Charles Scribner's Sons, 1971. In a book that provided a watershed for historians of early modern England, Thomas takes a largely anthropological approach to deal with many cultural and social dimensions of the reformation in England, including changing attitudes on providence, witchcraft, magical healing, astrology, ancient prophecies, ghosts and fairies, and times and omens.

7

Elizabethan England, 1558–1603

INTRODUCTION

The phrase "Elizabethan England" derives from the long reign of Elizabeth I, who occupied the throne from 1558 until 1603. The daughter of Henry VIII and Anne Boleyn, Elizabeth was born on September 7, 1533. She received a good education under the direction of Catherine Parr, her father's last wife, and became proficient in Latin, Greek, Italian, and French. During the reign of the Catholic Queen Mary (1533–1558), Elizabeth, who always embraced Protestantism, was briefly under suspicion for treason, but nothing was proven against her and she was released. Her succession in 1558 upon Mary's death was peaceful.

At the beginning of her reign, Elizabeth received great help from William Cecil (Lord Burghley), whom she appointed as her secretary and chief minister. A wily politician and devoted Protestant, Cecil was an able and trusted counselor to Elizabeth for forty years. He advised her to take the throne as a Protestant despite the domestic risk of antagonizing bishops and Scots, and the international risk of alienating Catholic foreign rulers. Papal supremacy, restored by Mary, was again abolished, and the spiritual powers Henry had held were given to her, although she was called supreme governor rather than supreme head. The Catholic mass was again outlawed, and the doctrine of transubstantiation (the idea that the wine and bread of communion actually become the blood and flesh of Christ during the sacrament) was officially denied.

Protestant sufferings under Mary between 1555 and 1558 were chronicled by John Foxe in a long book known commonly as the *Book of Martyrs*, which, in part, drew a connection between the Christian martyrs in

Queen Elizabeth I signed the death warrant for her cousin, Mary, Queen of Scots, in 1587. For many years the English have looked back with great favor upon the reign of Elizabeth ("Good Queen Bess"). In fact, the Elizabethan era was a rather perilous one for both the monarch and the country. In consigning her conniving cousin to the block, Elizabeth virtually ensured a hostile response from Spain, Europe's current superpower. (Reproduced from the Collections of the Library of Congress.)

Roman times and the contemporary Protestant martyrs. Despite its length, the book was popular after its publication in 1563, and copies were ordered to be placed in every church. No one who read of the terrifying accounts of torture and execution could fail to have great contempt for the Roman Catholic Church, an attitude that continued for three centuries. Still, Elizabeth was more tolerant and lenient toward religious extremists than her father or half-sister had been. Far fewer heretics were executed, and the queen, anxious to unite her nation, tried to be conciliatory.

The early years of Elizabeth's reign were much concerned with Scottish affairs. In 1558, Scotland was a poor country with a population of some 500,000. It remained Catholic under the rule of Mary, Queen of Scots, a teenaged ruler with close ties to France. The country was plagued by both a struggling economy, which caused many Scots to emigrate, and a church even more corrupt than the church in England had been before reformation. Indeed, in much of the country, religious practices were no longer to be found.

Scottish Protestants were more militant than their English counterparts had been, and they fomented a rebellion in 1547, seizing St. Andrews Castle and killing Cardinal David Beaton, the chancellor of Scotland. The French sent a fleet to Scotland and recaptured the castle, but the incident reflected the depth of feeling among Scottish Protestants. In 1559, Scottish Protestant leader John Knox incited another rebellion that spread quickly through the lowlands and into Edinburgh. When the French offered to help the government, the rebels appealed to Elizabeth for assistance. Although she disliked Knox, who did not favor women in government, she and Cecil saw this as a chance to secure Scotland for Protestantism and wrest it away from French (and Catholic) influence. Elizabeth first sent money and material support to Knox and then decided to intervene with her army. This was risky because her army was not strong, and she could not expect help from others. After a naval expedition in the winter of 1759–1760 only partly succeeded in delivering aid to the Scottish rebels, Elizabeth sent an 11,000-man army to Scotland in the spring. Her force laid siege to the French garrison at Leith. In the end, Cecil himself negotiated a treaty in which French troops left Scotland, and Scottish Protestants were free to establish their church.

They did so under John Knox's leadership, forming what came to be known as the Presbyterian Church, governed by local congregations. Attending Catholic mass was a crime. Queen Mary, who had been in France during the rebellion, returned in 1561 to find herself in the difficult position of being a Catholic queen in a Protestant country. She fended off several plots to depose her, but in 1567, her husband, Lord Darnley, was killed in a scandal in which the suspected murderer was the earl of Both-well, Mary's putative lover (whom she married just three months later). This was too much for Protestant leaders, who captured Mary and forced her to abdicate in favor of her baby son, who became James VI (and much later, James I of England). Mary spent a year in the island prison of Lochlaun, then escaped and raised an army to restore her to her throne. That army was defeated in battle at Langside, near Glasgow, and Mary fled to England, where Elizabeth granted her political asylum. For many years, Mary held out hope that Elizabeth would restore her to the Scottish throne, but that never happened, and in 1587, Mary was executed for her involvement in a plot against Elizabeth.

Relations between England and Spain had never been close during the early years of Elizabeth's reign, and when in 1585, she sent troops to the Netherlands to help the Dutch win their independence from Spain, relations worsened. The expedition was popularized by the heroic death of Sir Philip Sydney, an aristocrat, who was wounded in battle, made it back to camp, and then supposedly ordered water meant for him given to a more seriously wounded soldier.

In 1587, the execution of Mary brought great criticism from European Catholics, who had never stopped believing that Mary was still the rightful ruler of Scotland. Among the most upset was Philip of Spain, also angry about the English aid to the Dutch two years earlier. He decided to invade England and crush Elizabeth; this he attempted to do with the "Invincible Armada," that is known today as the Spanish Armada, a vast fleet of ships carrying 52,000 soldiers and 8,000 sailors. The plan was to land at Margate on the English Channel, march to London, overthrow Elizabeth, and proclaim Philip king of England. This was fine with the Catholic Church, which had excommunicated Elizabeth in 1570 and no longer recognized her as a queen. A more recent papal bull, or decree, had made Philip king of England in the eyes of the church.

The armada was defeated in the English Channel in the summer of 1588, and those ships not sunk were forced to withdraw. It was not the end of Anglo-Spanish conflict, however, which dragged on for sixteen more years in the Caribbean, the Atlantic, in Ireland, and in France.

Elizabeth's reign had cemented Protestantism in place in England and had seen the rise of England as a powerful and prosperous nation-state. A short-lived colony had been established in North America in a place named Virginia in her honor (Elizabeth, because she never married, was thought of as the "Virgin Queen"); it was the precursor to the first great British empire.

One of the side benefits of Protestantism and more secular thinking was the rise of the theater toward the end of Elizabeth's reign and the freedom of playwrights such as William Shakespeare to write and produce plays other than the religious morality dramas of the past.

INTERPRETIVE ESSAY
Connie Evans

In the early hours of March 24, 1603, the last Tudor monarch of England, Elizabeth I, lay dying at her palace of Richmond. Outside, her courtier, Robert Carey, awaited news of the queen's death, as he was anxious to be the first to carry it to the new king, James VI of Scotland. Though it is fairly certain that Elizabeth made no dying declaration as to her successor, it was also equally clear that no better candidate for the throne was on the horizon. Word reached James on March 26 and he began to make preparations to travel south to claim his new kingdom. What the legacy had been left to him by the woman who would give her name to the "Elizabethan Era"?

Elizabeth herself had in 1558 inherited a country rent by strife; few of her contemporaries put much faith in her ability to solve the problems she faced. Historical debate on Elizabeth in recent years has centered on the question of whether she was indeed able to salvage her country from its woes through her much vaunted skills or if she was just incredibly fortunate. Whatever the judgment may be, the era to which historians have given her name was, unquestionably, a time of extraordinary change and accomplishment.

The issue of religion was of immediate concern to Elizabeth on her accession, so much so that the first major act of her reign was the creation of the Elizabethan Religious Settlement, a series of statutes promulgated in 1559 that effectively established the modern Anglican church. While her father, Henry VIII, had separated the English church from that at Rome, religious practice remained Catholic. The brief reign of her brother, Edward VI, had seen a doctrinal reformation of the church that was intended to make it thoroughly Protestant. Their sister, Mary I, had tried to return the English church to the fold of the papacy at Rome, but had failed to do so, even at the cost of burning some three hundred "heretics." The incoherent national religious policy left many English subjects in a quandary; indeed, recent scholarship has shown that Protestantism, in terms of theological adherence, did not take hold in England until the 1570s, and many people continued their traditional religious practices, which were inherently Catholic in form. Elizabeth herself appeared to like—and, indeed, would retain—elements of Catholic ritual and practice in her own personal religious observance. She liked candles, permitted the use of some images, including the Catholic cross, and insisted that her clergy wear vestments similar to those of the Catholic priests. Elizabeth was known to dislike married clergy, which was reminiscent of Catholic belief, and prevailed on them to follow certain practices at odds with Protestant practice, such as having people kneel at communion.

Acknowledging her personal predilections and believing them to be those of a majority of her subjects, Elizabeth wished to create a moderate Anglican church—a via media—to which the majority of her subjects could pledge allegiance. Elizabeth was unwilling to bow to the small minority of radical Protestants in forming her church, but was equally unable to embrace Catholicism, as it deemed her a bastard. The queen, aware of the wide variety of religious beliefs among her subjects, also knew that most of them rejected the notion of the pope as their spiritual leader. The queen accepted—and took seriously—her role as supreme governor of the Church of England, and worked with Parliament to pass an Act of Uniformity as to church practice. Though the uniformity passed with the slimmest of margins, it allowed Elizabeth to sweep away the Marian reforms and reinstitute the Edwardian form of worship, in English. Edward's 1552 Book of Common Prayer set the parameters of the Elizabethan church service, although textual changes ensured sufficient ambiguity, especially on the issue of the Eucharist. These changes allowed the majority of the queen's subjects to worship in the Anglican church without offending their religious sensibilities. The Thirty-Nine Articles, created by the Convocation of the Clergy in 1563, laid down the doctrine of the reformed church. Elizabeth was determined that no further changes to her settlement would take place, although the tenor of the debate changed with her excommunication in 1570, thereby giving carte blanche to Catholics to dethrone her, presumably in favor of her younger, Catholic cousin, Mary, Queen of Scots.

Elizabeth was unwilling to go the route of her sister, Mary, and compel Catholics to conform to Anglican practice through persecution and punishment; instead, she put in place directives which kept punishment for nonconformity to a minimum. Unfortunately, her excommunication increased Catholic attempts to remove her from her throne, most notably in the Ridolfi Plot of 1571. The English were horrified by this attempt on the queen's life, and grew even more confirmed in anti-Catholic bias in the aftermath of the slaughter of their Protestant co-religionists in the St. Bartholomew's Day Massacre in France in August 1572. Elizabeth, to her regret, found herself unable to continue her relaxed attitude towards Catholics, particularly as determined Jesuits began to enter the country in an attempt to revive allegiance to Catholicism. However, Elizabeth's persecution and punishment of Catholics plotting against her was not done for religious reasons, but rather, on the grounds of treason, thereby making it a political crime. These prosecutions involved only a small minority of Elizabeth's Catholic subjects, as most continued to be loyal to her.

Indeed, in many ways, Puritans seemed to be more of a threat to the maintenance of Elizabeth's religious settlement than did Catholics. These were the Protestants who wished to purify the Anglican church of its Catholic elements and put more of an emphasis on preaching and communal activities that centered on godly pursuits. Elizabeth insisted that her clergy use approved sermons instead of writing their own and dictated an adherence to the 1559 Prayer Book.

In the 1560s, the queen began to bear pressure on nonconforming ministers and deprived many of them of their livings. Presbyterians were particularly troubling to the religious settlement, as they urged a reconstruction of the hierarchy of the Anglican church. This goal divided them from other Protestants, who only sought to reform church practice. Elizabeth found herself at odds with her Archbishop of Canterbury (from 1575), Edmund Grindal, who favored a more Puritan church, especially in terms of individual preaching. As a result, he spent most of his tenure as archbishop on suspension. The Presbyterian threat subsided in the aftermath of the Armada, as it became clear that the English, regardless of their religious beliefs, were solidly behind Elizabeth. The Armada threat also made it clear to many English that Protestant allegiance was their one best defense against the Spanish, and, by the end of Elizabeth's reign, one can consider that England was clearly in the Protestant column.

Therefore, despite the Catholic threats and the importunings of a growing Puritan/Presbyterian minority, Elizabeth was able to maintain her church as she established it and handed it down to her successors. Elizabeth is thus credited with the creation of the Anglican church that survives largely intact to the modern day.

When Elizabeth came to the throne, she also had to commit herself to a foreign policy that would maintain England's balance between the two great continental powers of France and Spain. By the mid-sixteenth century, England was in conflict with Spain, a conflict that would culminate in war by the end of the century. Elizabeth was fortunate in having the advice of her principal secretary, William Cecil (Lord Burghley), who functioned as her agent in foreign policy matters. His influence and those of his successors, notably Francis Walsingham, helped Elizabeth avoid war—which was costly both in terms of money and men (neither of which she could spare)—for the majority of her reign. Some historians have argued that Elizabeth's use of the office of the principal secretary for the management of foreign affairs prefigures the modern Foreign Office. By the last quarter of her reign, Elizabeth was finding it increasingly impossible to maintain a peaceful coexistence with Spain, which meant in practical terms that the queen had to commit to costly intervention in areas outside of her realm.

There is much debate on the importance of the Spanish Armada to the history of England and, indeed, to continental European history in general. Some historians think of it as being inflated into mythological proportions way beyond its actual impact, while others see it as one of the most pivotal battles in early modern history. Elizabeth's reputation as a strong leader of her people was solidified, and she needed that cachet as problems began to grow in the last years of her reign. The war did not end with the defeat of the Armada; indeed, it would be left to her successor, James I, to reach peace in 1604. The result of the war with Spain left England committed to protecting their Dutch brethren (something that Elizabeth personally disliked), and this intervention would eventually aid the Protestant Dutch in achieving independence in the seventeenth century.

One of the major legacies of the Armada was its impact on English finances; the cost of the war was staggering, and, for the balance of her reign, Elizabeth found herself scrambling for funds: bankruptcy became a real possibility. In any event, she left a significant debt to her successors, leaving the first two Stuart kings in a position of having to fight with Parliament about all of their funding, both for personal use and to run the country. While Elizabeth commanded enough respect to keep such battles to a minimum, James I and Charles I were faced with members of parliament who wanted a say in how their tax dollars were being spent; the Stuart kings found themselves in the position of having to dismiss Parliament for years at a time in order to thwart these demands.

The war with Spain left the English with a distaste for conflict, and this aversion began to be reflected in their parliamentary representatives, who often balked at voting funds for future military ventures. The war did keep Catholicism from being imposed over the whole of the continent, including England. In addition, initial contacts made in the New World by Elizabeth's explorers were put on hold while the queen's seadogs—Drake, Raleigh, and Hawkins among them—pursued privateering ventures against Spain that weakened that country's coffers while lining England's own treasury. Thus, initial colonization efforts were not expanded upon until the reign of James I. In any event, by defeating the great Spanish

Armada, the Elizabethan navy had scored a great coup. From that core of triumphant sailors came a British navy that would dominate the seas by the early nineteenth century.

Domestically, Elizabeth continued the policies of her predecessors in Ireland, wanting to subdue it, often without regard to cost. The English had essentially achieved dominance in Ireland by 1300, but the English who were among the original settlers there had become more Irish than the natives. By the 1580s, it was apparent that rebellion, which had as its object the overthrow of Protestant dominance in Ireland, was imminent. Elizabeth sent the young Earl of Essex, who was anxious to restore his damaged image, to attack Ulster to quell the rebels. Instead, Essex, acting on his own volition and without the queen's approval, entered into a treaty with the Earl of Tyrone. When Essex returned to London, he was punished by the queen for what, in her eyes, appeared to be treason. Essex's response to his exile was to lead a rebellion against the queen that ultimately led to his execution in 1601. The situation in Ireland, still in flux, was handed down to Elizabeth's successors. Eventually, Oliver Cromwell, who led England during the Interregnum, followed a course of bloody repression of the Irish; combined with William III's scorched earth approach to Jacobite adherents, this policy laid the foundations for the present day Irish conflicts between the now independent Republic and Northern Ireland.

Elizabeth's detention of her cousin, Mary, Queen of Scots, starting in 1568, left an infant king on the throne of Scotland, thus destabilizing that country well into Elizabeths's reign, leaving her free to deal with other matters. The Scots queen had spent the majority of her girlhood in France, first engaged to and then the wife of Francis II, successor to Henry II. This short-lived, unconsummated marriage ended in 1560, and Mary returned to rule a Scotland she barely knew. Early discretion came to an end with her marriage to Henry, Lord Darnley. Elizabeth had skillfully manipulated this marriage, knowing her cousin Henry to be a dissolute young man who would soon give his young wife much grief. After the birth of a son, Mary sought comfort in the arms of Lord Bothwell, who soon arranged the murder of Darnley. Her people's disgust at her behavior soon compelled Mary to throw herself on Elizabeth's mercy, thus allowing the English queen control of the most dangerous claimant to her throne. Mary's nineteen-year imprisonment led to many plots; finally, in 1587, Elizabeth's councilors convinced the queen to put her cousin on trial for treason. Mary was subsequently executed and her death gave Philip II the final excuse to launch the Armada against England.

One of the key components of Elizabeth's foreign policy was to put herself on offer as a marriage prospect, a game she played well into middle age. This bargaining chip of possible union with the "Virgin Queen" often kept Elizabeth's enemies at bay and her country out of war. Without question, this was one of the best of the queen's political strategies. Even in her first days as queen, she parried the approaches of her dead sister's husband, Philip, in an attempt to gain breathing room in which to establish herself on her throne. Her councilors were quite serious about the reality of a marriage in order to secure an heir to the throne, but many historians believe that Elizabeth herself only considered marriage seriously on two occasions. In the first years of her reign, her affection for Robert Dudley (later Lord Leicester) appeared destined to end in marriage. However, the death of Dudley's first wife under suspicious circumstances ended that possibility. In any event, Dudley had too many enemies at court to make him a viable candidate. In 1572, a middle-aged Elizabeth considered the suit of the French Duc d'Alencon, but found herself having to repudiate the match due to the St. Bartholomew's Day Massacre. Again, a possible marriage to a Catholic prince troubled her courtiers, but many would have been ready to swallow it to get an heir. In the event, Elizabeth remained unwed, and refused to name a successor to prevent plots against her on behalf of that person, and the succession to the Scottish king did proceed very smoothly.

In the political arena, Elizabeth continued her father's use of Parliament as a tool in passing legislation, the principle of the "queen in Parliament" becoming firmly entrenched in the political spectrum as the fount of legislation; the importance of Parliament rose concomitantly. Elizabeth herself preferred a more traditional relationship between monarch and Parliament than her father had favored, but she did not have such an earth-shattering issue as separation from the church at Rome to settle, as her father had. However, Henry's use of Parliament to help him achieve his goal of divorce from his first wife had strengthened its position in the governmental structure, and Parliamentary leaders were loath to retreat from that. They felt that they had established the parameters of a partnership, but Elizabeth's arguments with her parliaments over religion and the issue of her marriage made it clear that she was to be the final arbiter in those types of decisions. As noted earlier, the need to raise money for war brought Parliament back into prominence as taxpayers began to demand accountability for how their taxes were spent. The notion of what constituted the "royal prerogative" began to be debated, and the Stuart kings' attempts to block debate on such issues brought to the fore the question of traditional rights of free speech and a defense of parliamentary privilege. As the House of Lords in Elizabeth's reign was small in number, most of them were employed in her service in one way or another, thus preventing the jealousies that had undermined the reigns of some of her prede-cessors.

The queen also followed her father's practice of tapping "new men"—men of skill and competence—to serve as her advisers and bureaucrats, thus opening the door to a burgeoning middle class, growing both in wealth and importance, with merit as the first consideration in their service to the monarch. These new gentlemen began to fill the seats in Parliament, and their security made them much more likely to act independently than those members who had gone before. In addition, Elizabeth reduced the size of the Privy Council and used it as the organ through which her orders were transmitted across the country. The Privy Council saw to the administration of the day-to-day business of the country, setting a precedent for what today is called the Home Office.

Elizabeth also constantly reinforced the notion of the importance of being "English," both in her speeches and in her appearances around the country; the creation of the image of "Gloriana" was at once both a reflection of the queen's native vanity and her wish to present a brilliant monarch in which her people could take pride. Elizabeth emphasized the primacy of the English over all other nations and evoked a nascent nationalism that found its apogee in the creation of the later British empire. Knowing that—for her male subjects—her gender was a problem, Elizabeth presented herself in both ways—willing to don armor when her country was threatened, but also capable of wearing the most dazzling clothes and jewels to emphasize her femininity. Perhaps she deliberately chose to remain unwed in order to put herself on a pedestal above all other women; allusions to the Virgin Mary and to the mythological goddesses, especially Diana, were often made in connection with Elizabeth. The queen was determined that no one, especially her male subjects, see her as weak and inferior, and she was willing to invoke any image that would reject those characteristics. She also promoted herself as having the healing touch, a notion that linked her to someone having divine status in the eyes of the English, who could then use it to sell herself as chosen by God.

The Elizabethan Era saw changes in society as well, most notably in the treatment of the poor. By the mid-sixteenth century, there was a sea change in attitude toward the unemployed and disadvantaged subjects of the queen; economic downturns, increasing inflation, and the practice of enclosure put many out of work through no fault of their own. The Elizabethan government came to recognize that such people did not deserve the traditional response to the poor, which had generally been punitive. Starting in 1563, a series of statutes was passed that provided first voluntary, and eventually, compulsory collection of rates, or taxes, to provide for those unable to care for themselves. All of these statutes were incorporated in the great Elizabethan Poor Law of 1601, which made rates compulsory and directed the localities to take responsibility for the care of their poor. This law signaled a change in the belief that the poor were poor because they *chose* to be. However, punishments remained for those who were found not to be among the "deserving poor." In any event, this law remained in place until 1834, and provided a rudimentary welfare system; thus, the welfare state created in Britain in the twentieth century bears the hallmarks of its Elizabethan antecedents.

Elizabeth's use of "new men" in her government and bureaucracy contributed in part to the rise of urban society that began to come to prominence in the sixteenth century, along with the tradesmen, merchants, entrepreneurs, and artisans who sought new opportunities in London and other cities around the country. Urban life provided access to previously untapped ways in which to acquire a sizable fortune; along with this newly acquired wealth and status came a desire to give sons and heirs a better life, one that included an extensive education that might lead to positions in the government, the church, or law. Once again, promotion based on merit came to represent the modern model of government and other modes of service to the state. These men sought to express themselves through a new dedication to art, literature, theater, and music; literacy rose apace with this new type of expression.

Culturally, Elizabeth's reign was a time of high achievement in many arenas. The inculcation of humanist learning in schools and universities, with its emphasis on the liberal arts, produced scores of talented individuals whose native genius created what came to be known as the "Elizabethan Renaissance." Protestantism, which emphasized individual reading of Scripture, hastened the increase of literacy; printing of books, pamphlets, plays, and poetry fed the demand for secular reading material. The Elizabethans were eager patrons of poets, playwrights, and artists, and the emerging Elizabethan theaters and playhouses that opened their doors to the "penny public" spread the fame of these brilliant men far and wide. Actors became professional for the first time, and sought to change their "strolling" status to one of patronage that would allow them to settle down in one locale. Eventually, these patrons were supporting numbers of actors, who then formed a company under the patron's name: the Lord Chancellor's Men was a good example. These acting companies set the precedent for such groups in centuries to come.

Once companies were established, they looked for permanent venues in which to play; beginning with presentations in the yards of inns, the idea of professional theaters was developed and the first ones were built in the last quarter of the sixteenth century. Naturally, they were almost always outside city limits due to concerns of the populace; anywhere large crowds gathered, disease, crime and the possibility of fire were more likely to occur. Richer patrons established private theaters for smaller audiences within city limits.

New forms of poetry emerged, as well as plays, which reflected real life; these works resonated with the public at large, and especially with those men and women who served as Elizabeth's courtiers. Elizabeth, herself, encouraged and patronized these talented individuals, among them Christopher Marlowe, Edmund Spenser, and, most notably, William Shakespeare. These men clearly showed the effects of their humanistic education and developed a different style of writing that reflected both court life and life in the lanes and alleys. They were always careful to validate the hierarchical order of life; indeed, Shakespeare, in many ways, became a Tudor apologist, as his history plays always cast the dynasty in a favorable light. The contributions of this great genius of English writers are myriad: new words were invented, new ways of communication through plays were established, and the importance of the sonnet in the world of poetry was accepted unquestionably. Marlowe, who seemed to live life on the edge (dying in a knife fight at 29), made great contributions in the creation of blank verse, a technique that allows for very dramatic speech. Spenser's *Fairie Queene* imagined the perfect world overseen by the best of queens. Elizabeth's court thus became a center of cultural exposition that many other countries envied and sought to emulate; these achievements reinforced the idea that the English could be proud of their nation and of the queen who created an atmosphere at her court that not only encouraged but actively supported the efforts of her ablest subjects. Patronage, as always, formed the foundation for the creation of these great works. Beyond that, however, their work defined the monarch's image in such a way that people looked to the court as the best example of Renaissance culture, so much so that this period is referred to as the "Elizabethan Renaissance." It is clear that this emphasis on intellectual, cultural, artistic, and literary pursuits percolated down to the gentry class, and further, to the yeomanry, many of whom were literate by 1603. Their ballads, songs, and stories are evidence of the rising tide of interest in expressing one's self as eloquently as those persons further up the social scale.

At the behest of Sir Walter Raleigh and other courtiers, Elizabeth consented to the founding of a colony in the New World that would bear her name—Virginia. It was Raleigh who solicited the help of Richard Hakluyt in inflaming the imaginations of prospective colonists through his books on travel and planting. Additionally, Hakluyt aided Raleigh in mapping a strategy whereby Spain would be deprived of her colonies in the New World. Though the first permanent English colony would only be established under her successor, three successive attempts—most notably at Roanoke Island in what is now North Carolina—in the latter years of her reign spoke to Elizabeth's interest in expanding the dominions of her country beyond its shores. Her assent to the ventures of Raleigh and his cohorts meant that England now had a presence in the New World, one that eventually formed the basis of British settlement and domination in the American colonies up to the revolutionary era. This contact also opened up a trade in new foodstuffs and other products, most notably tobacco. While the great bulk of colonization falls under the Stuart umbrella, the Elizabethans must be given credit for planting the seeds of that effort.

The Elizabethan Era and the queen who symbolized it, regardless of the depth of her involvement in its creation, has had a profound and lasting impact on the modern world, and it is impossible to imagine a successful Britain without its Elizabethan antecedents.

SELECTED BIBLIOGRAPHY

Andrews, Kenneth R. *Trade, Plunder and Settlement: Maritime Enterprise and the Genesis of the British Empire, 1480-1630.* Cambridge: Cambridge University Press, 1984. Conveys all the excitement of the Elizabethan adventures on the sea.

Bassnett, Susan. *Elizabeth I: A Feminist Perspective.* New York: St. Martin's, 1988. As its title implies, a modern approach to the sixteenth-century queen.

Haigh, Christopher, ed., *The Reign of Elizabeth I.* Athens: University of Georgia Press, 1987. A revisionist approach to the efficacy of the queen in many areas of her reign.

Johnson, Paul. *Elizabeth I: A Study in Power and Intellect.* London: Wiedenfeld and Nicolson, 1974.

Levin, Carole. *The Reign of Elizabeth I.* Houndsmills, UK, and New York: Palgrave Press, 2002. A succinct overview of the queen's reign with historiographical notes.

MacCaffrey, W. T. *The Shaping of the Elizabethan Regime.* Princeton: Princeton University Press, 1968; *Queen Elizabeth and the Making of Policy 1572–1588.* Princeton: Princeton University Press, 1981; *Elizabeth I: War and Politics, 1588–1603.* Princeton: Princeton University Press, 1992. A trilogy primarily covering the politics of the reign, but with little attention to administrative issues.

Marvel, Laura, ed. *Elizabethan England.* San Diego, CA: Greenhaven Press, 2002. A series of articles on aspects of Elizabeth's reign offered both factual and interpretive standpoints.

Neale, J. E. *Queen Elizabeth.* New York: Doubleday, 1957 (London, 1934). The standard biography, flawed by his positive bias for his subject.

Palliser, D. M. *The Age of Elizabeth: England under the Later Tudors, 1547–1603.* London: 1983. Covers most of the topics associated with the Elizabethan era, but particularly strong on social and economic issues.

Perry, Maria. *The Word of a Prince: A Life of Elizabeth I from Contemporary Documents.* Rochester, NY: Boydell, 1990. A valuable collection for researcher seeking original documentation.

Rowse, A. L. *The Elizabethan Renaissance: The Cultural Achievement and The Life of the Society.* 2 vols. New York: Charles Scribner's Sons, 1972. Good overview of, as indicated, the society and culture of the Elizabethan period.

Smith, Lacey Baldwin. *Elizabeth Tudor: Biography of a Queen.* Boston: Little, Brown, 1975.

Somerset, Anne. *Elizabeth I.* London: Wiedenfeld and Nicolson, 1991. Explores the dichotomies of the queen's nature in light of her policies.

8

Civil War and Restoration, 1642–1660

INTRODUCTION

The course of English history between 1642 and 1660 is, to say the least, confusing. This period of rebellion against the monarchy and subsequent restoration of the monarchy features not one, but three civil wars, as well as the public execution of King Charles I, an eleven-year interregnum without monarch, and, finally, Charles II's accession to the throne in 1660.

Elizabeth I was succeeded by James VI of Scotland, who became James I of England. He was the son of the executed Mary, Queen of Scots. His rule in England from 1603 until 1625 was marked by peace in Europe until the outbreak of the Thirty Years' War toward the end of his reign, and by unresolved domestic problems, which probably made matters worse for his son and successor, Charles I.

Charles I was not a particularly industrious king, and his belief in the royal prerogative instilled in him a tendency toward autocracy. From 1629 to 1640, he ruled without benefit of Parliament, but he never seemed greatly interested in matters of state. One of the incidents that helped drive a wedge between Charles and Parliament during the 1630s was the so-called "popish plot," an apparent increase in Catholic influence at Charles' royal court between 1636 and 1642. In 1625, Charles had married Henrietta Maria, daughter of King Henri IV of France and a Catholic. In 1636, two Roman Catholic advisers, seen as papal agents, came to court and had much influence on the queen. They worked to mitigate restrictions on Catholics, carried out intrigues in Scotland and Ireland, and assisted in indirect ways the Catholic side in foreign affairs. Rumors of Catholic plots against Parliament were common and further damaged

King Charles I received the last rites before his execution in January 1649. Although possessed of a charming personality, Charles I was a political incompetent. His repeated mishandling of admittedly difficult political and religious questions resulted in civil war and, subsequently, his execution. (Reproduced from the Collections of the Library of Congress.)

relations with the king. In 1640, when Parliament reconvened, it took punitive action against certain Catholic leaders and enacted various anti-Catholic measures. In early 1642, the queen went to France, and Catholic influence in the royal household lessened. But by then, the first civil war was almost at hand.

Charles did see himself as God's representative in England, and, in 1637, when Scottish Presbyterians balked at accepting an Anglican form of worship, he decided to take a firm stand against the Scots. The resulting impasse led to the first civil war between the king and Parliament. When Charles was forced to convene Parliament in 1640 to obtain funds for the war, he and Parliament could not agree, principally because Charles' belief that he was a ruler by divine right convinced him that no compromise was possible. Likewise, some in Parliament believed compromise impossible. One parliamentary leader, the Puritan John Pym, had established a reputation as a staunch anti-Catholic back in the 1620s. During the 1630s, when Parliament was not in session, he worked with Puritan groups on colonization efforts. When Parliament reconvened, however, Pym again emerged as a major spokesman for parliamentary unity against the Catholic threat. An Irish rebellion in 1641 further crippled relations between king and Parliament, and when Charles attempted to arrest five opposition members of Parliament in January 1642, the break was complete. Pym and others managed to help Parliament unify against the king and work out an alliance with Scotland, and the first civil war formally began in May.

Although Charles had the initial military advantage, his forces failed to gain a quick victory. Indeed, parliamentary forces won a decisive victory at the battle of Marston Moor in 1644 that secured for them a strategic outpost in northern England. At about the same time, Oliver Cromwell emerged as the hard-headed practical military leader Parliament needed. Cromwell reorganized the army through the New Model Ordnance (1645) and the Self-Denying Ordnance (1646), by which members of Parliament (with a few exceptions, like Cromwell himself) denied themselves the opportunity of military command. The New Model Army, created in the 1645 ordinance, mostly draftees, consisted of 22,000 men and 2,300 officers. Its commander was Sir Thomas Fairfax, a good military leader with no significant political involvement. The New Model Army proved its worth at the battle of Naseby, although the king's small army helped ensure its own defeat by forcing the issue against a much larger force. After Naseby, the New Model Army continued to perform well in the second civil war and in conflicts with Scotland and Ireland. It was well-financed, supported and largely supplied by the commercial establishment in London, and led by a largely Puritan officer corps of exceptional zeal and a sense that they were involved in a divine mission. Second-in-command under Fairfax, Oliver Cromwell emerged as a great field commander, using a sincere expression of Puritan faith to gain the unqualified loyalty of his troops combined with a degree of tolerance that allowed Scots and other non-Puritans to fight with him.

The parliamentary forces sustained their momentum by virtue of a reasonably unified Parliament—the legacy of skillful political leader John Pym, who died in 1643—and by alliance with the Scottish army. The Scots agreed to fight for the promise of protection for their Presbyterian Church, a share of the military leadership in the war, and some financial subsidization. All of this was packaged together in a document called the Solemn League and Covenant.

The military turning point of the war was the battle of Naseby in June 1645, another parliamentary victory. The war continued on until May 1646, when the king surrendered to Scottish Covenanters, a group then managing affairs in Scotland. The next two and a half years were spent searching for some kind of settlement that might allow the king to resume his royal duties. But a plethora of competing and contentious factions prevented consensus: the army and Parliament often disagreed, as did those who became known as Independents, people who favored a kind of decentralized national church, and the more secular Levellers, focused on parliamentary reform toward greater democracy.

Meanwhile, a second civil war broke out when Scottish forces invaded England with the king's blessing. A force led by Oliver Cromwell defeated the Scots in 1648 and put down several royalist uprisings as well. As Charles seemed to be the inspiration, if not the direct cause, of these rebellions, the parliamentary army decided he should be tried, convicted, and executed for treason. He was brought to trial in January 1649, and although he presented a good and articulate defense, he was duly convicted. Seeing himself as a martyr, he died with dignity on January 30, 1649.

Charles's death precipitated a third civil war. A royalist army, nominally under the command of Charles's son (now, technically, Charles II), formed in Scotland and included German and Danish mercenaries. They began to march through Scotland on the spring of 1650 but were soon defeated in battle at Corbisdale. Following that fiasco, Charles himself came to Scotland and accepted the covenant that formally created the Scottish Presbyterian Church. Afraid that a unified Scotland under Charles would pose a dangerous threat, the New Model Army crossed the English-Scottish border on July 22, 1650. Early skirmishes were inconclusive, and the parliamentary forces withdrew to await reinforcements and supplies. The Scottish army unwisely pursued the parliamentary forces, found itself in an open space ideal for cavalry maneuvers, and were quickly overrun in a battle that the parliamentary army had neither sought nor anticipated.

The Scots regrouped, and in the summer of 1651, they moved south into England, hoping to find substantial royalist support. Although little help materialized, the Scots persevered until a battle at Worcester on September 3 at which the larger parliamentary force won a decisive victory and sent Charles' army fleeing in disarray back to Scotland.

Meanwhile, from 1649 to 1653, England was ruled by a Parliament shorn of those who had supported the second civil war. In late 1648, these members had been purged by being physically restrained from entering the House of Commons. The remaining members numbered as few as sixty, and many places in England lacked representation. Inelegantly called the "Rump" Parliament, it halted negotiations with Charles I, setting the stage for his trial and execution in January 1649. Following that, it managed the everyday affairs of state, while Cromwell's army roamed the countryside as well as Ireland, crushing royalist or Roman Catholic opposition. Scotland, which had broken its alliance with Cromwell to join in the second civil war, likewise felt Cromwell's wrath and fell under military occupation. The Rump Parliament also engineered a naval war with the Dutch (1652–1653) over commercial conflicts.

By early 1653, Cromwell had become impatient with the Rump Parliament and its uninspiring leadership and sent its members home. After several months of bickering with an appointed assembly that thought itself a parliament, Cromwell declared England a protectorate and himself lord protector. Legitimized through a document called *The Instrument of Government*, the Protectorate was to have a king-like head of state who would rule jointly with Parliament. However well meant, this new system failed to please everyone, and Cromwell could not prevent continual tinkering with it. Some were uncomfortable with the departure from the old royalist tradition (Cromwell could have been crowned king of England but declined the offer). Others were concerned with the issue of Cromwell's successor and with the army, which remained a powerful and politically influential force.

Oliver Cromwell died in September 1658 and was succeeded by his son Richard, who lacked his father's leadership skills and dedication. Richard Cromwell resigned after just seven months in power. The old Rump Parliament reassembled, and in February 1660, began negotiating with the army and its leader, General George Monck, for the restoration of the Stuart royal family to the English throne.

Charles II, beneficiary of the Restoration, had little to do with his return to the English throne, which came about through internal problems of the republic. Parliament was in limbo, hung up between the Rump and those who had been purged more than a decade earlier; the army had lost public support and was divided over the composition of parliament.

A Convention Parliament was elected that contained both royalists and parliament supporters, and this body invited Charles II to return as king. For his part, Charles issued the declaration of Breda in April 1660 as a way of allaying the fears of those who had opposed his father and supported Parliament during the civil war and interregnum. In the declaration, he pardoned everyone except any to whom Parliament might take exception. He promised religious toleration and accepted existing land titles, leaving Parliament to settle any disputes. This statement formed the basis for Charles' restoration, and he worked, with only limited success, to persuade Parliament to pass acts granting amnesty and providing for religious toleration. Charles returned to the throne without parliamentary preconditions, although his role was redefined both by the Convention Parliament and the Cavalier Parliament elected in early 1661. This new Parliament invalidated legislation passed since 1641, because nothing since then had been approved by a monarch. The Cavalier Parliament also passed various acts to strengthen the authority of the king, a reaction against the past twenty years of parliamentary and social disarray.

INTERPRETIVE ESSAY
William T. Walker

The era of the English Civil War and Restoration was a turbulent and violent period of conflict between Parliament and the king, resulted in the execution of Charles I, temporary elimination of the monarchy, and the dominance of Puritanism. The era concluded with restoration of the monarchy in the person of Charles II and the reestablishment of Anglicanism. Some historians have argued that this conflict was a "war of religion"—a Puritan revolution, while others have contended that it was a "civil war" between political, economic, and social forces affiliated with either the monarchy or the parliament. In fact, it was a civil war, a defining event in English history.

The English Civil War that began in 1642 resulted from a political and religious crisis that emerged clearly during the 1630s but had its roots in the 1580s and 1590s with the growing religious and political unrest during the closing years of Elizabeth I's reign. The Elizabethan Settlement in religion that limited the impact of the reform and supported an Anglican Church of England that was above all else loyal to the monarch, came under increasing criticism after 1580. However, Elizabeth I's popularity during this period of war against Catholic Spain prohibited any change in religion. That restriction was eliminated with Elizabeth's death in 1603 and the accession of James I (1603–1625) to the throne. From the outset James I was an unpopular monarch; he was a Scot, the son of Mary, Queen of Scots, who had been involved in several attempts to assassinate Elizabeth I. Nonetheless, Elizabeth recognized his right of succession. While his ancestry was held against him, his unpopularity resulted more from his policies and behavior. James I managed to alienate himself and the monarchy from several important sectors of English power. As an outspoken defender of the divine right of kings and absolutism in government (he wrote *The True Law of Free Monarchy* in 1601), James alienated those who advanced a view of government based on a partnership between the monarch and parliament. They argued that England had developed a unique approach to governing in this manner and that it was documented in the many charters that had been negotiated since the medieval period. James tended to ignore Parliament during most of his reign, dissolved the so-called Addled Parliament in 1614, and conspired with his counselors to rule without Parliament. Although, at the time of his succession, he encouraged almost everyone from Catholics to Puritans that he would support some accommodation in religion, it became quite apparent at the Hampton Court Conference (1605) that James I would support the status quo in religion. To James, the Church of England was more of a political prop than a separate religious entity. While the nation was moving away from the right, that is, Catholic, to the center and left of the religious reform pendulum, James's static view of religion resulted in his detachment on this issue. The king also found himself at odds with the English legal system; his ongoing battles with Sir Edward Coke, chief justice of the Court of Common Pleas, gave witness to his lack of understanding and support of English courts and law. Finally, James's erratic personal behavior was increasingly unpopular among the people; his support of favorites such as the hated duke of Buckingham brought about much criticism.

   This English crisis that led to civil war reflected itself in British diplomatic and economic policies with respect to the Thirty Years' War that was devastating the continent. The European war began in 1618, a conflict based on religious and political differences. The war ended in 1648 with the strictly political settlement known as the Peace of Westphalia. Between 1618 and his death in 1625, James I gave limited support to the Protestant

Bohemians who were confronting the power of the Catholic Habsburgs. His son, Charles I (1625–1649), was also restricted in his involvement in the struggle because of his lack of resources and the limited parliamentary support for his increasingly pro-Catholic preferences.

In 1625 James I died and was succeeded by Charles I. Charles advanced the same policies as his father but did not possess his political acumen, and, after a brief period of popularity, came under mounting criticism for both his domestic and foreign policies. After a series of unfortunate and reckless foreign exploits that included failed military operations against Spain and France, Charles I needed financial assistance from Parliament to pay debts and refit the military. In the Petition of Rights of June 1629 Charles agreed to recognize a set of parliamentary grievances (no taxes without Parliament's approval; no housing of troops in private homes; and no arbitrary arrest or detention) in exchange for financial subsidies. By the end of the same month Charles dissolved Parliament and initiated a prolonged period in which he attempted to govern without a Parliament. To his royalist supporters and to later sympathetic historians, this period is known as the "Era of Personal Rule," but to Parliamentarians and less sympathetic historians, it is known as "The Eleven Years' Tyranny." Basically, Charles was inclined to the absolutism that was becoming more attractive on the Continent and constituted a modern adaptation of the "Divine Right of Kings" concept. On the other hand, Parliament was asserting what it believed to be its traditional and historic role in governing the nation and demanded that the monarch affirm these historic and legal rights of Parliament. During these eleven years, Charles became increasingly sympathetic to the religious right; in Archbishop William Laud he found a church leader who shared his views. To most outward appearances, England appeared content with the regime; however, a strong undercurrent in opposition to "High Anglicanism," Laudism, and the authoritarian nature of Charles's government became evident in the late 1630s when the Scots resisted the imposition of English liturgical practices.

Scottish support for James I and Charles I had remained strong. After all, James was from Scotland, and his son was likewise identified as a Scot and was regarded with loyalty and some affection. However, the Scots, who were Presbyterians, were not willing to accept the Anglican liturgy that Archbishop Laud tried to force on them. In 1637, when the Anglicans attempted to read the English liturgy in Edinburgh, the Scots rioted. That incident resulted in organized resistance to the imposition of what the Scots identified as a Catholic-like liturgy. They signed a Solemn League and Covenant (1638) to defend their religious views, and in the same year the Covenanters, as they became known, denounced Anglicanism and formally established the Scottish Kirk (Church). In 1639 they organized an army and seized Edinburgh. Charles led an army to confront the rebels but before a battle could be fought, both sides agreed to disband their armies and to refer their differences to assemblies. This attempt at reconciliation was short-lived when the Scots continued to resist any accommodation with Anglicanism.

In 1640, Charles I, in need of financial resources, was forced to convene a Parliament. In April, the Short Parliament (it lasted only three weeks) met at Westminster. The anti-Stuart forces—Parliamentarians, Puritans, the legal and merchant communities, and others—seized control of the agenda and did not approve new subsidies for the king. Charles dissolved the Short Parliament but found his regime confronting another crisis in the summer of 1640. Not only had a Scottish force marched south and defeated some royalist units, English opposition was evident in London when Laud's palace was attacked. On October 26, 1640, Charles agreed to the Treaty of Ripon that specified that he would pay the occupying Scottish force a daily subsidy until he summoned another Parliament that could work toward a negotiated settlement.

This new parliament became the so-called Long Parliament, which first met on November 3, 1640. From its outset, this Parliament was determined to gain concessions from Charles before granting him funds and to take action against those it deemed responsible for the worst misdeeds during the eleven years when Parliament was not in session. What was surprising was the vigor and assertiveness of Parliament's strategy. Within weeks, Thomas Wentworth, earl of Stafford and one of Charles's closest advisers, and Archbishop William Laud were arrested and placed in the Tower of London. In March 1641 Stafford was tried and convicted; he was executed in May. Laud lingered in prison for three years before his trial and conviction in 1644 and his execution early the following year.

In addition to these actions against Charles's advisers, Parliament advanced radical political and religious agendas. Politically, Parliament passed the Triennial Act (May 1641) that required that Parliament would be convened every three years. Another measure, which Charles signed, specified that the Parliament could not be dissolved without giving its consent. In religion, the Root and Branch Bill (1641) was an attempt to eliminate bishops and the Episcopal order. While the bill failed to pass, it spawned other acts that reflected the Puritan strength in Parliament. These acts included, for example, ones that forbade playing sports on Sundays, and ordered the removal from churches of all pictures of the Virgin Mary. The gravity of the situation for Charles I became more apparent as the year progressed. During the summer, the High Commission and the

Court of the Star Chamber, two so-called "prerogative" courts, in which the monarchy had a great deal of authority, were eliminated. Parliament negotiated a settlement with the Scots, and Charles I found himself isolated. In December Parliament passed the Grand Remonstrance that constituted an indictment of all its grievances with the king. Although Charles made a fairly reasoned response to the remonstrance, he was angered when Parliament published the document. In early January, after hearing rumors that Parliament was considering impeaching the Catholic Queen Henrietta Maria, he attempted to seize control of the crisis by marching on Parliament to arrest its leaders. Parliament refused to surrender the accused to the king's men. When Charles returned to try again, the accused had left Westminster. And the result of the whole affair was important in turning public opinion even further against the king.

Emboldened by the public support it received after this incident, Parliament passed measures that eliminated the Episcopal system and required that the army be under its control. Charles I refused to comply and departed London for York. In June Parliament sent Charles I a document called the Nineteen Propositions for his assent; from Parliament's perspective, this was a final attempt to work with the king. The Nineteen Propositions called for Charles I to recognize Parliament's control over the army, religion, the appointment of the king's ministers and the guardians of his children, and membership in the House of Lords. This was a direct challenge to the substantive authority of the crown; Charles's acceptance of this ultimatum would have reduced the monarchy to a minor position in governing. As many had expected, Charles I refused to sign the Nineteen Propositions. Preparations for war began in June, and by August the English Civil War entered its military phase.

The English Civil War divided the nation between the royalists, also referred to as the Cavaliers, who supported the crown and came principally from northern and west-central England, and those who supported Parliament, who came from East Anglia and southern England, including London, and who later came to be called the Roundheads. Generally, the nobility and supporters of the Anglican Church supported Charles I, while the London merchants, Parliamentarians, and Puritans were aligned with Parliament. The English Civil War is actually three civil wars: the first, from 1642–1646, witnessed the military defeat of the Cavaliers; the second, from 1647–1648, was characterized by further radicalization of the political and religious agenda and by the decision that Charles would have to be eliminated; and the third (1649–1651) involved the remnants of royalist forces and Charles's son (who would become Charles II) making one last effort to prevail over the parliamentary army.

As could have been foreseen, 1642, the first year of the war, went well for Charles. With more experience and better equipment, the royalist forces won a series of battles and skirmishes at Edgehill, Bristol, and Chalgrove Field. However, none of these encounters was decisive. At the same time, Parliament appointed one of its members, Oliver Cromwell, to raise and equip an army. This force, which Parliament institutionalized as the New Model Army in 1645, developed quickly and matched anything that Charles I could put into the field. During 1643 fighting continued to be confined to skirmishes. At the same time, Cromwell worked on his army and the Puritans began an extensive debate on religious issues in the Westminster Assembly. In September 1643 Parliament supported another Solemn League and Covenant that required that religions in England, Scotland, and Ireland be reformed along Puritan principles. All military, religious, and political officials were required to sign this document; most complied but almost 2,500 Anglican clerics declined and lost their positions. The Scots agreed to support Parliament and sent an army into the field against Charles I in January 1644. Charles I, headquartered in Oxford, attempted unsuccessfully to pit Catholic Ireland against his enemies.

The tide was turning against the king. On July 2, 1644, the most important battle of the war was fought at Marston Moor. Cromwell and his army soundly defeated the king's army, under the leadership of his German nephew, Prince Rupert. With this victory, Parliament gained control over northern England. Charles I's forces did achieve some successes in Cornwall and in Scotland, but Cromwell and other leaders of Parliament's forces were able to counterattack and regain the initiative. During 1645 Parliament became more radical as Cromwell's influence and power increased. On June 14, 1645, Charles I's army was defeated in the battle of Naseby; this defeat was followed by the collapse of royalist resistance to Parliament. On May 5, 1646, Charles I surrendered to the Scots, who turned him over to Parliament in January 1647.

During most of 1647 Cromwell and his army were involved in open conflict with Parliament; the army refused to disband and prevailed. In December Parliament presented Charles I with four measures and demanded his assent. Charles was expected to recognize Parliament's control over the army for the next twenty years, and he was to recant all previous denunciations of Parliament and its role in governing the nation. His recent appointments to the House of Lords were to be invalidated, and both houses of Parliament were to have the power to control their dissolution. In November 1647, Charles left his house arrest near London and the following month, he entered into a secret alliance with the Scots, agreeing to reestablish Presbyterianism in Scotland in exchange for Scottish military support to restore him to power. With that agreement in hand, Charles I rejected Parliament's four bills. In January 1648 Parliament formally broke its allegiance with Charles I and the second English Civil War began. In March Cromwell and the Puritan-minded Independents determined to bring Charles to justice, while the more moderate Presbyterians, who held control of Parliament, were interested in negotiating with the king.

After a spring and summer of indecisive skirmishes and troop movements, Cromwell's forces defeated the royalists in August in the last major battle of the second Civil War at Preston. Charles I was arrested by the army on December 1, 1648. That humiliation was followed by Pride's Purge, in which Colonel Thomas Pride refused admission to Parliament to almost 200 Presbyterian members of the House of Commons; another 127 were either arrested or stayed away in protest. The resulting assembly, known as the Rump Parliament and consisting of about 150 members, acted quickly to try Charles I. When the House of Lords refused to participate in the trial, the Rump Parliament declared that the Commons possessed all legal authority. A High Court of Justice was established to hold the trial; it consisted of sixty-seven members. Charles I's trial lasted for seven days; multiple charges, including high treason, were brought against him, but Charles I refused to recognize the jurisdiction of this court. He was convicted and sentenced to death.

The execution of Charles I on January 30, 1649, persuaded many, including Cromwell, that not only had a king died but the monarchy had been eliminated, too. Charles I's death began another eleven-year period in English history; to the supporters of the monarchy, it is known as the Interregnum; to those opposed to the crown, it is known as the Commonwealth. The Commonwealth was a republican form of government with government by committee through the House of Commons. The House of Lords and the title and office of king were eliminated. From its beginning, the Commonwealth was under the influence of the power of Oliver Cromwell and his army.

During its first phase, 1649–1653, the Commonwealth was challenged by the Stuart claimant, Charles II, son of Charles I, who mounted a campaign in Scotland, usually referred to as the third Civil War, designed to reestablish the monarchy. Young Charles landed in Scotland in June 1650, and a royalist army under the command of David Leslie was created. The New Model Army was reassembled and reinforced, with Cromwell in command. John Lambert, major-general of the cavalry, was second in command. A decisive victory for Cromwell's forces at the battle of Dunbar in September 1650 seemed to mark the end of the war, but over the winter, Leslie's army regrouped and invaded England in the summer of 1651, hoping to enlist royalist support in the counties of northern England. Not much assistance was forthcoming, and the royalist forces, depleted by desertion and demoralized by the evident hopelessness of their situation, met final defeat at Worcester on September 3, 1651.

Once the country was at relative peace, Cromwell became disturbed with the ineffective government. After several months of political maneuvering, Cromwell and his supporters in Parliament established the Protectorate (December 16, 1653) through *The Instrument of Government,* the first and only written constitution in English history. Under the Instrument, the Lord Protector and a council of twenty-one would lead the government. Parliament was triennial (elected every three years) and composed of 460 members, including representatives from Scotland and Ireland. Once it was convened, Parliament had the power to levy taxes and make grants, and it could not be dissolved during its first five months. When Parliament was not in session, the lord protector and the council had the authority to make laws if necessary. The Instrument also specified that England would have a standing army of 30,000 men. Cromwell was named lord protector and the so-called Protectorate phase of the Commonwealth lasted for five years, during which Cromwell's rule was stern and arbitrary. He suppressed the traditional Anglican church in favor of a more reformed (Puritan) approach, dealt harshly with all opponents, censored the press, and created a cultural climate that was static, dismal, and failed to recognize the joy of life. In addition, Cromwell employed the army to eliminate an uprising in 1655 at Salisbury and taxed Anglican royalists at a high rate to support his military operations. In 1656 Parliament reduced some of the lord protector's powers and extended tolerance to most Christians except Anglicans and Catholics. In 1657, Parliament attempted to name Cromwell king, but he declined. Cromwell built up the navy and launched a lengthy and expensive war against Spain in the West Indies and the Low Countries in 1655. Cromwell remained as lord protector until his death on September 3, 1658.

Upon his father's death, Richard Cromwell was named lord protector and served until his resignation on May 25, 1659. The period from Oliver Cromwell's death to the spring of 1660 was chaotic, at times bordering on anarchy. Richard Cromwell was ineffectual and factions with the Parliament competed with one another for power. The army remained aloof until February 1660 when General George Monck brought it out of Scotland to stabilize the political situation in London by bringing about the restoration of the monarchy. By the spring, the nation and its leaders were exhausted by the Puritan experiment and longed for normalcy. Monck and a group of parliamentarians wrote to Charles II, exiled son of the executed Charles I, advancing the idea of his return as king. In reply, Charles issued the declaration of Breda in April 1660 that proved to be the means for the restoration of the monarchy and the Stuart dynasty. The Declaration of Breda meant the return of a constitutional monarchy, not a "divine right" or "absolutist" monarchy. Charles II was forced to recognize the role of Parliament in governing. Other terms agreed to in the declaration were: the restoration of the Anglican Bishops; the army was limited to a force of 5,000 men; Cromwell's suppression of Ireland was confirmed; the laws of 1640–1642 that Charles I had signed were to remain; and all involved in the civil war, except those who voted to execute Charles I, were not to be charged.

The Restoration designates not only the actual reestablishment of the monarchy, but it also applies to English politics, life, and culture during the reign of Charles II (1660–1685). Representative of the anti-Puritan measures exacted during the early years of the reign were the four components of the Clarendon Code (1661–1665). Named after Charles II's adviser, Edward Hyde, earl of Clarendon, these laws included: the Corporation Act (1661), in which magistrates were required to be members of the Church of England and to take an oath recognizing that it was illegal to try to overthrow the king; the Act of Uniformity (1662), which required all clergymen, professors, and teachers to accept everything in the *Book of Common Prayer;* the Conventicle Act (1664), which prohibited dissenters from worshiping in groups of more than five; and the Five-Mile Act (1665), which stated that dissenting preachers could not come within five miles of any incorporated town unless they had sworn allegiance to the king. These harsh measures were as difficult to enforce as had been some of the laws pronounced by Cromwell and the Puritans. However, they do reflect the sentiment of the period in their repudiation of the dark days of the 1650s.

On the whole, Charles II was willing and able at first to take advantage of this sense of repudiation, which reached its height when Cromwell's body was disinterred and hanged. He entered London on his thirtieth birthday, healthy and robust. Early on, he readily agreed to the various limitations Parliament placed on royal authority imposed in the Restoration settlement—the permanent elimination of the Star Chamber and other prerogative courts and royal taxation authority, for example. He spread the bounty of patronage to all factions, even Cromwellian supporters. And he blunted Parliament's efforts to punish most of the early opponents of monarchy; only those who had actually signed Charles I's death warrant were executed.

Although Parliament insisted on strict adherence to the Church of England in the Act of Uniformity and some of the other aspects of the Clarendon Code, Charles worked to instill some degree of religious toleration in England. He was largely unsuccessful in these efforts, but the attempt was good for his public image.

Yet England went through a serious, though bloodless revolution in 1688–1689, just three years after Charles II's death. How did this happen? How could the optimism surrounding Charles's restoration have become so unraveled in the space of a generation? Primarily, the problem stemmed from Charles's personality and chosen lifestyle. He lacked ambition as king, and he never articulated any long-term vision for England's future, preferring instead to sleep with countless mistresses, dabble in intellectual pursuits, and live in a quasi-mystical world that enabled him to believe that he could cure certain diseases by his touch. Most seriously, he gradually veered toward an open accommodation with Catholicism, the religion that most of the rest of his family, including his brother James, practiced.

As Charles II drifted away from those qualities that had made him popular in the first years of his reign, members of a Parliament without strong leadership likewise drifted. They quarreled among themselves over how to deal with the king, and they almost always preferred discussion to action. Thus Charles, almost despite himself, ruled as he chose without much organized opposition until February 1685, when, on his deathbed, he professed himself a Catholic and quietly passed into history.

SELECTED BIBLIOGRAPHY

Ashley, Maurice. *The English Civil War.* New York: St. Martin's, 1990. Ashley's study is perhaps still the best and most readable introduction to the English Civil War.

Ashton, Robert. *The English Civil War: Conservatism and Revolution, 1603–1649.* London: Weidenfeld and Nicolson, 1989. A reliable study of the polarizing forces in English political and religious life most evident during the struggle.

Aylmer, G. E., ed. *The Levellers in the English Revolution.* London: Thames and Hudson, 1975. A diverse selection of essays that introduce the complexities of the Puritan Levellers.

Bennett, Martyn. *The English Civil War, 1640–1649.* London: Longman, 1995. A solid survey of the English Civil War that provides a balanced approach incorporating political, religious, economic and social, and cultural considerations into an integrated study.

Carlin, Norah. *The Causes of the English Civil Wars.* Oxford, UK: Blackwell, 1999. A comprehensive and reliable study of the various factors that led to the English civil wars, with a good bibliography.

Cust, Richard, and Ann Hughes, eds. *The English Civil War.* London: Arnold, 1997. This collection of essays by prominent historians addresses various aspects of the English Civil War.

Emberton, Wilfrid. *The English Civil War, Day by Day.* Stroud, Gloucestershire, UK: Sutton, 1995. This chronological account of the war provides a wealth of detail and the diary format supplies an interesting perspective.

Gaunt, Peter, ed. *The English Civil War: The Essential Readings.* Oxford, UK: Blackwell, 2000. This anthology is particularly strong in providing primary source material on the Puritan/Parliament side of the struggle.

Hughes, Anne. *The Causes of the English Civil War,* 2nd ed. Basingstoke, UK: Macmillan, 1998. This is a reliable and detailed study on the factors and conditions that contributed to the outbreak of the English Civil War.

Keeble, N.H., ed. *The Cambridge Companion to Writing of the English Revolution.* Cambridge, UK: Cambridge University Press, 2001. A selection of essays on the historiography of the English Civil War.

Kenyon, J. P. *The Civil Wars of England.* London: Phoenix, 1996. A solid introduction to the English Civil War.

Lindley, Keith, ed. *The English Civil War and Revolution: A Sourcebook.* London: Routledge, 1998. A selection of primary and secondary sources on various aspects of the English Civil War.

Morrill, John. *The Nature of the English Revolution.* Harlow, UK: Longman, 1993. An important study on the meaning of the English Civil War by an outstanding historian.

Pocock, J. G. A. *The Ancient Constitution and the Feudal Law: A Study in English Historical Thought in the Seventeenth Century, A Reissue with Retrospect.* Cambridge, UK: Cambridge University Press, 1987. This seminal work by J. G. A. Pocock is a classic study of English historiography in the seventeenth century.

Razzell, Edward, and P.E. Razzell, eds. *The English Civil War: A Contemporary Account.* London: Caliban Books, 1996. A collection of primary materials that provide personal accounts of the English Civil War.

Russell, Conrad. *The Causes of the English Civil War.* Oxford, UK: Clarendon Press, 1990. Russell's account on the outbreak of the English Civil War provides a full discourse on the political divide between the parliament and the monarch.

Smith, Nigel. *Literature and Revolution in England, 1640–1660.* New Haven, CT: Yale University Press, 1994. A serious study in which Smith analyses the interrelationship of literature and the English Civil War.

Tomlinson, Howard, ed. *Before the English Civil War: Essays on Early Stuart Politics and Government.* New York: St. Martin's, 1983. A series of essays concerned with the mounting crisis in English politics during the period from 1603 to 1640.

Worden, Blair. *Roundhead Reputations: The English Civil Wars and the Passions of Posterity.* London: Allen Lane, 2001. An important study on the image and legacy of Puritan leaders in and since the seventeenth century.

Young, Peter, and Richard Holmes. *The English Civil War: A Military History of the Three Civil Wars, 1642–1651.* London: Eyre Methuen, 1974. Perhaps the best military history of the English Civil War for the general reader.

9

The Plague and the Fire, 1665–1666

INTRODUCTION

Bubonic plague may first have visited London around 166 or 167, when the town was called Londinium and was the center of Roman Britain. At that time, it was part of a general European epidemic, and although its true nature is not known with certainty, the sickness quite possibly was the plague. Archaeologists know that the rats that carry plague were in London by the third century, and probably earlier. Over its long history, London, like other great cities has had frequent epidemic diseases brought on by overcrowding, lack of sanitation and pest control, and no knowledge of preventive medicine. By the sixteenth century, London was one of the largest cities in the world, crowded with immigrants and subject to epidemics. An influenza virus killed many Londoners in 1558–1559, but plague came more often (and was never entirely absent) during the sixteenth and seventeenth centuries. An outbreak of plague in 1593 killed an estimated 18,000 people, and that of 1603 killed 30,000. But the worst of the plague epidemics, that of 1665, killed perhaps 65,000 to 110,000 people, although the exact figure can never be known.

Plague was difficult to diagnose in its early stages, because the symptoms varied among victims. Often, however, it started with a severe chill, followed in short order by convulsions and nausea, with protracted vomiting. Next came a period of malaise and depression, marked by severe headaches and loss of balance. At this point, some victims fell into a coma. Some died without regaining consciousness; others revived and in many cases, developed buboes (hence, the name *bubonic* plague). Buboes were purple, black, or red lumps that could appear in the groin, armpits, or less

Between September 2 and September 5, 1666, a fire destroyed about 80 percent of the buildings within the ancient city walls of London, including St. Paul's cathedral, many government buildings and guildhalls, and the Royal Exchange at the center of London's financial district. (Reproduced from the Collections of the Library of Congress.)

commonly, other parts of the body. These "plague tokens," as they were often called, were frequently accompanied by delirium, irrational activities, and a high fever, followed in short order by death. If a victim survived this stage of the disease, he or she might endure the buboes, sometimes as big as a person's fist, for weeks. Most efforts to remove or otherwise treat the buboes were more painful than the buboes themselves. The worst were the black ones, which gave rise to the term, "Black Death" to describe the plague; those with black buboes usually died within hours of their appearance.

From the early sixteenth century, the government had urged the London corporation—the city administration—to take measures to stem the spread of plague and other diseases. The usual suggested remedy was a form of quarantine, where the sick were not permitted to leave their houses. In the 1630s, the king's doctor, Theodore de Mayerne, wrote a report suggesting tighter control of the food supply, expulsion of vagrants, and general cleansing of the city. In addition, he recommended that a public health office be created, with authority over matters of hygiene, vagrants, and poor relief. Although de Mayerne enjoyed respect among the king's advisers, his proposals were quickly forgotten after the epidemic had passed. Deaths from plague were rare in the years after the mid-1640s, and the "pesthouses" where victims were kept in quarantine had been converted to other uses. By 1665, many doctors had never seen the characteristic symptoms of the plague, and London remained vulnerable.

That year, London was a sprawling city of nearly a half million inhabitants, situated entirely on the north side of the Thames River, with only scattered settlements on the south side. Still, its geographical area was quite large, and this meant that the plague and subsequent fire ravaged different parts of town, with some districts experiencing neither. The worst areas of plague infestation were largely spared by the fire, which, had it burned them, might have led to more sanitary and spacious buildings. The plague of 1665 began in May in St. Giles, one of the worst slum districts of London, and because St. Giles was known to be unhealthy, reports of plague cases there at first attracted little attention. By the end of the month, only forty-three deaths had been counted. A severe heat wave in early June, however, changed all that; the disease seemed to explode around the city, causing 267 deaths in the last week of June alone and causing those who could escape to the countryside to do so, including the king and his entourage, who moved to Hampton Court. To their credit, many city officials, including the lord mayor, stayed in town and carried out their official duties. The hot weather continued, and the death rate climbed: 1,000 per week in mid-July; 2,000 per week in early August; 7,000 per week at the epidemic's peak in early September.

The Royal College of Physicians, the licensing organization for doctors, had been chartered by Henry VIII and had been a prestigious body. But by 1665, its influence was much reduced because of its historical association with the monarchy, challenges from other organizations, such as the Society of Chemical Physicians, and the fact that not many Royal College doctors were practicing in London—and some practitioners could only be described as quacks whose licensing had been forced on the Royal College by King Charles. Still, when the plague epidemic struck, the Royal College recommended medicines and public health measures to ameliorate the crisis. The college also subsidized medicines for victims who could not afford them. New pesthouses were hastily built, and so-called "plague nurses" were hired to care for victims, although many believed that their principal concern was to hasten their death so they could rob them.

As was its practice, city authorities tried to combat the plague by driving vagrants and itinerant vendors off the streets, closing schools and courts, and enforcing a forty-day quarantine on victims and their families. The economic life of London was thrown into chaos, and thousands of dogs and cats were killed because of suspicions that they spread the disease. Official exterminators were used to kill dogs and cats and were paid two pence per animal. This was a generous wage in those days, and Daniel Defoe, who wrote an account of the epidemic, estimated that 40,000 dogs and 200,000 cats were put down. Most were killed either by clubbing or with poison, and often the corpses were left in the streets or thrown in the Thames, thus adding to the already horrid stench in the city. All of this helped the rat population thrive, since no one understood in 1665 that rats were the principal carriers of the disease.

In September, city leaders authorized the lighting of bonfires to drive the pestilence out of the air. So many were dying in such a short time that burying the dead became a major sanitation problem. Mass graves were dug, but an acute shortage of gravediggers left bodies literally stacked on the streets. Finally, when the weather cooled in October, the death rate declined and people began returning to the city. But the economic life of London was still moribund until after February 1666, when King Charles II finally returned to the city.

It is significant to note that although contemporaries linked the plague and the fire together as punishment from a wrathful God angered by the sins of Londoners, they really were quite separate incidents. After the end of the plague epidemic, Londoners enjoyed six or seven months of relatively normal life. But on the morning of September 2, they awoke to learn that their city was burning. A baker's house on Pudding Lane had caught fire after its occupant, one Thomas Farriner (sometimes spelled Farynor) had not extinguished the fire under his oven the night before. Wind blew sparks from Farriner's house to others in the neighborhood, and although the lord mayor, Thomas Bludworth, dismissed the fire with the comment, "A woman might piss it out!", it spread quickly during the night. By Monday, September 3, Samuel Pepys, the diarist who lived through the fire and wrote a contemporary account of it, noted that residents were fleeing to the Thames River, and John Evelyn, another writer, described how the entire south side of the city (that part nearest the Thames) was ablaze. The next day, September 4, was even worse, as entire districts on the north side of the city were destroyed, and St. Paul's cathedral burned. That day, efforts were made to prevent the fire from spreading further by demolishing structures in its path, but this did not prove effective until the next day, and then only because the wind died down. By midnight on September 5, the fire was under control.

Roy Porter, a historian of London, concludes that the fire was as bad as it was because it early on reached warehouses full of flammable goods near the river. Winds from the east pushed the fire into crowded neighborhoods to the west, and the lord mayor waited too long to implement a demolition plan, tearing down buildings to create firebreaks. Amazingly, only eight people died in the fire, but thousands were made homeless. Some 80 percent of the city was burned out, including St. Paul's cathedral and 87 other churches, as well as many government buildings, private businesses, and more than 13,000 houses. Although some, like the architect Christopher Wren, wanted to take advantage of the devastation by creating a new street plan for London, this did not happen, and most streets were left as they had been. A few streets were widened, and the riverfront was improved, with a long dock between the Tower of London and London Bridge.

More important, however, were the regulations put in place that mandated the use of brick or stone instead of wood as the building material of choice, and a code establishing four classes of houses that could be built in the city. Most of London, except for St. Paul's and some other significantly large buildings, was rebuilt in a decade, with homeowners footing the bill for their houses in a day before fire insurance and federal disaster relief programs. A coal tax paid for much of the cost of rebuilding public property—streets, prisons, gates, and government buildings.

INTERPRETIVE ESSAY
Robert Landrum

Insofar as this volume is concerned with *transformation,* the devastating visitation of plague on London in 1665 and the "Great Fire" of 1666 are unlikely choices for discussion. While the outbreak of 1665 took more than 50,000 lives, it simply accelerated demographic trends that had long been at work in England and the city. Likewise, though the fire ravaged most of London proper and large swaths of the suburbs, Londoners responded with the resiliency they are famous for, rebuilding their houses, shops, and churches on the old street pattern. London endured the pestilence and rose from the ashes, never surrendering its role as the unchallenged center of the English economy, the seat of government, law, and trade, and (soon) the largest city in Europe. It remained a place where the ambitious and the unscrupulous sought their fortunes, a place where the new commercial economy reigned, and a place where England's mercantile and imperial future might be seen in the present. London is and was no stranger to misfortune but, like the phoenix, the city emerged from repeated catastrophes, constantly reborn yet ever recognizable.

If we are to understand London's recovery in the 1660s, a short review of the city's past is necessary. More than many ancient cities, London's history contains alternating episodes of disaster and recovery. London endures, though, through advantages of site and the human capital it attracts. The city was founded by the commerce-savvy Romans, and it has always been a trading community. It lies forty miles from the sea, on the Thames, at a point where the river is wide enough to accommodate ocean-going ships and narrow enough to be bridged. Caesar encountered the place during his incursion of 54 B.C.E. and may have built a bridge. When the legions returned in 43 C.E., though, they certainly did so. The bridge attracted settlers and merchants and soon became the focal point of trade routes within Britain and across the channel. In the new province of Britannia, all roads led to Londinium.

London's pattern of demise and rebirth began in 60 C.E. In that year, Boudicca, queen of the Iceni, rallied the British tribes against Roman rule. Governor Suetonius Paulinus was campaigning in Anglesey when the Celtic warriors burned the city and slaughtered its inhabitants. On news of the disaster, Paulinus returned to defeat Boudicca; London, not for the last time, rose from the ruins. Indeed, the city soon became the provincial capital and boasted all the hallmarks of Roman civilization: a forum, basilica, amphitheater, temples, baths, and a theater. A Roman fort was erected and the walls were finished around 200.

Britannia was a stable and prosperous part of the Roman world for nearly four centuries. During the fourth century, though, heavy barbarian pressure elsewhere forced Roman officials to draw down Britannia's three legions. In the collapse of the fifth century, the Romans cast off the provinces in the effort to protect Italy. In 410 Emperor Honorius instructed the Britons to look to their own defenses. The legions were gone, and with them went imperial trade and stability—London's life-blood.

The sixth century was therefore London's darkest hour. The Saxons came to England after the departure of the Romans, first as marauders and mercenaries, later as settlers. A warring and farming people, the Saxons had little need for trade and none for cities. For nearly a century Londinium was little more than an abandoned shell. With the slow revival of trade though, the Saxons recolonized the site, and the city gradually regained its status as a crossroads of the north. Writing from a Northumbrian monastery, the Venerable Bede, an early writer and historian, called eighth-century London "a market for many people coming by land and sea."

Unbeknownst to Bede, though, another dark period was at hand. From 834 to 886, Danish and Norse Vikings repeatedly raided the city, leaving it a smoking ruin and destroying the nearby abbey of Westminster. London was saved by the actions of King Alfred, who reestablished British rule over the area, and organized the citizens in self-defense. In the 1040s King

Edward sought to rebuild the abbey and moved his household to West-minster to oversee the project. The migration of the crown represented a challenge to London's centrality, but allowed it to develop outside of royal oversight. This independence was confirmed in 1066, when King William recognized London's charter and built a defensive castle, the Tower, to protect and overawe the city. By the time of Magna Carta, the difficult, autonomous city could not be disregarded. It was a source of wealth and could be a source of power, provided it was ruled appropriately and that its jealously guarded liberties were respected.

This last was an insight that rulers ignored to their peril. Charles I's commercial policies annoyed London's merchants while his conservative religious pretensions enraged the city's Puritans. When his impasse with Parliament reached a nadir in 1642, Charles abandoned his capital in favor of the solidly royalist north. He discovered, however, that city support was crucial in the ensuing civil war. The wartime alliance between Parliament and London lasted long enough to defeat Charles, but Cromwell and his generals soon found that governing the "stiffe-necked town" was as difficult for the saints as it had been for the Stuarts.

By the mid-seventeenth century, then, London had assumed a central place in the English state. It was the linchpin of the English economy; the focal point of English trade, and the country's most important manufacturing center. It was a seat of the Church and, with the suburbs, of government. It was the only place where young lawyers could learn their trade and the best craftsmen plied theirs. It had weathered burnings, plagues, sieges, and freezes. The twin crises of 1665–1666 tested the city; as before, though, London endured, emerging triumphant from the ashes.

The plague first came to London via Bristol in 1349. That visitation—the Black Death—killed at least one-third and perhaps as many as one-half the citizens. Later afflictions were no less severe: in 1563, some 17,500 souls—a fifth of the city—perished; 23,000 died in 1593; in 1603, 37,000 Londoners died; in 1625, 35,000. Medieval medicine was in no way prepared to cope with such a pestilence. Victims were purged or bled, prescribed elaborate placebos or told to avoid exertion. Many were advised to detoxify their breath by smoking tobacco, and to avoid swamps and other sources of dank air. Magistrates served the same purpose with smoky fires at street corners. Roughly 40 percent of those who contracted it in the original blood-borne bubonic form recovered, but when one contracted the pneumonic (airborne) form, it was invariably fatal. The means of transmission, rats and fleas, remained a mystery for five centuries.

Faced with an implacable and inscrutable foe, Londoners adopted methods of self-preservation developed by the Italian city-states—quarantine and flight. When plague was discovered in the city, the infected were restricted to their houses for forty days, time enough for the disease to sort out the living and the dead. On the continent, a skull and crossed bones identified infected towns or buildings, in seventeenth-century London, a red cross and the legend "Lord have mercy upon us" was painted on the walls. Food could be brought to the afflicted, and the hour from nine to ten was reserved for the sick to "go abroad for air," but otherwise the quarantine was enforced by watchmen. When the pest was abroad, towns expelled visitors within their bounds and limited entry; travelers would be forced to camp outside the walls for a period of several days, long enough for symptoms to be visible.

These measures sometimes halted the transmission of disease, but they were by no means universally successful. The movement of people can be restricted, but fleas do not recognize human law, so plague still spread. When quarantine failed, citizens simply left the source of infection: Parliaments were prorogued, courts ceased their sessions, tradesmen shut their shops. Those who had the means retreated to isolated country estates. Those who had friends and relations elsewhere made do as best they could. Only the truly destitute and the duty bound remained in London during the once-a-generation epidemics.

The plague of 1665 grew slowly from the endemic bubonic deaths that haunted the city. Reports surfaced of "the sicknesse" in April, confined to the slums of St. Giles parish. In June, however, the pestilence crossed the walls into the teeming city and an epidemic began. The diarist Samuel Pepys, a navy official who had to remain near the dockyards, has left an account of London during the plague. His entries tell of lengthening "Mortality Bills" and the sudden deaths of friends and neighbors. Parliament decamped from Westminster. The entire Court—excepting only George Monck, duke of Albemarle—left for Salisbury. By late June "all the towne [was] out of towne." Pepys revised his will and sent his wife and servants to lodgings in Woolwich.

The death-rolls peaked in September, when in a single week 7,000 died. The corporation could do little outside of paying for bonfires to dispel the air and assigning watchmen to enforce quarantines. Bodies accumulated in the streets as death overwhelmed the graveyards. Pepys found himself stumbling over abandoned corpses in the night, and the corporation eventually resorted to mass graves. National authorities outside the city could do nothing.

Pepys survived the summer of 1665, and his diary recounts the gradual return of Londoners and the gradual recovery of London. With cooler weather, the appalling harvest receded, tradesmen returned, followed by lawyers and bankers, followed (in February) by the Court. The official toll was 68,000 deaths to plague, ineffective reporting by the outlying parishes means the actual figure is quite likely higher.

One searches in vain for changes caused by the 1665 plague. London endured a frightful calamity, but a longstanding pattern of metropolitan growth continued unabated, despite repeated outbreaks of the pestilence. From 120,000 in 1560, the metropolis grew to 200,000 in 1600. That number doubled to 400,000 by 1660, then vaulted—despite plague—to 575,000 by 1700. Against this background of growth, plagues appear as brief pauses. For centuries London acted as a demographic "sink" to the rest of England, and 1665 was just a part of this pattern. Simply stated, early modern and medieval cities were filthy, fetid, and overcrowded—disease and opportunity rubbed shoulders within them. Deaths in the city always outnumbered births. London's phenomenal growth was therefore fueled by immigration from the provinces. Ambitious young English men and women—in the seventeenth century no less than the twenty-first—sought their fortunes in the capital. The pull of the Court brought the aspiring lawyer Thomas Cromwell to serve Henry VIII; the pull of the London stage brought young William Shakespeare from Stratford; Dickens' Oliver Twist had no destination in mind, but he arrived in the Bermondsey district of London nonetheless. The arrivals brought tradesmen and shopkeepers in their wake. All of them, though, faced reduced life expectancies in the unhealthy streets of London.

If plague failed to reverse the flow of people into the metropolis, it did accelerate trends within the city. Population in the area bounded by the walls—London proper—was in decline through the last half of the seventeenth century. From a peak of 135,000 in 1640, "the city" shrank to about 105,000 in 1660. Propelled by the calamities of 1665–1666, this figure fell to 80,000 in 1695. Growth in London was therefore restricted to the suburbs, while overcrowding was eased in the disease- and fire-prone tenements of the city itself. The corporation, which governed only the city, was understandably concerned for its preeminence and responded with an ever-vigilant protection of the city's privileges and monopolies—rigorously enforcing chartered "liberties" such as market days and work rules.

Change was also noticeably absent in the responses to disease. Methods of quarantine had been developed in Italy and adapted locally since the fourteenth century; likewise the flight to uninfected areas that left London empty of people. The one innovation that the corporation attempted was the eradication of cats and dogs, under the mistaken belief that they spread the disease. Pepys estimated that 40,000 dogs and 200,000 cats were killed, which, like much premodern medicine, only inflamed the situation. The new predator-free London made an ideal environment for a booming rat population.

London's plague of 1665, though, was the last major outbreak. This owes little to any positive advances in treatment and much to the fire. The brick and stone city that replaced the wooden city of 1665 was a healthier place. The new buildings housed fewer people and far fewer rats. More-over, the building ordinances of 1667 and 1671 mandated the construction of gutters and drains to eliminate sewage running in open passages in the middle of the streets and forbade "noxious trades" in the city itself. Taken together, these measures resulted in a safer human environment.

Londoners reacted to the pestilence in 1665 much as they reacted to eleven earlier outbreaks; they understood it in terms of the will of God. According to Calvinist notions of Providence, an omnipotent God is inti-mately involved with events on earth. Plague was one of the tools in his inscrutable scheme: a judgment on those who died, a mercy to those who lived, and a warning to society at large. Though many of his acquaintances died, Pepys rejoiced in the Lord's charity for his own survival, and hoped that it might continue. The Crown sought divine clemency by declaring public fast days; the corporation followed suit, forbidding public enter-tainments and private celebrations and restricting "disorderly tippling" at pubs and coffee houses. A flood of moralizing literature attempted to dis-cern "God's design in sending the plague amongst us," with a score of con-tradictory conclusions. Some saw it as a partial expression of the Lord's anger, and unless the sins of the people were recognized and addressed, more might follow. The Lord, one said, had yet to "empty his quiver of wrath." Cavalier diarist John Evelyn understood it as judgment on the sins of the Court and the nation's ingratitude for the restoration of church and Crown. Exactly what pleased and displeased the Lord could be debated, as might the remedy. Providential thinkers were convinced of one surety— the wrath of God. Some even interpreted it as a harbinger of the end of days foretold in the Book of Revelation—Armageddon.

Providence notwithstanding, the plague of 1665 ended with the winter. Colder temperatures brought relief, and by February most of those Lon-doners who fled had returned. Evelyn celebrated God's "infinite mercy in preserving us" after his family's seven-month absence. Pepys found it "a delightful thing...to see the towne full of people again" and the return to coffeehouse and tavern sociability. After some 70,000 deaths, London recovered quickly. The city's mortality bills recorded plague deaths through 1666, but by September, the worst of God's wrath was transferred to the sinful sailing communities of Deal and Deptford. For the immediate future, Armageddon was averted.

The citizens' relief was short-lived, and visions of brimstone returned in a new form. Early in the morning of September 2, 1666, a fire broke out at Thomas Farriner's bakeshop in Pudding Lane. After a dry summer and a windy week, conditions were ripe, and by 3 A.M. the fire had spread to several neighboring structures. When he arrived at the site, though, Lord Mayor Thomas Bludworth refused to tear down five adjoining houses in a fire-line, citing rebuilding costs. "A woman," he quipped, "could piss it out." Fanned by the winds, the fire spread to Thames Street, where the warehouses were full of combustible naval stores: pitch, tar, hemp, flax, wood, and coal. Within hours the opportunity to fight the fire was lost.

By seven that morning, the fire had consumed 300 houses. Charles II overrode the dithering mayor, gave royal weight to widespread demolition and placed his brother James, duke of York, in charge of firefighting. Over the next two days, James brought in troops to contain looting and placed firelines well ahead of the blaze. The lines at Cornhill and the Queenhithe marketplace failed to contain the fire, but elsewhere there were some limited successes. At the Tower, cannoneers employed gunpowder against nearby houses, blasting a firebreak at the walls. The fire advanced to the gates, but the castle itself was saved. Similarly, fire lines based on the ancient city walls usually, though not always, held. The bucket brigades and water engines were less successful, though, because the water sources failed. Flames destroyed the Thames-driven wheel that brought water up at London bridge. At the same time, desperate householders broke through the streets to gain access to the elm-wood water mains. The improvised taps robbed the system of pressure and the water supply ran dry throughout the city. Partially contained but not extinguished, the fire ceased when the winds that drove it died. By Thursday morning, Europe's greatest city was "a smoking mass of lamentable ruins."

Lamentable, indeed. Over 200,000 homeless inhabitants thronged the open fields surrounding the city, driven out of the 13,200 destroyed multistoried tenements. A total of 436 urban acres, 400 streets, and more than 80 churches were obliterated. Among these was that bulwark of the west London skyline, St. Paul's, where heat collapsed the leaden roof, and molten metal poured onto the goods stored inside by local householders and the Company of Stationers. The centers of commerce, the Guildhall and Royal Exchange, went up in flames, as did Newgate prison, the Session House and forty-four livery halls. Evelyn wrote: "London was, but is no more."

Evelyn was wrong. Physical London, the houses and the churches, was indeed destroyed, but cities are composed of citizens, and London itself extended outside the jurisdiction of the corporation. Londoners, the soul of the city and the source of its resilience, survived. Only eight people died in the conflagration. Moreover, damage was limited to the city proper. Relatively little burned beyond the walls and across the river, in the suburbs and Westminster.

Sullen embers steamed for several weeks, but rebuilding began even before the flames died. The first orders of business were to reestablish order against looters and thieves, and to see to the refugees camped on every piece of open ground near the city. Within four days nearly all these "burnt Londoners" had found shelter. Many roomed with family and friends in the undamaged suburbs, while others left for English colonies in America or the Caribbean. A stubborn few returned to the sites where their homes had been, defiantly setting up shanties of rubble and charred timbers. The squatters and claimants to city lots necessarily slowed the work of demolition that had to be completed before the work of rebuilding could begin.

Rebuilding was on many minds. The Corporation, naturally, hoped to accelerate the process so that businesses might return and commerce might not be lost permanently to the suburbs. The Crown promised a "much more beautiful city" than that which had burned. Given encouragement, a legion of amateur city planners emerged with utopian visions for the phoenix city. John Evelyn, long an advocate of redevelopment, produced a plan within days. Another less scrupulous visionary, Valentine Knight, earned an arrest for prefacing his rebuilding scheme with the suggestion that the Crown might draw a benefit from the catastrophe. Most significant was the plan put forward to Charles II and his council by the royal architect Sir Christopher Wren. Wren's plan envisioned a magnificent London, a thoroughly modern planned city situated on broad avenues, proud piazzas, and rational traffic patterns.

In typically English muddling-through fashion, and with typical English attention to legalities, the grand schemes for a rebuilt London came to naught. The accumulated layers of land claims meant that any comprehensive transformation would lead to endless wrangling in courts, as limitless claimants cited burned titles to rezoned tracts. Instead, Parliament passed legislation to allow efficient hearing of cases and expedite rebuilding. The "Fire Courts" established a shortcut hearing of tenants' and titleholders' cases, bypassing the notoriously slow Chancery and Exchequer courts. Meanwhile, the Rebuilding Act set binding construction standards for all rebuilt structures. Hereafter, buildings would be of prescribed heights, their exteriors would be brick or stone, and the practice of jettying—creating additional floor space by oversailing successive

storeys into the streets—was forbidden. The Rebuilding Act also mandated acceptable prices for material and required that suppliers bring
goods into the city to market. The Act set new minimum widths for streets
and alleys, stipulated an open quay along the Thames, the widening of
several of the major thoroughfares, and the construction of a new King
Street connecting the Guildhall and Cheapside. This was to be the extent
of basic change. Much of the city remained on the medieval plan, along
the streets originally plotted by the Romans.

This absence of change and the failure of the grand visions for London
disguises what was actually accomplished in the years following the fire.
The great public structures, such as the Royal Exchange, the Guildhall,
and the Customs House, were slated for speedy reconstruction. Charles II
himself laid the first stone of the Exchange on October 23, 1667; by 1670
the customs officers were working from their new building. The Fire
Court did its work, too, and by the end of 1670 more than 7,000 house-sites
had been surveyed. Most importantly, the city was rebuilt according to the
restrictions set out in the Rebuilding Act. The use of wood and thatch in
exteriors was abandoned, as was jettying. Uniformity was not quite
achieved, but stone and brick exteriors were, and with wider streets the
rebuilt London was considerably safer from fire.

The most striking part of the new London skyline, however, were
Wren's new churches. The royal architect was frustrated in his effort to
rationalize the city as a whole, but he nevertheless won the commission to
rebuild St. Paul's and fifty-one parish churches. Church construction was
slow and dependent on the receipts from a new duty on sea-coals, but the
work was truly inspired. By 1679, thirteen were finished; the last were
begun in 1686. The steeples that defined Wren's stately churches came
later, when funds came available in the early eighteenth century. Construction of the new St. Paul's began in 1675, with Wren constantly revis-
ing plans. Thirty-five years later, the aged architect's son attended the
opening of the completed cathedral. Emblazoned on the south transept
was the figure of a phoenix: the symbol of the burned city reborn.

What emerged from the rebuilding was indeed a new city. Some
thought it a masterpiece. One minister celebrated the city for its new uniformity, "the streets broader, the houses of one form," the buildings were,
"infinitely more beautiful, more commodious, and more solid." On the
other hand, those who expected a "convenient, regular, well-built city"
were disappointed. Nicholas Hawksmoor condemned it as "a chaos of
dirty rotten sheds, always tumbling or taking fire, with winding crooked
passages (scarce practicable), lakes of mud, and rills of stinking mire running through them." The critics were disappointed that the London street

plan emerged much as it had been, or annoyed, like John Evelyn, that their own pet rebuilding scheme went unheeded. Most of these plans, though, were untenable. The Corporation demanded that business return to usual. The crown demanded the return of trade and customs revenue. Landlords demanded the use of their sites, and tenants demanded their homes, shops, and pubs. Britain did not have the luxury of Russia, where a capital could be carved out of a wilderness; or of France, where the ruler's presence served as capital and court. Neither money nor time permitted a master-planned transformation. One important change, though, went unheralded. The city was rebuilt in vermin-proof brick and stone, assuring that the rats and their plague would never return on the same scale again.

The rebuilding that did take place also reveals ongoing demographic and economic patterns. The city proper shrank as the suburbs grew. By 1672, only 8,000 of the 13,200 burned houses were replaced, and these were difficult to lease. The Corporation relaxed guild and citizenship restrictions, but not all the tradesmen returned. Dissenters migrated to villages where they might worship without legal impediments, while wealthy residents sought the newly fashionable west end. In a pattern familiar to the twentieth century, the city became a place where people worked, the suburbs where they lived. London's breakneck growth continued throughout the following centuries, but after the fire, "London" meant city and suburbs, not just the precincts under the Corporation. In this case, the catastrophes of 1665–1666 accelerated trends that were already in place.

As population shifted in the metropolis, so too did London's economic profile. Though it would be wrong to draw too strong a distinction between pre- and post-fire London, some changes can be discerned. Before the apocalypse of the 1660s, London was England's financial and manufacturing center, as it would remain. In the decades and centuries following 1666, though, manufacturing declined relative to services. Georgian London emerged as a leader in banking and exchange, insurance, and retailing—the services one might expect of an international and imperial center.

Founded on commerce, London remained wedded to trade. In 1650, London was the greatest inbound market and outbound manufacturing center in England. Port facilities and seaborne commerce naturally attracted the subsidiary trades: makers of masts, ropes, and sails were all a part of the larger shipbuilding yards. Other industries followed the growing market, but not all were welcome. In *Fumifugium* (1661), John Evelyn complained of the smells and smokes of the "noxious" trades carried on within city limits. Evelyn and others recognized the salt-, sugar-, and soap-boilers, slaughterhouses, dyers, tanners, and glue makers who poured their by-products into the air and into the Thames as sources of pollution. The disruption of the fire and rebuilding forced these and other industries to relocate, and the Rebuilding Act promised that those "whose trades are carried on by smoke" would be confined to "a quarter assigned to them." Though mitigated, pollution remained a problem. Polluting trades gravitated toward the London market, despite post-fire restrictions. Moreover, the citizens—tanners and tailors as much as lawyers and clerks—depended on sulphurous Newcastle coal for heat, and a pall of smoke usually enveloped the city.

The pace of industrial change can be overstated. Not until the mid-eighteenth century did independent mining and textile centers emerge in the north. Shipbuilding gradually migrated to Clydeside and Tyneside, cutlery to Sheffield, engineering to Birmingham, and textiles to Manchester. The Industrial Revolution was still a century in the future, but London would experience it as a spectator, not a participant. London, however, remained the indispensable center of consumption in Britain. The capital boasted a unique high-wage, high-skill service and craft economy, and led the world in banking, insurance, and retailing. London's broad-based prosperity was centered, as it had been under the Romans, on the Thames and on an outward-facing empire.

One emblem of the new economy was the creation of novel forms of service and intangible products. Post-fire London became a center for the international insurance business, based on the underwriters who met at Edward Lloyd's Coffee House on Tower Street. The Lloyd's agents specialized in seaborne trade, but at the same time other insurance products were developed. The great London developer Dr. Nicholas Barbon, who bought up scores of devastated properties at bargain prices in the aftermath of the fire, devised what might be called the first modern fire insurance scheme. For a fee, Barbon insured the value of the structure and provided the protection of supplemental fire-fighting teams. Competitors soon emerged, at least three by 1700, six more by 1725.

Barbon is an interesting character, and the "fire companies" are a colorful footnote in eighteenth-century urban history, but there is something more to this. Insurance is, by its very nature, a rejection of the Providential worldview. It is predicated on the idea that disasters are not the work of a vengeful and incomprehensible deity; rather, fire, storms, plague, and the like are the product of natural forces. Human misfortune, according to this new ethos, was somewhat predictable and subject to what the modern era might call "risk management." This serves as a backdrop to the publication of Isaac Newton's *Principia* (1689), which banished Calvin's irrational God (and most other gods) to the celestial sidelines, excluding Him from active involvement in His rational, predictable, earthly creation. The unscrupulous Barbon was too busy with property speculation for hand-wringing piety. This is made all the more poignant when one recalls that he was the only son of Praisegod Barbon, the interregnum Puritan fanatic who gave his name to Cromwell's short-lived enthusiast Parliament. The Barbons, father and son, provide a illuminating contrast, from unrealizable Puritan idealism to pragmatic hypercapitalism in a single generation.

The calamities that afflicted London in the 1660s can hardly be imagined as the source of economic and demographic changes. Indeed, those changes often proceeded in defiance of fire and plague. London was neither destroyed nor rationalized in the 1660s, largely because of the stubborn attachment of Londoners to their homes. This attachment frustrated architects, who understood 1666 as an opportunity missed. As haphazard as it was, though, the resurrection of London enabled the city to reassume its place at the center of English (and later, British) society. Some three centuries later, Hitler's *Luftwaffe* brought London yet another Armageddon, destroying some 130,000 London houses and damaging 1.25 million more. Patrick Abercrombie stepped forward as the twentieth century's Wren in two government-sponsored reports, the *Greater London Plan* (1943). This program envisioned a green belt surrounding London, beyond which all subsequent development would be situated. The green belt has actually been enforced, but the relocation of industry and population never followed the planner's visions, and lack of means prevented the wholesale transformation that Abercrombie called for. In 1945, as in 1666, Londoners rebuilt their irrational, congested, overcrowded, and beloved city along the lines laid out by Roman surveyors. London was reborn again, and took on the task of reinventing itself—no longer the favored child of an outward-facing empire and the center of North Atlantic trade. This time, the phoenix emerged from the ashes to find the world changed by the fire.

SELECTED BIBLIOGRAPHY

Primary Sources

Defoe, Daniel. *A Journal of the Plague Year.* New York: Modern Library, 2001. The most recent edition of this classic work, with an introduction by Jason Goodwin. Defoe disguises historical fiction as personal recollection. Even so, his account is master storytelling close to the event.

Evelyn, John. *The Diary of John Evelyn.* Rochester, NY: Boydell, 1996. There are many editions of this work; this is the most recent one-volume edition, edited by Guy de la Bedeyere. Evelyn's diary is not nearly so personal as that of Pepys but provides an especially effective description of the fire.

Pepys, Samuel. *The Diary of Samuel Pepys.* 11 vols. Edited by Robert Latham and William Matthews. Berkeley: University of California Press, 1970–1983. The quintessential diarist: insightful, honest, and thoroughly human.

Secondary Sources

Ackroyd, Peter. *London: The Biography.* London: Chatto & Winders, 2001. Portrays London as a living organism.

Bell, Walter G. *The Great Fire of London in 1666.* Westport, CT: Greenwood Press, 1971; and *The Great Plague of London in 1665.* New York: AMS Press, 1979. Originally published in 1951 and thus somewhat dated, but still useful.

Hibbert, Christopher. *London: The Biography of a City.* New York: Morrow, 1970; rev. ed. London: Allen Lane, 1977. The survey from the doyen of London historians.

Picard, Liza. *Restoration London.* New York: St. Martin's, 1998. A useful and readable general history.

Porter, Roy. *London: A Social History.* Cambridge, MA: Harvard University Press, 1995. An intimate panorama of Londoners, their built environment, and their neighborhoods over twenty-one centuries.

Porter, Stephen. *The Great Fire of London.* Stroud, Gloucestershire, UK: Sutton, 1996. A succinct recent account.

Saunders, Ann. *The Art and Architecture of London: An Illustrated Guide.* Oxford, UK: Phaedon, 1984. A guidebook to connect the modern observer with physical London.

Slack, Paul. *The Impact of Plague in Tudor and Stuart England.* London: Routledge, 1985. The best study of the plague epidemics.

Tinniswood, Adrian. *His Invention so Fertile: A Life of Christopher Wren.* New York: Oxford University Press, 2001. The most recent comprehensive biography of the renaissance man who rebuilt London.

10

The Glorious Revolution, 1688–1689

INTRODUCTION

On May 30, 1660, his thirtieth birthday, Charles Stuart returned to London from his French exile to be crowned Charles II, king of England. Eleven years earlier, his father, Charles I, had been executed at the conclusion of the English Civil War, and England had come under the sway of the victorious Oliver Cromwell and his Roundheads. Cromwell's rule subsequently degenerated into a military dictatorship and the extremely straitlaced Christians who surrounded him, derisively referred to as the "saints," dominated everyday life in England. The English soon tired of military rule and a rigid morality, and when Cromwell died in 1658 the desire to restore the monarchy became irresistible. Little wonder then that London erupted in joy when Charles returned; the sound of ringing bells filled the air, the citizenry cheered the progress of the new king's entourage, and wine flowed freely from the city's fountains.

Charles II was tall, dark, but not particularly handsome. He was highly intelligent, but he was also lazy, cynical, and debauched. His court ran on wit, charm, gossip, and licentiousness, and Charles led the pack with his numerous mistresses and a slew of royal bastards. While Charles rarely exerted himself, he showed great determination never to resume what he referred to as his "travels," that is, his exile from England. Nevertheless, the great question that had undone his father remained: who was to rule, the king in an absolute manner or the representatives of landed and merchant England assembled in the Parliament?

Although Charles had no love for the men who had executed his father, he realized that he had to accommodate them if he hoped to succeed. The

Landing of William 3rd at Torbay

William III

William III, together with his wife Mary, became joint rulers of England in 1689 after driving his father-in-law, James II, from the throne. The replacement of the absolutist James II with the more conciliatory William and Mary marked a crucial development in England's Glorious Revolution that established Parliament's ascendancy over the Crown. (Reproduced from the Collections of the Library of Congress.)

new king made it plain from the start of his reign that he did not seek retribution against those who had put his father to death. Furthermore, the 1660 Act of Indemnity and Oblivion had the effect of regularizing the land transactions that had occurred during the Interregnum. While land directly confiscated by the revolutionary government was returned to its former owners—the king, the Anglican Church, and monarchist gentry— other lands that the king's supporters had been forced to sell to ambitious beneficiaries of the revolution in order to pay taxes and fines remained with the new owners, thereby demonstrating the king's solicitude for a now wealthy and powerful portion of the English population. Impoverished loyalists who had expected Charles to restore their land to them bitterly condemned what they called "the Act of Indemnity for the King's Enemies and Oblivion for His Friends."

Both his sloth and his desire to have someone else "out front" on the issues prompted Charles to work through his advisers. Initially, his most important minister was competent Edward Hyde, earl of Clarendon, although it should be noted that Hyde's continual criticism of the court's moral shortcomings annoyed Charles to no end and—as with all his advisers—Charles was willing to jettison Clarendon when the latter attracted too much criticism from Parliament. Charles was also fortunate that in 1661 the first parliamentary election after his return resulted in a royalist landslide. Knowing that he was unlikely to ever have a more supportive Parliament, Charles kept the so-called Cavalier Parliament in session for eighteen years.

Nevertheless, tension between Parliament and Crown continued. For example, the issue of religion seemed never ending. The Cavalier Parliament and its successors strongly favored the traditional Church of England. They held both Roman Catholics and Dissenters (Protestants outside the Church of England such as Puritans, Presbyterians, and Unitarians) in contempt. The ironically named Clarendon Code, a series of discriminatory measures aimed at Dissenters and Roman Catholics passed by Parliament against the earl of Clarendon's wishes, was the most visible consequence of this attitude. Charles, on the other hand, favored religious toleration as a way to both constrain religious passions that threatened his realm's tranquility and provide protection for the Roman Catholicism that he personally, yet quietly, embraced.

Finances was another area where Charles and his Parliament failed to see eye to eye. To its credit, the Cavalier Parliament tried to establish a more regular flow of income for the monarchy. It ended the confusing and sometimes contradictory maze of feudal dues and obligations that had provided the bulk of the king's income, and substituted an annual payment of more than £1,000,000. As generous as this sum appeared, it was not enough to cover the state's expenditures. The unhappy Charles was loath to petition the Parliament for money to make up the difference because he valued his independence and viewed any subordination to Parliament as undermining his royal prerogative.

The impasse over money led to yet another serious disagreement. The English nation, including its Parliament, had long regarded France as its "natural" enemy; it both hated and feared the France of Louis XIV. However, Charles regarded Louis and his court at Versailles with affection and admiration. His mother was a French princess, Louis was his cousin, he had spent more than a decade in exile at the French court, and his sister was married to Louis' younger brother. In terms of culture, manner, and religious preference, Charles appeared to be more French than English. Consequently, when Louis offered the impecunious Charles what amounted to a yearly subsidy to free him of financial dependence on Parliament, Charles readily accepted. The 1670 Treaty of Dover provided Charles with his much-needed funds in return for which the king brought England into Louis' struggle with Holland on the side of the French and, secretly, promised to return England to Roman Catholicism—a pledge never fulfilled but one nevertheless bound to outrage the vast majority of Englishmen if it were to become public.

One further issue divided Charles from most of his subjects. As it became more apparent that Charles would father no legitimate heir, attention began to shift to the man who would inherit the crown upon Charles' death, his younger brother James. As historian Lacy Baldwin Smith has noted, if Charles was lazy, intelligent, and possessed a sense of humor, James was hard working, stupid, and humorless. Moreover, James was a devout Roman Catholic, and religion meant much in this era. As early as 1673, the staunchly Anglican Parliament took aim at James. In that year it passed the Test Act that effectively barred both Roman Catholics and Dissenters from holding office. As a consequence, James was forced to resign his position as lord high admiral.

During the latter years of his reign, Charles, who now actively engaged in the political warfare of the day, found himself increasingly at odds with Parliament. New elections failed to bring in the parliamentary majority that the king had hoped for; nevertheless, Charles remained popular with most Englishmen. When Charles' parliamentary opponents continued to demand the exclusion of James from the line of succession and subsequently overplayed their hand, Charles capitalized on this miscue to prorogue Parliament and to make himself appear to his subjects as the indispensable man for maintaining the realm's peace and prosperity. At the time of his death in 1685, Charles was ruling in a quasi-absolutist manner.

Thus, when James Stuart, duke of York, received the crown as James II, he found himself in an advantageous position. However, in less than four years he managed to squander the power and good will that his brother had bequeathed to him and was forced into exile. Fifty-three-year-old James was a political fool of the first magnitude. An ultraroyalist, he was dogmatic, obstinate, rigid, and shortsighted. Perhaps most importantly, he was a devout Roman Catholic who made no attempt to hide his desire to return England to Catholicism. This dream and the steps he took to accomplish it quickly alienated the new king from his subjects, but most of all from the Anglican squires who controlled Parliament. These country gentlemen might well have tolerated James' absolutist approach to governing, but they could not abide either a direct attack on the Church of England or its subversion by the forces of Roman Catholicism.

During his short reign, James committed one blunder after another. He effectively dismantled the Test Act in a highhanded manner certain to antagonize Parliament. He intervened in the electoral process and stationed a standing army near London in order to intimidate the capital. James subverted the justice system and ignored parliamentary decrees. He behaved arbitrarily and capriciously, and initiated a personal rule by fiat. In an act of colossal stupidity, he expelled the powerful gentry from their positions of local overlordship and governance, replacing them with nonentities subservient to the throne. Most egregiously, James enthusiastically promoted Roman Catholicism at the expense of the Church of England. Roman Catholics replaced Anglicans in the officer corps of the army and the navy, the royal administration, the universities, and within the Church of England itself.

While James rapidly alienated virtually every segment of conscious English society, memories of the civil war and Cromwell's rule remained fresh and served to stay the hand of those who would openly challenge James for fear of provoking a new civil conflict. Moreover, James was aging and his Protestant daughters were his only heirs. Obviously, if England could hold out for a few more years James would disappear and a more reasonable figure would occupy the throne.

This vision of the future exploded in June 1688 when James' second wife, the Italian Catholic Mary of Modena, gave birth to a boy. The infant's claim to the throne superseded that of his older half-sisters. Clearly, the child would be raised a Catholic in a court that regarded absolute royal authority as a right bestowed by God, and Parliament as an inconvenience at best and a traitorous usurper of royal power at worst.

This birth galvanized the already substantial and growing opposition to James' rule. By the end of June, a courier was on his way to Holland with a letter signed by seven prominent Englishmen, including the bishop of London and the leaders of all factions of Parliament, inviting Prince William of Orange, the stadtholder of Holland, and Mary, his wife and James' older daughter, to come to England and replace James II as monarch.

On November 5, 1688, William and a considerable force landed at Torbay. Virtually no one rallied to James' side, and before the end of the year he along with his wife and son fled to France and the court of Louis XIV. There they would spend the rest of their lives. William and Mary, confirmed Protestants and deferential toward Parliament, now ruled jointly.

However, the story is not yet complete. Elections brought a new Parliament, the so-called Convention Parliament, which convened on January 22, 1689. This Parliament offered the crown to William and Mary, but it also obliged the royal couple to accept certain conditions. These conditions, originally called the Declaration of Rights but later expanded to become the famous English Bill of Rights, constituted what is sometimes called the "Revolution Settlement." Above all, the Bill of Rights clearly but indirectly established once and for all that the monarchy was beholden to Parliament and not to God.

In specific terms, the Bill of Rights made it illegal for the monarchy to tamper with juries or impose unreasonable bail or fines, rig elections, keep a standing army without Parliament's consent, collect monies without Parliament's assent, or issue decrees with the force of law. Englishmen were confirmed in their right to bear arms and to petition the crown for redress of grievances. Members of Parliament were granted freedom from prosecution for what they might say during debates. Subsequent acts either directly or indirectly provided for an independent judiciary, regular meetings of Parliament, and regular elections of new Parliaments. Quite significantly, Parliament's control of the purse strings was recognized and strengthened.

The Revolution Settlement also dealt with the question of succession by vesting the subsequent right to the throne in William and Mary's children, then Anne (Mary's younger sister) and her children, and finally in William's children should he choose if Mary died to marry again and father children. The infant James Stuart was excluded from the line of succession by the provision that barred any Roman Catholic from inheriting the English crown.

Finally, the Revolution Settlement provided a solution to the vexatious question of religion. The Anglicans, who controlled Parliament, swallowed their pride and principles to the extent that for all practical purposes they now accepted the notion of religious toleration for all Protestants, even though non-Anglican Protestants remained barred from the realm's highest offices. In this manner, the Dissenters were brought on board. However, the previous disabilities placed on England's Roman Catholics were tacitly confirmed and remained in place well into the nineteenth century.

INTERPRETIVE ESSAY
Steven E. Siry

The Glorious Revolution, which involved the last successful invasion of England, produced more consequences of enduring significance than any other European revolution of the early modern period. In addition, the Declaration of Rights, later changed into statutory form as the Bill of Rights, expressed the goals and ideas of the Glorious Revolution more than any other document. The Declaration was adopted by the Convention Parliament, which was a revolutionary body created to resolve the crisis caused by Prince William of Orange's invasion of England and King James II's subsequent flight to France. Although the Declaration asserted no doctrine of parliamentary supremacy; nevertheless, it is arguably the seventeenth-century's most significant constitutional document. It described James II's alleged and real abuses of royal prerogative, resolved that he had abdicated the throne, declared William and Mary to be king and queen of England, established the succession to the crown, set forth new oaths of allegiance, and stated what were claimed to be ancient rights and liberties of the English people. In particular, the Declaration asserted the rights of individuals to bear arms and to petition the king without fear of reprisals, as well as to be protected against excessive bail, exorbitant fines, and cruel and unusual punishments. Moreover, the document declared illegal the levying of taxes and the suspending of laws without Parliament's consent. It also further strengthened Parliament by claiming the rights of free speech, free elections, free debate, and frequent meetings. Finally, the Declaration broke new constitutional ground by banning the creation or maintenance of any army in peacetime without Parliament's consent.

The "radical" Whigs in the Convention Parliament insisted that the claim of rights be linked to the offer of the throne to William and Mary. The Declaration of Rights was subsequently read to William and Mary immediately before Parliament offered them the Crown, and thirty-eight-year-old William, who was James II's nephew and son-in-law, asserted: "As I had no other intention in coming hither than to preserve your religion, laws, and liberties, so you may be sure that I shall endeavor to support them."

The Glorious Revolution therefore marked a watershed in relations between Crown and Parliament. Though the Crown retained quite significant authority and influence, the Glorious Revolution had clearly ended the possibility of establishing some form of absolutist monarchy in England, and thus confirmed Parliament's legislative sovereignty.

In addition to this significant shift in the constitutional balance of power as a part of the Revolution Settlement, other constraints on the Crown's powers were established after 1689. The Triennial Act (1694) asserted that no more than three years should pass without a Parliament, but no Parliament was to exist for more than three years in order to lessen the effects of ministerial and Crown patronage on Parliament. Furthermore, to protect political opposition to the Crown, the Trial of Treason Act (1696) provided procedural safeguards for individuals accused of treason. These safeguards included legal representation, a copy of the charge to the accused, and the need for independent testimony from at least two eyewitnesses to obtain a conviction. Moreover, in 1701 the Act of Settlement clarified the line of succession after Anne, the younger daughter of James II. It further declared that any future monarch had to be a member of the Church of England and could not leave England nor involve the nation in war without Parliament's approval. The act also banned foreign nationals from becoming privy councilors, holding any other offices under the Crown, or sitting in the House of Commons. Beyond these provisions, the act asserted that judges' tenure in office depended on good behavior rather than at the Crown's pleasure, and that judges could be removed only through action by both houses of Parliament.

The Bill of Rights and subsequent legislation substantially altered the balance of power between Crown and Parliament, but this new relationship was primarily upheld by the financial settlement that occurred in the 1690s. Distrust of the monarchy led the House of Commons to curb the power of the king and his ministers. Despite accepting William's offer to give up the unpopular hearth tax, which had been granted in perpetuity, Parliament initially extended the customs revenue for the Crown only until 1694. William therefore became the first monarch since the fifteenth century (except for Charles I) to be denied the customs tax for life. Since the king no longer had an independent source of royal revenue, the House of Commons could potentially force its programs and policies on the Crown by withholding revenue. During the eighteenth century, Parliament gradually emerged as the real authority in Britain's system of constitutional monarchy.

In the late 1600s, political revolution also raised the possibility of ecclesiastical revolution. In 1688–1689 many people wanted a dramatic revision of the Church settlement of the 1660s. Some hoped for a really comprehensive national church. Some, especially the Presbyterians, felt a reconciliation to the Anglican Church was a better possibility than at any time since the beginning of the century. Those known as the Dissenters believed that the Word of God could be understood by men without the assistance of a hierarchical church establishment with roots in the medieval period. The Anglican leadership, however, would not allow any change to the Church's hierarchical and episcopalian structure. Instead, the Dissenters were given the Toleration Act of 1689, which granted freedom of worship to Protestant nonconformists in places licensed by Anglican bishops if the nonconformists accepted the basic doctrines expressed in the Thirty-Nine Articles and approved by the Act of Uniformity (1662). Though this seemed to fall far short of the freedom held out to Dissenters by James II's Declaration of Indulgence, the Toleration Act established an unprecedented security for some Dissenters who had faced persecution. In particular, it exempted Presbyterians and those who believed in the Trinity from the penalties of the 1673 Test Act. It did nothing, however, for the Unitarians, the Quakers, or the Jews. In addition, Roman Catholics were more vulnerable than before. Nevertheless, the Toleration Act did represent a departure in English history because the government in the future would persecute few people for religious reasons.

Probably most of the revolutionaries in 1688 did not recognize the potential effects of their actions on England's foreign relations. The consequences, however, would soon become evident. Prior to the Glorious Revolution, English leaders from Oliver Cromwell to James II had pursued a largely pro-French and anti-Dutch policy. But William III was primarily a continentalist who had been seeking any means to block French expansion since Louis XIV's advance into the Netherlands in 1672. He wanted to maintain a balance of power between the Habsburgs and the Bourbons, the two principal European dynasties. Thus, in May 1689 England declared war against France. In short, France essentially became the permanent enemy and overseas rival of England, which assumed a leading role in a "Grand Alliance" with Austria, the Netherlands, and other smaller European states to counter French ambitions.

The War of the League of Augsburg (1688–1697) and the War of the Spanish Succession (1702–1713) involved England in continental and colonial warfare as it had not experienced since the Elizabethan conflict with

Spain. Strategically, England pursued an interventionist policy to challenge Louis XIV's expansionist efforts in the Low Countries and to stop the creation of a powerful new Bourbon empire comprising the French and Spanish monarchies. Britain's concern with France intensified in 1701 when Louis XIV recognized James II's son as the rightful heir to the English Crown. In addition, England pursued its "right" of access to markets and resources in the Spanish empire. Overall, Britain's interventionist policy eventually led to great military success, especially in the War of the Spanish Succession as the Duke of Marlborough achieved triumphs at the Battles of Blenheim and Ramilles, and the British navy gained victories at Gibraltar and Minorca. The Treaty of Utrecht (1713) made Great Britain into an important player in continental politics, a major power in the Mediterranean, and a constant colonial competitor with France. But to establish that peace Britain had withdrawn its troops from the front, negotiated without informing its allies, and shared military secrets with the French. Indeed, feeling betrayed, Britain's allies were indignant.

In addition to providing England with increased influence in continental Europe, the wars during 1689–1713 allowed England to uphold its domination over Ireland and Scotland. In 1689 the Scots were not united in their attitude toward James II's forced abdication. He retained strong support in Scotland, especially among Highland chiefs and the Episcopalians. In response, William III relied on support from the Presbyterians who were dominant in the lowland areas. In July 1689 Highland forces won a victory at Killiecrankie but were defeated a month later at Dunkeld, and soon the Lowland forces were attempting to establish domination over the Highlands. Fully recognizing his dependence on Presbyterian support, William accepted the Scots' reestablishing of Presbyterianism, the abolishing of the royally appointed Episcopalian ministers, and the establishing of a Parliament and a Church in Scotland more independent than ever of England.

Nevertheless, Anglo-Scottish relations rapidly deteriorated. The Scottish Parliament eventually passed legislation for a separate foreign policy and a separate line of succession to the Scottish Crown. In response, the English government enacted provisions that would establish a trade embargo and would seize all Scottish assets in England if the Scottish Parliament did not accept the Hanoverian line of succession and if union discussions were not held. The resulting Act of Union in 1707 ended the possibility of a Jacobite takeover in Scotland. The Scots retained their own church and law courts, but gave up legislative authority while receiving representation in the British Parliament and gaining access to England's colonial and domestic markets.

As William dealt with Scotland, he also had to face the danger of a French-supported invasion from Ireland. On March 12, 1689, James II landed in southwestern Ireland where he was greeted by a rising tide of Irish Catholic nationalism. The "Patriot Parliament" meeting in Dublin in May passed anti-English legislation that proclaimed Ireland's legislative and jurisdictional independence of England. William responded by sending a force of 10,000 soldiers to aid Ulster Protestants. Disease and inadequate supplies, however, claimed half of the force, which resulted in William's personal intervention as he led English forces to victory at the Battle of the Boyne in July 1690. Within a year the complete conquest of Ireland had been achieved. Though the Irish campaign clearly distracted William from his efforts to create an anti-French alliance, the Irish situation did help him to convince many of the English that a campaign against France, which continued to support James II, was important for protecting England's security.

As Ireland and Scotland were being drawn more closely into England's orbit, imperial control was being tightened for the mainland American colonies.

Indeed, the Glorious Revolution was a major turning point in the constitutional and political life of the American colonies. The colonists jubilantly received the news of the Protestant William III replacing the Catholic James II, who had established the Dominion of New England. This dominion had eventually brought all of the New England colonies, as well as New York and New Jersey, under one governor who governed without a legislature. In 1690 William and Mary acquiesced in the abolishing of the Dominion of New England, and the colonies revived their representative assemblies. Moreover, the colonists wrote and talked extensively about their rights as Englishmen while praising the Bill of Rights. They failed to understand, however, that this bill was primarily an expression of parliamentary authority rather than a statement about individual rights. In short, divine kingship had been replaced by a new institution, the king in parliament, which would eventually exercise its own forceful type of authority that increasingly strained relations between the British government and the colonies after the end of the Seven Years' War in 1763.

William III in 1696 created the Board of Trade to enforce the navigation laws and to evaluate the colonial laws before sending them to the Privy Council for action. Parliament also applied to the colonies an act that regulated the customs. In particular, revenue officers could use writs of assistance, which allowed access to any places where the officers suspected smuggling. Moreover, vice-admiralty courts, which had no jury, were established in Virginia, Maryland, Pennsylvania, New York, and Massachusetts to ensure more convictions for smuggling and other infractions of the trade laws.

After 1689, agents of the English government increasingly had to adhere to a code of conduct in America. An act of Parliament in 1700 permitted the prosecution of governors who oppressed the colonists under their authority. Three years later, to prevent the use of bribes, the Privy Council declared that colonial officials could not accept presents from the assemblies, and expenditures by the colonial officials were to be monitored with detailed reports sent to the Treasury.

Overall, the English government after the Glorious Revolution revised the methods for governing England's colonial empire. Imperial leaders moved away from delegating authority to proprietors and began to implement a strategy for the English government's direct administrative control of the colonies. As a result, colonial wars, which prior to 1689 had been localized, now became a part of much wider conflicts.

Warfare has always been an expensive activity, but the adoption of gunpowder weaponry beginning in the sixteenth century eventually led many European countries to significantly increase the size of their military forces, which resulted in a massive increase in the cost of warfare. By 1694, as England was escalating its military operations against France, Parliament allocated funds to support about 93,000 soldiers. By 1712, however, Parliament set aside funds for almost 171,000 soldiers and 48,000 sailors and marines. This occurred when the adult male population of England and Wales was less than a million and a half. Altogether, the wars during 1689–1713 cost Great Britain almost £150 million in an age when peacetime expenditures usually totaled less than £2 million per year.

The wartime expenditures led to a substantial increase in taxation. During William's reign, the average annual taxation yield of approximately £4 million was twice the amount James II had been able to raise. This, however, proved insufficient to pay for all outlays. The English government, badly in need of cash and willing to mortgage the incomes of future taxpayers, borrowed funds to cover approximately one-third of its expenditures, which primarily involved the interest charge on the national debt. Indeed, the use of borrowing in conjunction with taxation to pay for war initiated a new era in English government finance.

A partial explanation of the popular support for increased expenditures and government borrowing is that the policy changes were accompanied by a shift in power from the Crown to Parliament. In addition, support grew when the Licensing Act lapsed in 1695. This unleashed the power of the press to mobilize Protestant public opinion behind the war effort, and that mobilization mostly occurred after England began to achieve victories.

Prior to 1688, England's government and society had been controlled by landowners, but after the Glorious Revolution bankers and other financiers, who were providing enormous amounts of money to the government, saw their power and influence dramatically increase. Initially an angry and suspicious landed elite refused to accept these new power brokers. Eventually, however, a process of assimilation resulted in the absorption of the monied men into a now united and more diversified ruling class that embraced a new culture that emphasized urbanity and luxury. But old-fashioned moralists denounced so much worldly display. In response, Bernard de Mandeville, who had moved from Holland to England to work as a physician, wrote *The Grumbling Hive* (1705), known later by the title of *The Fable of the Bees*. This story describes a hive of greedy, ostentatious, and dishonest bees who became prosperous as a result of their behavior. When the bees increasingly complained about all the dishonesty, God made everyone in the hive virtuous and honest. This, however, led to a rise in unemployment, a loss of trade, and a decline in prosperity, which made the hive so vulnerable to its enemies that the bees were forced to retreat to the hollow of a tree, where they lived miserably. Mandeville's moral was that private vices created public benefits and to tamper with that arrangement could lead to negative results for society.

To raise money and to create an effective military, the British government after the Glorious Revolution increasingly relied on the services of more civil servants, known as "placemen." The number of permanent officials increased from about 4,000 in 1689 to approximately 12,000 in the mid-1720s, which does not include the many part-time and temporary employees of the post office, customs, and royal dockyards. Like the expansion of the army and navy, the proliferation of placemen after 1689 led to fears that too much power was being placed in the hands of the government and that the independence of Parliament was endangered. These were key issues as the Whig and Tory parties were transformed.

After 1689 men's political views were divided in two ways: Whig versus Tory and Court versus Country. But these two divisions did not necessarily coincide. During the 1690s, in comparison to the following decade, political party issues seldom emerged; rather, the major division was between Court and Country as various new issues arose largely due to the War of the League of Augsburg and the anxiety it caused for the Country members of Parliament (MPs) who distrusted those wielding power and who feared the creation of standing armies and the rise of the monied interests. The Court-Country division, however, did not crystal-

lize into a formal system because patronage or party loyalty could lead a
Country MP to support an issue that went against Country principles. The
Whig-Tory division was different, especially after 1702 during the reign of
Queen Anne when party issues were important and MPs exhibited a party
loyalty not evident in the 1690s. Furthermore, the great influence of polit-
ical parties affected many aspects of English culture. There were clubs,
theaters, race meetings, and even doctors associated with the Whigs or
Tories. The party identities thus acquired a permanence and an organization in both Houses of Parliament that had never been associated with the
Court and Country.

After the Glorious Revolution, the Tories continued to espouse the idea
of a divinely ordained royal prerogative and to promote the Anglican
church as England's only church. But the Whig party, which favored a limited monarchy, Protestant succession, the containment of France, the protection of property, and the promotion of commerce, formed an alliance
with the Dissenters.

The major political theorist of this alliance was John Locke. His *Two
Treatises on Government* (1690) denounced the divine right of kings and
asserted that succession should be subject to reason since men were
rational and wise. Indeed, Locke espoused the theory that government
rested on the consent of the governed and the protection of natural (God-
given) rights. This view of government came to be seen as closely representing the events of 1688–1689, and therefore Locke emerged as the
philosopher of the Glorious Revolution whose theories in the eighteenth
century inspired new groups of revolutionaries.

When Queen Mary, who had acted as co-ruler with William, died in
1694, a group of Whig leaders, known as the Junto, were selected to act in
the king's absence. The Whig Junto thus wielded significant power
because William, conducting wars and diplomacy, spent a third of his
reign abroad. But William resented many of the restrictions that the Whigs
imposed on the king. The earl of Sunderland, however, once remarked to
William: "It is true that the Tories are better friends to monarchy than the
Whigs are, but then your majesty is to consider that you are not their
monarch."

When Anne became queen in 1702, she greatly disliked and distrusted
the Whigs, who she believed had tried to dominate William, had been
rude to her at times, and had been a threat to the Church of England due
to their connection to the Dissenters. Nevertheless, Whigs gradually
secured positions in the administration during the early years of Anne's
reign. But in 1710–1711 the Tories won control of Parliament as public
opinion swung against the Whigs.

During Queen Anne's reign, Henry St. John, raised to the peerage in 1712 as Viscount Bolingbroke, became the leader of the country gentry against the Whig alliance. In 1711 Jonathan Swift described St. John as "the greatest young man I ever knew, wit, capacity, beauty, quickness of apprehension, good learning, and an excellent taste. The best orator in the House of Commons." When he became secretary of state in 1710, St. John was determined to fill the ranks of government with Tories. He also wanted to end the war with France and therefore played a leading role in the negotiations that culminated with the Treaty of Utrecht. The conclusion of the conflict started a new political crisis that centered on the succession issue, but additionally involved taxation, voting rights, and religion. In 1711 the Tory-controlled Parliament made only large landholders eligible for election to the House of Commons. Other wealth, like stock holdings and bank deposits, did not count. And in 1713 Parliament significantly lowered the tax on land. Moreover, in 1711 the Tories continued their religious intolerance by banning the practice of occasional conformity to avoid the Test Act, and in 1714 they gave the Anglican church control over secondary education.

But in early 1714 it also became clear that Queen Anne, who suffered from edema and a bad heart, would not live much longer, and thus attention turned to the succession. Anne had been pregnant eighteen times, but she had twelve miscarriages, one stillbirth, and four children who died as infants. When her fifth child, the eleven-year-old duke of Gloucester, died in 1700, it became apparent that Parliament would once again be required to settle the issue of succession to the throne. In 1701 Parliament passed the Act of Settlement that provided for the succession of the Hanoverian line, which was the closest Protestant branch of the Stuarts. The death in June 1714 of Sophia of the Palatinate left her son, George, who was the elector of the German state of Hanover and a great-grandson of James I, as the direct heir of Queen Anne.

On July 27 Bolingbroke defeated the earl of Oxford for control of the Tory ministry, but Bolingbroke had only four days to use his triumph because Queen Anne, the last of the Stuart monarchs, died on August 1. Writing to Jonathan Swift, Dr. John Arbuthnot asserted: "I believe sleep was never more welcome to a weary traveler than death was to her." Since the Tories remained quite divided when Anne died, they could not offer a viable alternative to a Whig ministry. Until the elector of Hanover arrived in England, a regency council, dominated by Whigs, governed the country and began to make preparations for the Hanoverian succession.

Great Britain's resources were substantial when George I became king in August 1714, though its population was smaller than that of France or the Austrian Habsburg dominions. Britain had 8.5 million people, including 6 million in England and Wales, 1 million in Scotland, and 1.5 million in Ireland. Furthermore, Dublin had emerged as the second most populous city in the British Isles after London.

Britain's profitable trade benefited from the kingdom's geographical position and its colonial empire. While the domestic market was the most important, Britain's exports continued to grow. This was true not only of woolen cloth, which had long been England's leading export, but also tobacco, coffee, tea, and sugar, commodities that Britain shipped in increasing amounts to both European and world markets. Furthermore, England's western ports quickly developed with the slave-contract obtained from Spain in 1713. In addition, the warfare after 1689 had fostered manufacturing. Industrial towns such Birmingham and Manchester prospered as they produced goods for domestic and foreign markets. Moreover, the Anglo-French wars that ended in 1713 had left Britain with a significant naval superiority over France, which had primarily expanded its armies. Indeed, Britain's commercial expansion depended on its naval superiority.

As British trade continued to expand, the Whig party dominated the Hanoverian political world. George I had little sympathy for the Tories since he believed they had abandoned Britain's allies by negotiating the Treaty of Utrecht. George also understood that he had become king through the Whigs' support. Consequently, he appointed Whigs to most of the significant positions. Some of the Tories became Whigs in order to gain office. Many Tories, however, became staunch opponents of the Whig ministries, which they defined as corrupt and too expensive.

A few Tories, including Bolingbroke, gave their support to James II's son, James Stuart, known as the Pretender. As a result of discontent in the British Isles, the earl of Mar raised the Jacobite standard in Scotland on September 6, 1715, and 5,000 men led by 18 lords took up arms. An immediate offensive in Scotland might have been successful and allowed for a march into England, but Mar delayed as he tried to raise more men. Eventually, on November 13, he fought an indecisive battle against forces led by the duke of Argyll. In England significant support for James Stuart developed only in Northumberland and Lancashire. Furthermore, the Pretender did not arrive in Scotland until just after Christmas, and he brought insufficient money and men. At this point his cause was rapidly fading, and he failed to revive it. Indeed, the rule of George I never lost its credibility among a substantial percentage of the traditional ruling class. As a result of military factors and the lack of widespread popular unrest, by early the next year the forces of George I ended the rebellion (later known as the "Fifteen"). On February 4, 1716, the Pretender and the earl of Mar sailed for France.

Overall, the years 1713–1715 encompassed another watershed in British history as they signaled the end of a quarter-century of wars that made Britain into a major sea power and completed and secured the changes initiated in 1688–1689. The Revolution Settlement was not actually safe until the Hanoverian succession occurred and the Jacobite rebellion failed, but after 1715 the Revolution Settlement was never in serious danger and it became the structure for Britain's Augustan Age.

England, a small peripheral country that had usually played an insignificant role in sixteenth and seventeenth-century Europe, emerged in the eighteenth century as a major international power. The key to this transformation was the reshaping of England's military, government, and economy after the Glorious Revolution. The resulting new fiscal-military state eventually made England into a great naval power with an immense empire. None of these changes had been inevitable, but they were enduring.

SELECTED BIBLIOGRAPHY

Baxter, Stephen B. *William III and the Defense of European Liberty, 1650–1702.* New York: Harcourt, Brace & World, 1966. Portrays William III as a staunch defender of Protestantism and political and economic liberty against French aggression.

Black, Jeremy. *A History of the British Isles.* New York: St. Martin's Press, 1997. Describes the impact of the Glorious Revolution on the four principal peoples of the British Isles: English, Scots, Irish, and Welsh. The Glorious Revolution is crucial to the Whig interpretation of history, which portrays Great Britain's past as the unfolding of progress and liberty, but, as Black demonstrates, the Glorious Revolution was also a violent crisis that brought suffering to Ireland and Scotland.

Brewer, John. *The Sinews of Power: War, Money, and the English State, 1688–1783.* Cambridge, MA: Harvard University Press, 1990. Provides a brilliant analysis of the transformation of England into a major international power in the eighteenth century.

Coward, Barry. *The Stuart Age, 1603–1714.* 2nd ed. London and New York: Longman, 1994. Argues that the fundamental constitutional changes that occurred in England during 1689–1714 were products of England's involvement in the European wars rather than results of the pronouncements or legislation of 1689.

Cruickshanks, Eveline. *The Glorious Revolution.* New York: St. Martin's Press, 2000. This major reassessment of the Glorious Revolution asserts that James II was a revolutionary king who granted complete religious toleration because he considered it morally right. However, Tories opposed him, and treasonous actions by prominent noblemen and military officers allowed

William of Orange to gain the throne and to use England to create an anti-French coalition in Europe.

Dickson, P. G. M. *The Financial Revolution in England: A Study of the Development of Public Credit, 1688–1756.* New York: St. Martin's Press, 1967. A detailed analysis of the system of governmental borrowing for the seventy years after the Glorious Revolution.

Harris, Tim. *Politics Under the Later Stuarts: Party Conflict in a Divided Society, 1660–1715.* London and New York: Longman, 1973. A major work on English party politics during the later Stuart period from Charles II to Anne. It traces the origins of parties back to the failure of the Restoration settlement of 1660 to resolve the issue of how much power the monarchy should be allowed.

Hatton, Ragnhild. *George I: Elector and King.* Cambridge, MA: Harvard University Press, 1978. Asserts that George I was the most politically imaginative and competent of the Hanoverian kings in Britain.

Hoffer, Peter Charles. *The Brave New World: A History of Early America.* Boston: Houghton Mifflin, 2000. Includes a brief analytical account of the Glorious Revolution's impact on England's North American colonies.

Jones, D. W. *War and Economy in the Age of William III and Marlborough.* New York: Blackwell, 1988. Describes how the English economy supported two decades of warfare that resulted in England becoming a major power.

Langford, Paul. "The Eighteenth Century (1688–1789)." In *The Oxford Illustrated History of Britain,* pp. 352–418. Edited by Kenneth O. Morgan. Oxford and New York: Oxford University Press, 1984. A balanced overview of developments during this period.

Lovejoy, David S. *The Glorious Revolution in America.* New York: Harper & Row, 1972. Provides a detailed account of the Glorious Revolution's impact on England's North American colonies.

Middleton, Richard. *Colonial America: A History, 1585–1776.* 2nd ed. Cambridge, MA: Blackwell, 1996. Offers some useful insights on the Glorious Revolution in America.

Miller, John. *The Glorious Revolution.* 2nd ed. London and New York: Longman, 1997. Argues that much short-term continuity followed the Glorious Revolution, but that the revolution led to significant long-term change.

Newton, Diana. *Papists, Protestants, and Puritans, 1559–1714.* Cambridge: Cambridge University Press, 1998. Includes a brief overview of religious conditions in England before and after the Glorious Revolution.

O'Gorman, Frank. *The Long Eighteenth Century: British Political & Social History, 1688–1832.* London: Arnold, 1997. Discusses British political history from the Glorious Revolution to the Reform Act of 1832. It also describes the significant economic and social inequalities of late Stuart and Hanoverian Britain.

Plumb, J. H. *The Growth of Political Stability in England, 1675–1725.* London: Macmillan, 1967. The classic study of politics in late Stuart and early Hanoverian England.

Prest, Wilfrid. *Albion Ascendant: English History, 1660–1815.* Oxford and New York: Oxford University Press, 1998. Describes England's transformation into the greatest superpower the world had yet seen.

Schwoerer, Lois. *The Declaration of Rights, 1689.* Baltimore, MD: Johns Hopkins University Press, 1981. A comprehensive study of the Declaration of Rights that emphasizes the document's great constitutional significance.

Smith, Lacey Baldwin. *This Realm of England, 1399–1688.* 8th ed. Boston: Houghton Mifflin, 2000. Provides a general background to the Glorious Revolution and gives a brief analysis of the revolution's development.

Stone, Lawrence, ed. *An Imperial State at War: Britain from 1689 to 1815.* London and New York: Routledge, 1994. Contains several essays that analyze the Glorious Revolution's impact on England and its empire.

Taylor, John A. *British Monarchy, English Church Establishment, and Civil Liberty.* Westport, CT and London: Greenwood, 1996. Includes a chapter on the issue of civil liberty in connection with the Glorious Revolution.

Willcox, William B., and Walter L. Arnstein. *The Age of Aristocracy, 1688–1830.* 5th ed. Lexington, MA, and Toronto: D. C. Heath, 1988. Provides an overview of politics during 1688–1714.

Appendix A

Glossary

absolutism. A term referring to a system of government where absolute, or total, power rests in the person of the monarch.

Angevin. A variant of the word *Anjou*, an old French noble family, some of whose descendants ruled England as Plantagenet kings. Other Angevins ruled the duchy of Anjou in France, and in Naples and Sicily.

Aquinas, Saint Thomas (1225–1274). A Dominican monk who became a noted philosopher and theologian and who was later elevated to sainthood.

Aristotle (384–322 B.C.E.). Aristotle was an ancient Greek philosopher based in Athens. When Aristotle's ideas about human beings and the world in which they live were rediscovered in the twelfth century, they greatly influenced the course of subsequent European history.

assize. A "petty plea," or a legal device developed by Henry II to allow commoners to settle claims and disputes in a quick and just manner.

Baronial Council of Twenty-Five. According to Clause 61 of Magna Carta, a committee of twenty-five barons was to oversee the king's actions and to take remedial action if the king, in their opinion, acted contrary to the best interests of the country.

Bede, Venerable (c. 673–735). The most notable Latin writer and historian of Anglo-Saxon England. His *Ecclesiastical History of the English People* (731) is a valuable history of England from the end of the Roman presence to Bede's own time. He also wrote biblical commentaries, poetry, and flattering biographies of saints.

Boudicca, Queen of the Iceni (d. 61 C.E.). The Iceni were a tribe living in what is now Norfolk and part of Suffolk. Boudicca became queen following the death of her husband and led a destructive revolt against the Romans, who crushed it without mercy in 61 C.E.

Calvinism. Named for John Calvin, an important Protestant reformer, Calvinism emphasized predestination; certain individuals were the elect and should affirm their election (to heaven) through good works.

Cavalier Parliament (1661–1679). Summoned by Charles II in 1661, this Parliament worked to restore royal authority in England after the interregnum but disagreed with the king on certain ecclesiastical matters. In the 1670s, open conflict with Charles II led him to dissolve this Parliament in 1679. The term *cavalier* is a loose synonym for royalist.

Charter of the Forest (1217). A legal document setting out regulations regarding the use and abuse of English forests outside of those owned by the monarch.

Convention Parliament. The name given to two different Parliaments. The first was called into session in 1660 and brought about the restoration of the monarchy in the person of Charles II, and the second was in session at the time of and immediately after the Glorious Revolution.

courts in eyre. The name given to courts held by justices in eyre, or itinerant justices who rode a circuit to hold court in different counties.

De Donis statute (1290). This law established the practice of entail—the practice wherein land was granted to a tenant and his heirs. The tenant could not dispose of the land; he and his heirs simply had perpetual use of it until the family line ran out, at which time the land reverted to the lord.

Dissenters. A term applied in seventeenth-century England to a wide variety of Protestants who did not agree with some or all of the practices and beliefs of the Church of England.

dower. When a married man died in feudal England, his widow received the use of his dower, or his property, for the rest of her life.

Fairfax, Thomas, Lord (1612–1671). Commander of the New Model Army, Fairfax was a career military officer who managed to keep himself largely free from political controversy during the civil wars in the 1640s and 1650s.

fealty. A term that refers to the fidelity or loyalty owed by a tenant or vassal to his lord.

fief. The name given to an estate under the system of feudalism.

Fisher, John (1469–1535). The bishop of Rochester after 1504, Fisher was the principal defender of Catholicism during the early years of Henry VIII's reign, and he was Catherine of Aragon's most important religious adviser. In 1535, he was convicted of treason and executed for his opposition to the English Reformation.

Great Schism (1378–1417). A serious political split in the Roman Catholic Church, during which two rival popes, one based in Rome and the other in Avignon, France, attempted to rule the church. International politics often determined to which pope a particular monarch would give his loyalty.

Guildhall. London's "city hall," the seat of local government, built between 1411 and 1431. Parts of it survived the fire of 1666 and the German bombing of 1940 and still stand today.

Hardrada, Harald (1015–1066). King of Norway after 1047, Harald Hardrada invaded England in 1066 and allied with Harold II's brother Tostig, to wrest the crown from Harold. His forces lost and he was killed at the battle of Stamford Bridge.

homage. A term that refers to the act of a vassal submitting to the control of and pledging loyalty and service to his feudal lord.

interdict. To forbid, often by religious or legal sanction. In the Roman Catholic religion, it refers to the practice of denying offenders the right to partake in most sacraments.

Interregnum. A term referring in general to a period of time between two reigns, and specifically, to the years between 1649 and 1660 in England, when Oliver Cromwell and others loyal to Parliament managed the national government.

Jacobite. The term Jacobite describes those who continued to support the Stuarts after the Glorious Revolution of 1688–1689.

justiciar. A powerful position established by Norman kings after 1066. The person occupying the position of justiciar ruled in England in the king's name whenever the king was abroad. The practice of appointing a justiciar ended in 1265.

liege lord. A synonym for feudal lord.

maritagium. A term referring to the property of whatever description that a woman brought with her to her marriage, now usually termed "dowry."

Midlands. A geographical region of England that includes the current counties of Derbyshire, Nottinghamshire, Leicestershire, Rutlandshire, Northamptonshire, Warwickshire, and Staffordshire. Important cities in the Midlands include Birmingham, Coventry, Leicester, and Derby. This region coincides roughly with the Anglian kingdom of Mercia.

More, Thomas (1478–1535). A lawyer in his early years, More rose to a position of influence in the early years of Henry VIII's reign, particularly as a defender of Catholicism. He replaced Thomas Wolsey as lord chancellor in 1529, but his failure to support Henry's divorce from Catherine or the English Reformation generally led to his execution in 1535.

Naseby, Battle of (1645). The battle, fought in June 1645, pitted the Parliament's New Model Army, led by Sir Thomas Fairfax, against the army of Charles I. A victory for Fairfax and the New Model Army, the battle persuaded parliamentary leaders that they could defeat Charles without an alliance with Scotland.

Newton, Isaac (1642–1727). The most noted English scientist of his day, Newton was an astronomer and mathematician who made important contributions related to the theories of motion, gravity, and thermodynamics.

Normandy. A province in northern France whose duke became William the Conqueror in England in 1066. Normandy remained in English hands until 1204, when the French reoccupied it, although the English did not formally cede it to France until 1259. Those who came from Normandy were called *Normans.*

occasional conformity. This term describes the practice of dissenters who took communion in the Church of England just once a year in order to qualify for government service or other privileges reserved for Anglicans.

Papal Curia. A term used to refer to the central administration of the Roman Catholic Church.

Pilgrimage of Grace (1536–1537). A series of uprisings against Henry VIII in the north of England that stemmed from religious and economic grievances. Lacking the support of the great landowners, the Pilgrimage forces were defeated and the English Reformation continued.

Plantagenet. Family name associated with the House of Anjou (or Angevin). Plantagenet kings ruled England from 1154 to 1399, when the Lancasters come to power.

Popish Plot (1636–1642). Charles I's increasing association with Catholicism after his marriage in 1625 to Henrietta Maria of France fed fears that the court was plotting to make England Catholic again. Ultimately, it was a major cause of the first civil war between Charles and Parliament.

primogeniture. The legal practice, employed in England, wherein the eldest child (or the eldest son) inherits the entire estate of the family.

Provisions of Oxford (1258). Actually a petition of grievance by leading English barons, this document limited the power of the monarchy by establishing, in part, a council of fifteen to serve as a permanent advisory body to the king. King Henry III reluctantly agreed to this.

Puritans. Name given to those Protestants who stressed biblical teaching and good works over ritual and liturgy; many believed that the English Reformation had not gone far enough.

relief. An inheritance tax paid by heirs in feudal England.

roundheads. A derogatory term applied to those who favored Parliament and fought with its army during the English civil wars. The term apparently derives from the short hair that many favored at this time.

Scottish Covenanters (1638). A group of Scottish landowners and Presbyterians who protested the introduction of the "Anglican Book of Common Prayer" into their churches and emerged as the de facto government of Scotland until 1648.

scutage. A cash payment that excused one from military service and allowed kings to hire mercenaries.

Self-Denying Ordinance (1644). An act of Parliament, passed during the first civil war, that barred members of either house of Parliament from military or civil office during the war. The provisions of the act were applied to the New Model Army, created early in 1645.

shire. In Anglo-Saxon England, a shire was the geographical area around which local government was organized. The king's representative in a shire was, first, the ealdorman, and later, the sheriff. After 1066, local government based on counties replaced the shire system.

Statutes of the Realm. Written laws that applied to all of England.

Stuarts. Ruling royal family of Scotland from 1371 to 1714 and of England from 1603 to 1714. Famous Stuarts include James I, Charles I, and James II.

Ten Articles [of Religion] (1536). This was the first statement of religious principles seated in the English Reformation. The articles also represent an attempt to create a bond with German Lutheranism.

Thirty-Nine Articles (1563). A document that laid out the fundamental tenets of the Protestant church under Elizabeth I and that remains the principal doctrinal statement of the Anglican Church today.

Tower of London. Built about 1078, this fortress on the Thames River served for many years as a royal residence and the most important English prison.

Tyndale, William (c. 1494–1536). Tyndale was an early sympathizer with the Protestant Reformation in Europe. His 1526 translation of the New Testament into English was declared heretical and he was persecuted.

vassal. A person who is maintained and protected by a feudal lord. In return, the vassal pledges his allegiance to the lord.

wardship. If a minor inherited his father's estate, the king held custody or guardianship over the estate until the heir reached adulthood.

Whig. From the end of the seventeenth century until the middle of the nineteenth, the name given one of the two major English political parties. Whigs tended to favor change and were inclined to restrict the power of the monarch.

Wolsey, Thomas (c. 1472–1530). Oxford-educated scholar who became a cardinal in the Catholic church and chief minister to Henry VIII from about 1515 until 1529, when he fell out of favor for failing to secure the annulment of Henry's marriage to Catherine of Aragon.

Wycliffe, John (c. 1330–1384). A maverick Catholic cleric in England who rejected papal authority and transubstantiation and believed that the Church had too much wealth and power. He inspired a movement called Lollardy, an early forerunner of the English Reformation.

Appendix B

Ruling Houses and Dynasties

Prior to the Norman Conquest

871–899	Alfred the Great
1016–1035	Canute
1042–1066	Edward the Confessor
1066	Harold II

Normans

1066–1087	William I, the Conqueror
1087–1100	William II, Rufus
1100–1135	Henry I
1135–1154	Stephen

Angevins/Plantagenets

1154–1189	Henry II
1189–1199	Richard I, the Lion-Hearted
1199–1216	John
1216–1272	Henry III
1272–1307	Edward I
1307–1327	Edward II
1327–1377	Edward III
1377–1399	Richard II

Lancastrians

1399–1413	Henry IV
1413–1422	Henry V
1422–1461	Henry VI

Yorkists
1461–1483	Edward IV
1483	Edward V
1483–1485	Richard III

Tudors
1485–1509	Henry VII
1509–1547	Henry VIII
1547–1553	Edward VI
1553–1558	Mary I, Bloody Mary
1558–1603	Elizabeth I

Stuarts
1603–1625	James I
1625–1649	Charles I

Interregnum
1649–1653	The Commonwealth
1653–1660	The Protectorate

Stuarts (Restored)
1660–1685	Charles II
1685–1689	James II
1689–1694	William III and Mary II
1694–1702	William III
1702–1714	Anne

Index

Abercrombie, Patrick, 162
absolutism, 137–38, 144, 172
Act of Accord, 87
Act of Indemnity and Oblivion, 167
Act of Settlement, 172, 179
Act of Supremacy, 99, 102
Act of Uniformity, 99, 120, 144–45, 173
Act of Union, 174
Addled Parliament, 137
Agincourt, Battle of, 57, 61
agriculture, 1
Alfred, 3, 152
Anglican Church. *See* Church of
   England
Anglo-Normans, 13–14
Anglo-Saxon Chronicle, 10
Anglo-Saxon England, 3, 7
Anglo-Saxons, 3, 39, 152
Anne I, 178–79
Aquinas, Thomas, 51
architecture, 159–60, 162
aristocracy, 19, 23–24, 46, 68, 71, 75
Armagnacs, 61
army, 49, 117, 140, 143, 177
Assize of Clarendon, 21
Austria, 167

Babylonian Captivity, 70
Barbon, Nicholas, 161–62

Barnet, Battle of, 80, 89
barons, 26–28, 40, 47, 49
Barons' Wars, 47–48
bastard feudalism, 83–84, 86, 90
Bayeux Tapestry, 6, 10
Beaufort family, 78–79, 85, 90
Black Plague, 60, 63–64, 147–51,
   153–56
Black Prince, 59–60, 67, 77
Blenheim, Battle of, 174
Bludworth, Thomas, 150, 157
Board of Trade, 175
Boleyn, Anne, 96–98, 100–101,
   105, 115
Bolingbroke, Henry. *See* Henry IV
Bolingbroke, Henry (St. John), 179
Book of Common Prayer, 98–99,
   106–7, 120, 144
Book of Martyrs (Foxe), 115
Bosworth Field, Battle of, 76, 90–91
Bourbons, 173–74
Bouvines, Battle of, 23, 47
Boyne, Battle of the, 175
Bretigny, Treaty of, 59, 68, 71
Bretwealdas (warlords), 3
Bunyan, John, 112
burgesses, 46, 51–53
burghers, 41–42
Burgundians, 61–62, 67, 89

Cade, Jack, 84–85
Calvinism, 108–10, 156
Canute (Cnut), 4
Castillion, 72
Catherine of Aragon, 96–98, 100–101,
    105, 109
Catholicism, 97–106, 110–12, 120,
    167–69, 171, 173
Cavalier Parliament, 136, 167–68
Cavaliers, 140
Cecil, William, 115, 117, 121
Charles I, 34, 131–34, 138–42, 153, 165
Charles I (of Spain), 109
Charles II, 34, 134–36, 142, 144–45,
    149, 156–59, 165, 167–69
Charles V, 60
Charles VI, 61, 78
Charles VII, 67
Chaucer, Geoffrey, 14–15, 66
Christianity, 3
Church of England, 98–102, 104–5,
    108–9, 112, 120, 137, 145, 172–73,
    178; in Elizabethan England,
    119–20; relationship to Parliament,
    34, 167, 169–70
Clarendon Code, 144–45, 167
cloth, 57, 180
Coke, Edward, 137
Colet, John, 103
colonies, 128, 175–76
commerce. See trade
Commissions of the Peace, 68
common law, 12
Commonwealth, 142
Confirmation of the Charters, 42
Congregationalists. See Protestantism
Conventicle Act, 144
Convention Parliament, 136, 164–65
Corporation Act, 144
Covenanters, 134, 138
Cranmer, Thomas, 97–98, 100–102,
    105–6
Crécy, Battle of, 57, 59, 61, 67
Cromwell, Oliver, 34, 123, 133–35,
    141–44, 153, 165, 169, 173
Cromwell, Richard, 135, 143
Cromwell, Thomas, 97–98, 100–103, 155
Crusades, 22, 95

dauphin, the. See Charles VII
Declaration of Breda, 136, 144
Declaration of Indulgence, 173
De Donis statute, 33
Defense of the Seven Sacraments (King
    Henry VIII), 96
de Mandeville, Bernard, 177
de Montfort, Simon, 40–41, 48, 50
Denmark, 3–4
Dictum of Kenilworth, 28
Dissenters, 167–68, 170, 173, 177
divine right monarchy, 137–38, 144,
    175, 178
Domesday Book, 6, 9–11
Dominion of New England, 175
Dover, Treaty of, 168
dower, widows. See "reasonable"
    dower
Duke of Clarence, 88–89
Duke of Somerset, 78–79, 83, 86–87
Duke William of Normandy. See Wil-
    liam the Conqueror
Dunbar, Battle of, 142–43

Edmund, Earl of Cambridge, 65
Edmund of Langley, 71
Edward, duke of York, 79–80, 87. See
    also Edward IV
Edward, Prince of Wales, 79, 85, 87–89
Edward I, 13, 24, 27–29, 48–49, 69, 77;
    and development of Parliament, 16,
    32, 41, 43, 54; and English presence
    in France, 58, 62; and militarization
    of gentry, 64, 71
Edward II, 52, 64, 77
Edward III, 27–29, 33, 52, 58–59, 62,
    64–71, 77–78, 85
Edward IV, 62, 80, 83, 88–89, 91. See
    also Edward, duke of York
Edward V, 81, 89
Edward VI, 98, 100, 102–3, 105–6, 119
Edward the Confessor, 4, 7, 10
Eleanor of Aquitane, 21
The Eleven Years' Tyranny, 138
Elizabeth I, 33, 99–100, 105–8, 110,
    115–28, 137
Elizabethan England, 115–28
Elizabethan Poor Law, 126

Elizabethan Religious Settlement, 119, 137
Elizabethan Renaissance, 126
English Civil War, 54, 112, 131–45, 165
English General Baptists, 112
English language, changes in, 14–16
English Reformation, 95–113
Episcopalians, 174
Era of Personal Rule, 138
Evelyn, John, 150, 156–58, 161
Evesham, Battle of, 48
Exchequer, 11

The Fable of the Bees (de Mandeville), 177
Fairfax, Thomas, 133–34
feudalism, 9, 12, 19, 46, 58
Fire Courts, 158–59
Fisher, John, 103–4
Five-Mile Act, 144
Five Wounds of Christ, 104
Foxe, John, 111, 115
France, 11, 90, 120, 138, 168, 173–76, 178–81; English presence in, 22–23, 58–63; and Hundred Years' War, 42, 57–63, 65–67, 109
Free Companies, 66
French, as official language of England, 14–16

Gardiner, Stephen, bishop of Winchester, 100, 105
Gascony, 50, 58–59, 62–63
George I, 179–80
Glorious Revolution, 34, 54, 165–71
Godwin, earl of Essex, 4
grain, 1
Grand Alliance, 173
Grand Remonstrance, 140
Great Fire, 150–51, 162–68
Great Plague. *See* Black Plague
Great Schism, 70
guilds, 45
Gunpowder Plot, 111

Habsburgs, 173
Hadrian's Wall, 1
Hampton Court Conference, 137

Harald Hadrada, 4–5, 7, 15
Harold, 2, 4–8, 10, 15, 72
Hastings, Battle of, 2, 5–6, 8–10, 15–16
Hawkwood, John, 65
head tax. *See* poll tax
Henry I, 11, 19
Henry II, 12–13, 16, 21
Henry III, 40, 47–49, 52, 77
Henry IV, 43, 61, 69, 77, 85
Henry V, 61, 65, 67, 77–78, 83, 86
Henry VI, 61, 71, 78–80, 83–89
Henry VII, 52, 62, 81–82, 90–91
Henry VIII, 13, 53, 96–105, 108–10, 115, 119, 149
Holland, 168, 170
Hooker, Richard, 109
House of Commons, 34, 42–43, 68, 70, 148, 172
House of Lords, 42–43, 140–42
Huguenots, 110
humanism, 96, 104, 126
Hundred Years' War, 11, 42, 52, 58–72, 79, 110
Hyde, Edward, earl of Clarendon, 144, 167

Independents, 134
Interregnum, 142, 167
Instrument of Government, 135, 143
Ireland, 110, 121, 131, 133, 141, 143–44; English presence in, 13–14, 174–75, 180

Jacobites, 180–81
James I, 34, 111, 118, 131, 136–38
James II, 34, 166, 169–73, 175–76
James VI. *See* James I
James, duke of York, 157
Joan of Arc, 62, 67
John I, 12–13, 16, 40, 47–49, 52, 77; and Magna Carta, 19–20, 22–23, 26
John II (John the Good), 59, 66, 71
John, Duke of Bedford, 67
John of Gaunt, 77–78, 85
Junto, 178

King's Book, 102
knights of the shire, 32, 40–42, 44, 50

Knolles, Robert, 65
Knox, John, 110, 117

Lambeth Articles, 108
Lancaster, House of, 43, 77
Lancastrian kings, 43, 52
Lancastrians, 77–82, 86–89
Langton, Stephen, 23–24
Laud, William, 138–39
Leslie, David, 142–43
Levellers, 134
Lewes, Battle of, 48
Licensing Act, 176
Lionel of Antwerp, 71
Locke, John, 35, 178
Lollard heresy, 70
London, 147–62
longbow, 59
Long Parliament, 139
Lord Burghley. See Cecil, William
Louis XIV, 168, 170, 173–74

Magna Carta, 6, 12, 19–36, 41–42,
    46–47, 52
Margaret of Anjou, 78–80, 84–85,
    87–89
Marston Moor, 133
Martin Luther, 95–96, 100, 103
Mary I, 98–99, 105–7, 110, 115
Mary, Queen of Scots, 99, 110–11,
    116–18, 120, 123, 131
merchants, 45–46, 48, 86, 126,
    140, 153
Mercia, kingdom of, 3–4
middle class, 46, 53–54, 125
Model Parliament, 41, 50
monarchy, 19, 119, 124, 125, 131, 136,
    142, 144
Monck, George, 143–44
More, Thomas, 97–98, 100–101
Mortimer's Cross, Battle of, 87
motte and bailey castles, 10

Naseby, 133, 141
nationalism, 63, 125, 143, 177,
    180–81
navy, 117, 123, 143, 173, 180
Netherlands, 118

Neville, Richard, earl of Warwick,
    79–80, 84, 86–89
New Model Army, 133–34, 141–42
New Model Ordnance, 133
New World, 122, 127, 128
Nineteen Propositions, 140
nobility. See aristocracy
Norman Conquest, 1–16, 19, 58, 62
Norman Great Council, 39–41
Normandy, 7–8, 11, 47
Northampton, Battle of, 87
Northumbria, kingdom of, 3–4

Ordinances of 1311, 27–28
Ordinances of Walton, 67
Orleanists, 61

papists, 107–8
Parliament, 84–85, 87–88, 131, 133–45,
    153–54, 166–72, 175–79; evolution
    of, 13, 16, 39–54, 68–71; relationship
    to the crown, 34, 60, 63, 120, 122,
    124, 125, 133, 135–45, 172, 176; and
    religion, 34, 97, 99, 101–2, 104, 107,
    167, 169–72; Scottish representation
    in, 143, 174
Parliamentarians, 138–40
Parr, Catherine, 102, 115
Patriot Parliament, 175
Peace of Westphalia, 137
peasants, 46, 68
Peasants' Revolt, 69. See also Wat
    Tyler's Rebellion
Pepys, Samuel, 150, 154–56
Petition of Rights, 138
Philip II (of Spain), 110, 118
Philip VI, 59
Philip Augustus, 21–23
Philip the Fair, 50, 57
Pilgrimage of Grace, 98, 104
Pilgrim's Progress (Bunyan), 112
"placemen," 177
Poitiers, Battle of, 57, 59, 61, 66–67
poll tax, 60, 69
Pope Clement VII, 109
Pope Julius II, 95
Presbyterian Church, 117, 134
Presbyterianism, 142, 167, 173

Pretender, the, 180–81
Pride's Purge, 142
Prince Edward. *See* Black Prince
Privy Council, 169–70
Protectorate, 135, 143
Protestantism, 97–99, 110–12, 115, 117–19, 126, 171
Protestant Reformation, 95–96, 98
Protestant separatists, 107–8, 111
Provisions of Oxford, 27–28, 32, 47–48
Puritanism, 133, 136, 141
Puritans, 34, 100, 108, 110–12, 139–40, 144, 153, 167
Pym, John, 133–34

Quakers, 173

Raleigh, Walter, 122, 127, 128
Ramilles, Battle of, 174
"reasonable" dower, 30–31, 33
Rebuilding Act, 158–59, 161
Restoration, 136, 144–45
"Revolution Settlement," 170, 172, 181
Richard I, 21
Richard II, 33, 43, 60–61, 69, 71, 77, 85, 90
Richard III, 76, 81–82, 89–91
Richard, duke of Gloucester. *See* Richard III
Richard of York, 78–79, 83–86
Ripon, Treaty of, 139
Roman Catholic Church, 23, 95, 103, 117–18
Romans, and conquest of Britain, 1, 3, 152
Root and Branch Bill, 139
Roundheads, 140, 165
Royal College of Physicians, 149
Rump Parliament, 135–36, 142
Runnymede, 12

Saxons. *See* Anglo-Saxons
Scotland, 57, 90, 110, 117, 118, 119, 123, 137, 133–35, 174; English domination of, 14; religion in, 117, 138–39, 141–42, 174; representation in British Parliament, 143, 174
Scottish Reformation, 105, 107, 110

Self-Denying Ordnance, 133
Seven Years' War, 175
Shakespeare, William, 61, 66, 77, 81–82, 119, 127, 155
Short Parliament, 139
Six Articles, 101–2, 106
slavery, 180
Sluys, Battle of, 59
Solemn League and Covenant, 134, 138, 141
Spain, 109–11, 118, 120, 138, 143, 180
Spanish Armada, 110, 118, 122
St. Albans, Battle of, 79, 86
Stamford Bridge, Battle of, 4–5, 8, 15
Star Chamber, 140, 144
Statute of Laborers, 33
Statute of Merton, 27–28
Statute of Praemunire, 70
Statute of Provisors, 70
St. Bartholomew's Day Massacre, 111
St. Giles, 149, 154
St. John, Henry, 179
St. Paul's Cathedral, 150–51, 157, 159
Stuart, Charles. *See* Charles II
Stuart, James, duke of York. *See* James II
Stuart, Mary, 34, 53, 170–71, 175, 178
Stuart kings, 14, 44, 53, 179
Swift, Jonathan, 179
Swynford, Catherine, 78, 85

taxation, 6, 29, 42, 49–50, 52–54, 143, 172, 176; direct and indirect, 69, 71
Ten Articles, 101
Test Act, 168–69, 173, 179
Tewkesbury, Battle of, 80, 89
Thirty-Nine Articles, 108, 120
Thirty Years' War, 131, 137
tobacco, 128, 180
Toleration Act, 173
Tories, 177–80
Tostig, earl of Northumbria, 4–5, 7–8
Tower of London, 10, 80–81, 89, 151
Towton Moor, Battle of, 79–80, 87–88
trade, 45, 66, 86, 152, 161–62, 180
Trial of Treason Act, 172
Triennial Act, 139, 172
Troyes, Treaty of, 61, 71

Tudor, Henry. *See* Henry VII
Tudor kings, 44, 52–53, 81–82, 90
Two Treatises on Government (Locke),
    178
Tyndale, William, 96, 101, 105

Unitarians, 167, 173
United Kingdom, 14
Utrecht, Treaty of, 174, 179–80

Vestarian Controversy, 99

Wakefield, Battle of, 87
Wales, 46, 49, 110
Walter, Hubert, 23
War of the League of Augsburg, 173,
    177
War of the Spanish Succession, 173–74
Wars of the Roses, 62, 75–91
Warwick. *See* Neville, Richard, earl of
    Warwick
Wat Tyler's Rebellion, 60. *See also*
    Peasants' Revolt

weaponry, 59, 176
Wentworth, Thomas, 139
Wessex, kingdom of, 3–4
Westminster Abbey, 4, 152–53
Whigs, 34, 171, 177–80
White Company, 65
William II, 19
William III, 21, 34, 53, 166, 170–72,
    173–76, 178
William, Prince of Orange. *See* William III
William of Normandy. *See* William the
    Conqueror
William the Conqueror, 2, 4–14, 19, 72,
    75
witenagemot, 39
Wolsey, Thomas, 96–97, 100, 104
Woodville family, 80, 88
wool, 45, 57
Wren, Christopher, 151, 157, 159

Yorkist kings, 44, 52, 69
Yorkists, 78–80, 82, 86–89

ABOUT THE EDITORS AND CONTRIBUTORS

DOUGLAS BIGGS is associate professor of history at Waldorf College. He received his Ph.D. from the University of Minnesota and coauthored *Henry IV: The Establishment of the Regime, 1399-1406* with G. Dodd (2003). He has published articles in *The English Historical Review* and *The Journal of Medieval Military History*. He specializes in the study of early fifteenth-century England.

KENNETH L. CAMPBELL received his Ph.D. from the University of Delaware and is currently the Associate Dean of the School of Humanities and Social Sciences at Monmouth University in West Long Branch, New Jersey. He is the author of *The Intellectual Struggle of the English Papists in the Seventeenth Century* (1987) and is currently working on a book on religious nonconformity in England and a textbook on western civilization in a world perspective.

CONNIE EVANS is associate professor of history at Baldwin-Wallace College in Berea, Ohio. She earned her Ph.D. at Louisiana State University. She has published in the journal *Albion* and contributed an essay on the Spanish Armada to *Events That Changed the World through the Sixteenth Century*. She is currently researching the link between poverty and philanthropy in early modern Exeter.

JOHN E. FINDLING is professor of history at Indiana University Southeast. He earned his Ph.D. at the University of Texas and has pursued research interests in world's fairs and the Olympic movement for nearly twenty years. With Frank W. Thackeray, he edited *Statesmen Who Changed the World* (1993) and the *Events That Changed the World* and the *Events That Changed America* series. His latest book, *Encyclopedia of the Modern Olympic Movement*, co-edited with Kimberly D. Pelle, will be published in 2004.

ROBERT LANDRUM is assistant professor of history at the University of South Carolina, Beaufort. He earned his Ph.D. at the University of Wisconsin. He has published articles in *The Historian, Innes Review,* and *Aberdeen University Quarterly.* Currently he is researching topics dealing with mid-seventeenth-century Scotland.

LINDA E. MITCHELL received her Ph.D. from Indiana University. She is professor of history at Alfred University and recently published *Portraits of Medieval Women: Family, Marriage, and Politics in England, 1225–1350* (2003). Her current research focuses on the relationship between extended family, matrilineal alliances, and the development of the English political community in the thirteenth and fourteenth centuries.

STEVEN E. SIRY is professor of history at Baldwin-Wallace College in Berea, Ohio. He earned his Ph.D. at the University of Cincinnati and has published articles in *The Journal of the Early Republic, Locus,* and the *Theodore Roosevelt Association Journal.* He contributed an essay on the age of European expansion to *Events That Changed the World through the Sixteenth Century.*

FREDERICK SUPPE is associate professor of history at Ball State University. He received his Ph.D. from the University of Minnesota and is the author of *Military Institutions on the Welsh Marches* (1994). He has also published in *The Welsh History Review* and *The Haskins Society Journal.* His research interests include the Celtic world and medieval Europe.

FRANK W. THACKERAY is professor of history at Indiana University Southeast. He received his Ph.D. from Temple University. He is the author of *Antecedents of Revolution: Alexander I and the Polish Congress Kingdom* (1980) as well as articles on Russian-Polish relations in the nineteenth century. With John E. Findling, he edited *Statesmen Who Changed the World* (1993) and the *Events That Changed the World* and the *Events That Changed America* series. He is a former Fulbright scholar in Poland.

MARK K. VAUGHN currently holds the rank of major, United States Army Civil Affairs, and is serving in Iraq. He earned his Ph.D. at the United Kingdom's University of Reading. His current research interests are medieval military logistics and the impact of logistics on governments and their populations. He has served as a consultant for Lion Television Productions (UK).

WILLIAM T. WALKER received his Ph.D. from the University of South Carolina. Currently he is professor of history and vice president for academic affairs at Chestnut Hill College. He has contributed to *Events That Changed the World in the Seventeenth Century* and *Great Lives in History, British and Commonwealth Series*.

KRISTEN POST WALTON is assistant professor of history at Salisbury University. She earned her Ph.D. at the University of Wisconsin–Madison. She is currently completing her first book, *Catholic Queen, Protestant Patriarchy: Mary Queen of Scots and the Politics of Gender and Religion, 1561-73*. Her chief research interest is sixteenth-century English and Scottish social, intellectual, and political history.